FACTS PLUS™

Activity Book

Susan C. Anthony

Instructional Resources Company
1013 E. Dimond Blvd. #188
Anchorage, Alaska 99515-2099

Attention: Schools and Educational Organizations

This *Facts Plus Activity Book* was designed for use with *Facts Plus: An Almanac of Essential Information,* also by Susan C. Anthony (ISBN 1-879478-03-X). *Facts Plus* is recommended for use by students as a desk reference or text alternative. Contact Instructional Resources Company at one of the addresses below for information on quantity discounts for classroom sets of *Facts Plus*.

Instructional Resources Company
1013 E. Dimond Blvd. #188
Anchorage, Alaska 99515-2099
(907) 345-6689

Instructional Resources Company
3235 Garland
Wheat Ridge, CO 80033

ISBN 1-879478-02-1

NOTE TO THE TEACHER

Dear Fellow Educator:

I congratulate and honor you for your choice of profession. Day after day, year after year, you touch the lives of your students and influence their futures. The impact of your work extends far beyond the school year and your tenure as a teacher.

I wrote the *Facts Plus Activity Book* to *save you time* and to share tested ideas which sparked my students' interest in reference books and in learning. Most teachers who see the reference book, *Facts Plus: An Almanac of Essential Information,* quickly think of dozens of ways to use it in their classrooms. They have plenty of ideas, but rarely the time to develop supportive materials. And why *should* everyone have to reinvent the wheel?

The activities in this book are yours to do with as you wish. Although they're ready-to-use, feel free to change and adapt them to fit your unique situation. The suggestions are just that, suggestions. Some are "seeds" which may lead you to your own much better ideas. Be creative! Have fun! And please, I want to hear from you! Call or write and tell me what's working for you and for your students! Write to me in care of Instructional Resources Company, 1013 E. Dimond Blvd. #188, Anchorage, Alaska 99515-2099 or call 907-345-6689.

Susan C. Anthony

My Philosophy About Facts

1. Facts are building blocks for both creative and critical thinking.
2. The ability to find the facts one needs at the time one needs them is more crucial today than at any time in the past. This is a skill *distinctly* different from memorization.
3. The majority of facts which can be found in reference resources need not be memorized.
4. Some facts should be committed to memory. People who do not "know" these things may have difficulty understanding what they read and may appear to others to be uneducated. Continually having to look up basic and commonly-known facts is a waste of time.
5. People who enjoy memorizing facts should be encouraged to do so.
6. Facts are best learned in the context of rich and varied experiences, including literature, hands-on activities, and discussion. Isolated and unconnected facts can be worse than useless.
7. To be meaningful, new learning must be connected to what a person already knows. *Facts Plus* is intended to be used in building a schematic framework to help students connect and make sense of what they learn in all areas of study.
8. The more ways one organizes and views a set of facts, the greater the possibility of seeing patterns and relationships.
9. A person is more likely to learn a fact if it is needed to answer a question stemming from his/her own curiosity or if it relates to a current interest or concern.
10. Facts are fun and *fascinating!*

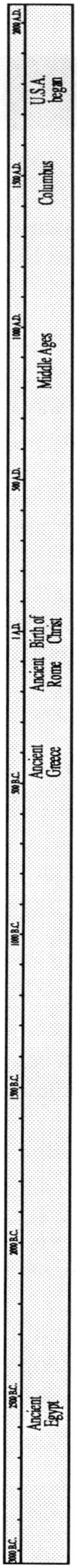

A Ready-Reference Classroom

Just as students immersed in quality literature will come to enjoy and appreciate it, students surrounded by reference materials will learn the habit of consulting them when questions arise. Any or all of the following items in your classroom will facilitate the teaching of lessons and concepts in this Activity Book.

Alphabet Cards which are generally used as handwriting examples can also help students learn to locate entries in a dictionary or index quickly. See Activity Book p. 2 and 7.

Time Line of World History. This can be hung high in the classroom and left there throughout the year for reference. I do not know of any commercially made time lines I would recommend. You can make your own out of a 30' long piece of butcher paper, cut to a 10" width with a black line 2½" from the top. Make "tick marks" on the line every 7 inches (for every 100 years), starting about three inches from the left. Number 3000 B.C., 2500 B.C., etc. by 500 year increments to 2000 A.D. as shown at left. Pictures can illustrate major eras or events. Dates for eras are approximate.

Ancient Egypt, 3000 B.C. to 715 B.C.
    Picture of Sphinx or Pyramids
Ancient Greece, 800 B.C. to 300 B.C.
    Picture of the Parthenon
Ancient Rome, 500 B.C. to 455 A.D.
    Picture of Roman Colosseum
Birth of Christ, c. 1 A.D.
    Picture of nativity scene
Middle Ages, 476 A.D. to 1450 A.D.
    Pictures of castles
Columbus, 1492 A.D.
    Picture of Columbus' ships
U.S.A. began, 1776 A.D.
    Picture of Liberty Bell or U.S. flag

Memorizing the general sequence of events on the time line gives students a framework for learning about cultures and histories of people around the world. See Activity Book p. 91.

Large Wall Maps make wonderful bulletin boards that can and should be left up all the time. Maps should be large enough to be seen from anywhere in the classroom and should always be visible. Children as well as teachers are more likely to refer to maps to clarify small points if they are easy to access. The following National Geographic maps are great for this purpose:

World Map, product number 02690, size 75" x 49", paper flat, price $12.95.
United States Map, product number 02208, size 70" x 49", paper flat, price $12.95.

Order from National Geographic, 1145 17th St. NW, Washington, D.C. 20036. 1-800-638-4077. $4.75 shipping for one map, $5.75 for both. If possible, also get a large map of your state and a map of Europe, as its countries are difficult to see on the world map.

Facts Plus: An Almanac of Essential Information for each student. Schools ordering class sets of 25 or more almanacs directly from the publisher qualify for a 25% discount.

The World Book Encyclopedia. Contact your local World Book representative about the "Partners in Excellence" program, which enables schools to obtain current encyclopedias at a discount.

Dictionary for each student.

World atlas, local telephone book, large calendar.

Facts Plus ACROSS THE CURRICULUM

Facts Plus: An Almanac of Essential Information is not only useful for teaching reference skills, but also most other areas of the curriculum. Ideally, students will use it as a "real" reference book, a ready source of information for answering questions as they arise. *Facts Plus* can enable you as a teacher to be flexible in instruction to take advantage of student interests and current events. The ideas here are starting points for using *Facts Plus* to integrate the curriculum and enhance instruction in basic school subjects.

Reading

— **Building Background.** Use *Facts Plus* to build background concepts necessary for understanding literature. For example, have students look up the location of a story on a map, find its place in history on the time line, etc. Tie literature to subject areas by reading related background information in the almanac. When I taught *The Cricket in Times Square*, my Alaskan students looked up information about New York City: its location, its population, and the height of the Empire State Building, Statue of Liberty and World Trade Center. They compared New York City to their own environment, and created a mental picture of the big city in preparation for reading.

— **Types of Literature Wheel.** Use *Facts Plus* p. 158 to introduce or review types of literature. Copy the wheel (copyright permission granted for this) and have students color in "spokes" to represent their reading selections. Try to scatter the spokes around the wheel.

— **Book lists.** Use lists of books on pages 159-162 of *Facts Plus* as a starting point for book sharing. For example, each child might choose a book from the Newbery list, read it, and share it with classmates.

— **Vocabulary improvement.** The lists of roots, prefixes and suffixes on pages 178-180 of *Facts Plus* may be helpful. Also, have students act out the synonyms given on p. 153: amble, stride, scurry, etc.

Computer Education

— **Database.** Have students create a computerized database using information from *Facts Plus,* such as states (p. 94-101) or volcanoes (p. 30). Rearrange information by sorting alphabetically, numerically, or by time.

— **Word Processing.** Students may use addresses for creating form letters. Lists of addresses include state tourist offices (p. 102) and national parks (p. 106-109).

— **Spreadsheet.** The information about countries (*Facts Plus* p. 53-69) may be used to create a spreadsheet. Enter formulas for figuring population density from area and population, for calculating next year's estimated population based on population growth rate, and for finding total GNP by multiplying per capita GNP by population, for example.

Writing

— **Writing Process.** Use *Facts Plus* p. 186 and 188-189 to teach the writing process.

— **Ideas for Writing** are on p. 187 and 194-195 of *Facts Plus.*

— **Letters.** Students may refer to *Facts Plus* p. 192-193 for proper letter form. Postal abbreviations are on p. 101. Addresses are on pages 20, 102, 106-109, 128-129 and 192.

— **Proofreading** help is on pages 167-171 and 190 of *Facts Plus.*

Spelling

— **Spelling Study Method.** A study procedure is outlined on page 175 of *Facts Plus,* along with five spelling "rules" which have few exceptions.

— **Challenge Spelling Lists.** Keep top spellers challenged. Below are sample lists of words. The teacher may find others pertaining to specific units of study. Students can study and take challenge tests at their convenience for special rewards or recognition if tests are tape recorded. All page numbers given are from *Facts Plus*. Students should locate geographical words they learn on a map.

- Frequently misspelled words, p. 176-177
- Planets, p. 17
- Forms of energy, p. 33
- Elements, p. 34
- Vitamins & minerals, p. 44-45
- Types of drugs, p. 46
- Oceans, p. 48
- Lakes (especially Great Lakes), p. 48
- Seas, p. 49
- Important rivers, p. 50
- Continents, p. 51
- Important mountain peaks, p. 52
- Countries, p. 53-69
- Inventions, p. 84-87
- Religions, p. 91-92
- States, p. 94-101
- State capital cities, p. 94-101
- Major cities, p. 103-105
- Indian tribes, p. 110-111
- Presidents, p. 130
- Subjects in Library of Congress classification system, p. 147
- Words in the Mini Thesaurus, p. 153
- Homonyms and troublesome words, p. 172-174
- Irregular verbs, p. 183
- Musical instruments, p. 197
- Geometric terms & figures, p. 208-209

Choose and tailor lists for *your* students!

Mathematics

Here are a few examples of how *Facts Plus* can be used in math. Integrate math with subject area units and set up challenges for top learners. Page numbers are from *Facts Plus*.

— **Place Value and Reading Large Numbers.** Page 201 can be used to teach place value. Have students read populations and areas of countries or states, areas of national parks, etc.

— **Ordering Numbers.** List large cities in order of area, pages 103-105. List state capitals in order of population, pages 94-101. List dams in order of height or capacity, page 90. List states in order of per capita income, pages 94-101.

— **Rounding.** Round the populations of states to the nearest million, the nearest thousand. Round the areas of national parks to the nearest unit, nearest thousand.

— **Addition.** Add the populations of the largest cities in Texas shown on pages 103-105. Calculate the combined areas of all national parks in Alaska or California from pages 106-109.

— **Subtraction.** Figure the approximate ages of notable people or presidents when they died, pages 78-83. Find the range of elevation (lowest to highest) for states and cities, pages 94-105. Find the difference between melting points and boiling points of elements, page 35. (Caution or teach students about negative numbers.)

— **Calculator division.** Figure population densities of cities, pages 103-105.

— **Word Problems.** Use the charts, graphs and statistics in *Facts Plus* to have students write their own word problems related to units of study. Students may exchange problems and solve them.

— **Measurement.** Measure the greatest snowfall and rainfall, page 25, the largest and smallest animals, page 38.

— **Graphing.** Graph the heights of waterfalls, volcanoes, skyscrapers, dams.

TABLE OF CONTENTS

Major sections are in bold type. Individual activities are in italics with page numbers for *all* pages needed for the activity.

FINDING FACTS FAST

The following activities are intended to introduce students to *Facts Plus: An Almanac of Essential Information* and to reference books in general. Students will gain experience in using the index and scanning for specific information. These activities will help students master the skills needed to do other activities in this book.

How Reference Books Are Organized

Materials:

Facts Plus class set
Optional: dictionary, atlas, encyclopedias

Background Information:

Literature is generally classified as fiction or nonfiction. A reference book is a special type of nonfiction book. Unlike fiction and most nonfiction, reference books are not intended to be read from cover to cover, but to be consulted for specific information. Reference books include dictionaries, atlases, almanacs, encyclopedias, telephone books and catalogs.

The first thing to do when looking at a reference book is to figure out how it is organized. There are five, and only five, basic ways to organize information. Knowing them is a key to not only understanding reference materials, but to organizing your own ideas.

1. **Alphabetical** (A to Z) such as the dictionary, encyclopedia, or white pages of a telephone book.
2. **Time** (old to new) such as a time line, journal or chronicle.
3. **Location** such as a map, atlas or travel guide.
4. **Categories** such as school subjects, body systems, or types of rocks. Categories are used to organize items of the same or similar importance. Colors rather than numbers would generally be used to identify categories.
5. **Continuum** (numerically, first to last, smallest to largest, fastest to slowest). Organizing information on a continuum is useful for making comparisons.

Suggested procedure:

1. Have pairs of students explore *Facts Plus* looking for an example of each of the five methods of organizing information. Note that information may be organized first by category and then alphabetically, as in the yellow pages of the phone book.
2. While students are searching, make a column on the board for each of the ways of organizing information. When students are ready to share, list their examples in the appropriate columns. Some examples:
   Alphabetical: countries, p. 53-69, index, p. 233-250.
   Time: time line, p. 72-77, Newbery books, p. 161.
   Location: maps, p. 131-140, Indians, p. 110-111.
   Category: geometric figures, p. 209.
   Continuum: lakes, p. 48, waterfalls, p. 49.
3. If time allows, have students look at other reference books to determine their basic method of organization. Find examples which combine two or more methods of organization.

Reorganizing Reference Information

Have students take information which is organized alphabetically, such as Important Dams on *Facts Plus* p. 90 and reorganize it by height, capacity or time. Often such reorganization can yield insights or make patterns apparent.

Parts of a Book

Materials:
Facts Plus, p. 148-150

Suggested procedure:

1. Have students read pages 148-150 for background information.
2. Find the front matter, text, and back matter in *Facts Plus*. Notice that *Facts Plus* includes:
   Front Matter: title page, copyright page, introduction, table of contents
   Text
   Back Matter: Sources and Notes, bibliography, index
3. Look for these parts in other books.

Scanning

Materials:
Facts Plus, p. 72-87 or any pages

Background information:
After using the index to find pages on which there is information about a subject, students must be able to scan the page to find that information. To scan, move eyes quickly over the page looking for key words, numbers or even capital letters, then read carefully on both sides of key words when located.

Suggested procedure:
Have students open their books to page 73. Tell them to scan the page as quickly as possible to find information about Cleopatra. Do this with any page and any key word on that page until students can scan easily.

Alphabetical Order & The Index

Materials:
Facts Plus, p. 233-250
Activity Book p. 7, cut into sections and used one at a time for as long as needed
Answers on Activity Book p. 8

Background Information:
The index is the *key* to finding information in an almanac. It is so important that some adult almanacs have moved it into the front matter.

Suggested Procedure:

1. Students start with *Facts Plus* closed. The teacher names a letter. Students open their books and search for key words in the index beginning with that letter. Start by thinking, "Is it in the first third, middle third, or last third of the alphabet?" Use the alphabet cards on the classroom wall as a reference if needed to check whether to search forward or backward. Students raise their hands when successful. Assist students who have trouble and allow everyone to succeed before going on. Continue with this activity until all students can find key words beginning with any letter without much trouble. Make this a "race" or game.
2. Next, the teacher names a guide word. Students "race" to find the guide word and raise their hands as before. Proceed with different guide words until all students are comfortable doing this.
3. Now, have students locate an entry word on a particular page. For example, find the entry word "Opera" on page 244. Name other words on various pages until students can locate them easily.
4. Next, name any word in the index. Students find it as quickly as possible and raise their hands when successful. Use a stopwatch for extra motivation and tell students their times.
5. Finally, students work on their own to locate 10 words in 10 minutes using one section of Activity Book p. 7 a day until proficiency is gained. Students note the page numbers shown in the index for each entry word. Use a stopwatch so that when students finish in *less* than 10 minutes, you can give them their times. This will keep faster students motivated.
6. Follow up by doing this activity with dictionaries. Students note page and column numbers on which an entry word is found.

Reading a Table

Materials:

Facts Plus, p. 130
42 copies of the worksheet on Activity Book, p. 5
Transparency of worksheet on p. 5
4 x 6 ruled index cards
Optional: Photos of U.S. presidents. These may be ordered from Giant Photos in Rockford, Illinois 61105, telephone 815-964-7927. A complete set costs $4.50.

Background information:

This activity is easy enough to do during the first month of school. It results in a great Back-to-School bulletin board if cards done by the students are displayed with photos of the presidents and surrounded by plenty of red, white and blue.

Suggested procedure:

1. Have students use the index to find the information about United States presidents on page 130 of *Facts Plus*. Allow them to make observations, then ask questions such as, "When did George Washington die?" "Where was Abraham Lincoln born?" "Do any of the presidents have the same birthday as you?" Have students ask and answer questions based on the table.
2. Pass out copies of the worksheet on page 5 of the Activity Book. Demonstrate filling in the information for a selected president on the transparency, then copy the paragraph (indented) onto an index card with good handwriting. Student's name should go at the bottom of the card.
3. Give each student a photo of a president. He/she fills in the worksheet for that president and has it checked by the teacher before copying the paragraph neatly onto an index card. When the card is finished, the student submits it to the teacher with the photo and is given the photo of a different president. This continues until all presidents have been done or time is up. Some students may finish only one card, some may finish several.

Note-Taking & Paraphrasing

Materials:

Facts Plus, p. 222, 226, 90, 37

Background information:

Once information has been located, students will generally need to take notes. They should paraphrase, or put information into their own words, to avoid plagiarism, which is illegal copyright infringement.

Suggested procedure:

1. Read page 222 of *Facts Plus* for background information on taking notes. Also read page 226, section IV.
2. Have students turn to a chart, such as the chart of important canals on page 88. Have them brainstorm several sentences which include information from the chart concerning the Suez Canal. For example, "The Suez Canal is in Egypt. It is 117.9 miles long and has no locks. It was opened in 1869." Have students write sentences using information from other charts until this becomes easy.
3. Have students turn to a section with text, such as page 37. Have them brainstorm other ways of presenting some of the information given in the first two paragraphs. For example: "There are two main groups of animals, vertebrates and invertebrates. Vertebrates have backbones and invertebrates do not."

Student Stumpers

Materials:

Facts Plus
3 x 5 index cards

Suggested procedure:

1. Have students make up questions they think will "stump" the other students and write them on individual index cards.
2. Post the questions on a bulletin board or read them aloud in the morning. Students can use free time to search for the answers in reference books or the library.

One Paragraph Reports

Materials:
Facts Plus

Background information:
Once students are adept at locating information and paraphrasing, and before they do independent reports, they can practice one-paragraph reports.

Suggested procedure:

1. Have everyone look up "Elephants" in the index and note the page numbers.
2. Look up information on each page and "take notes." Teacher can write paraphrased notes or sentences on the board.
3. Organize the information into a cohesive paragraph (indented). One example might be: "The elephant is an endangered large animal. The African elephant is the largest land animal in the world. It usually weighs about 6.5 tons. The largest weighed 13.5 tons! That's a lot, but in an average lifetime an American eats the combined weight of five elephants! The Republican Party chose the elephant as its special symbol in 1874."
4. Have students independently do one-paragraph reports on one of the following subjects: Aconcagua, Aluminum, Appalachians, Bears, Bristlecone Pine Trees, Calcium, Eagle, Samuel F. B. Morse, Mount Rainier, Television.
5. Read two or three paragraphs by different students on the same subject and compare how the information is presented.
6. Students may try again with a different subject.

Crossnumber Puzzle

Materials:
Facts Plus
Copies of Activity Book, p. 9
Answers on Activity Book p. 10

Suggested procedure:
Students do the puzzle independently.

Reading and Interpreting a Table

Materials:
Facts Plus p. 51, 52
Copies of Activity Book p. 11
Answers below

Background information:
Some of these questions require interpretation of information and calculation. Students should be sure to *label* answers if necessary, i.e. *feet, sq. miles*. Information on units may be at the *top* of a column.

Answers:
1) Himalayas, 2) Mount Mitchell, 3) Andes, 4) 3,000 miles long, 5) Europe, 6) Godwin Austin (K-2), 7) 778 feet (calculate 29,028 – 28,250), 8) 16,864 feet, 9) Cotopaxi, 10) 796 feet (calculate 20,320 – 19,524), 11) 12,388 feet, 12) Cascades, 13) Mt. Cook, 14) 2,511 feet (calculate 22,831 – 20,320), 15) Mt. Elbrus, 16) Sahara Desert, 17) about 500,000 sq. miles, 18) Asia, 19) Greenland, 20) 84,550 sq. miles, 21) Pacific, 22) Madagascar, 23) 8,129 sq. mi. (calculate 83,896 – 75,767), 24) Everest – 29,028, Godwin Austen (K-2) – 28,250, Kanchenjunga – 28,208, Annapurna – 26,504, Aconcagua – 22,831, Mt. McKinley – 20,320

Scavenger Hunt

Materials:
Facts Plus
Copies of *Facts Plus* Scavenger Hunt, Activity Book p. 12. Page #'s below.

Background information:
Because this is a scavenger hunt, there may be more than one correct answer to most questions.

Suggested procedure:
Alone or in pairs, students find as many of the items requested as possible within a stated length of time. Any who finish early may try the challenge questions. Compare answers.

Page numbers: 1) 46, 2) 106-109, 3) 19, 4) 38, 5) 13, 6) 94-101, 7) 85-87, 8) 34, 9) 53-69, 10) 20, 11) 179, 12) 129, 13) 17, Venus, 14) 44, 15) 94-101, 16) 50, 17) 103-105, 18) 111, 19) 89, 20) 15, 21) 35 & 17, 22) 35 & 17, 23) 130, 24) 212 & 130, 25) 61, 94-101

Crossword Puzzle

Materials:

Facts Plus

Copies of Activity Book, p. 13

Answers on Activity Book p. 14

Suggested procedure:

Have students work independently or in groups to complete the crossword.

Write Your Own Reference Book

Suggested procedure:

Have students brainstorm what could be included in a "Class Book of Records." A time line of birthdays, a neighborhood map showing homes, graphs showing favorite foods, list of the fastest runners, accounts of unique experiences? Compile the book, with contents and an index, and publish to share!

Teachers: To prepare the worksheet below, make two copies of this page. Fold one copy in half and slip it over the top of the second copy to make a master having two worksheets per page.

Tiny Trivia Books

Materials:

Facts Plus

Copies of Activity Book, p. 15 and/or 16

Answers below

Suggested procedure:

1. First make the books. Have students carefully fold the paper in half, then in half again, then in half again. Unfold and carefully cut along the dotted line. Fold in half lengthwise. Spread the cut portion and fold so that the cover is in front.
2. Have students work in pairs or groups to find the answers. Some require students to problem-solve and tally or process information. The Perpetual Calendar on p. 4-5 of *Facts Plus* is needed to answer #6.
3. Students may make their own books using the master on Activity Book p. 16.

Answers:

1) Japan, 2) Alaska, 3) Cardinal, 4) Venezuela, 5) Four, 6) Thursday (Johnson, Nixon, Bush)

__________________ (full name of president) was our __________________ (first, second, third, etc.) president. He was born in __________________ (state of birth) on __________________ (date of birth).

He was president from __________ (year term began) to __________ (year term ended). He died on

__________________ (date of death).

__________________ (student's name)

Months	Ordinal Numbers			
January	first	twelfth	twenty-third	thirty-third
February	second	thirteenth	twenty-fourth	thirty-fourth
March	third	fourteenth	twenty-fifth	thirty-fifth
April	fourth	fifteenth	twenty-sixth	thirty-sixth
May	fifth	sixteenth	twenty-seventh	thirty-seventh
June	sixth	seventeenth	twenty-eighth	thirty-eighth
July	seventh	eighteenth	twenty-ninth	thirty-ninth
August	eighth	nineteenth	thirtieth	fortieth
September	ninth	twentieth	thirty-first	forty-first
October	tenth	twenty-first	thirty-second	forty-second
November	eleventh	twenty-second		
December				

Teachers: Lesson plan p. 3

Mini Reports

Materials:
Facts Plus, p. 226-227
Optional: photos of these notable people are available from Giant Photos in Rockford, IL 61105

Suggested procedure:
Have students do numerous mini-reports throughout the year. For a mini-report, they might be asked to find the ten most interesting things they can about a topic and write ten sentences in list form. All persons listed have individual articles in *The World Book Encyclopedia.* Other possible mini-report topics include:

National Parks
Indian tribes
Presidents
Cities
Inventions
Volcanoes
Planets

* Not in the index of *Facts Plus*

Explorers
Amundsen, Roald
Balboa, Vasco de
Byrd, Richard B.
Cabot, John Sebastian
Champlain, Samuel de
Clark, William
Columbus, Christopher
Cook, Captain James
Cortés, Hernando
De Soto, Hernando
Drake, Sir Francis
Ericson, Leif
Hillary, Sir Edmund
Hudson, Henry
La Salle, Sieur de
Lewis, Meriwether
Livingstone, David
Magellan, Ferdinand
Peary, Robert
Pizarro, Francisco
Polo, Marco
Ponce de León, Juan
Raleigh, Sir Walter
Shackleton, Sir Ernest
Smith, John
Stanley, Henry Morton
Vespucci, Amerigo
Bering, Vitus*
Cabral, Pedro Alvarez*
Cabrillo, Juan Rodriguez*
Cartier, Jacques*
Coronado, Francisco de*
Mackenzie, Alexander*
Prince Henry the Navigator*

Frontiersmen
Appleseed, Johnny
Austin, Stephen
Baca, Elfego
Bean, Judge Roy
Boone, Daniel
Bridger, James
Buffalo Bill Cody
Calamity Jane
Carson, Kit
Crockett, Davy
Earp, Wyatt
Fink, Mike
Hickok, Wild Bill
Jones, Casey
Oakley, Annie
Love, Nat*

Outlaws
Arnold, Benedict
Billy the Kid
Blackbeard
Booth, John Wilkes
Capone, Al
Dillinger, John
Greaves, Captain
James, Jesse
Kidd, William
Laffite, Jean
Robin Hood
Villa, Pancho
Bass, Sam*
Morgan, Sir Henry*
Roy, Rob*
Starr, Belle*
Turpin, Dick*

American Indians
Black Hawk
Black Kettle
Brant, Joseph
Captain Jack
Cochise
Crazy Horse
Deloria, Vine, Jr.
Dorion, Marie
Gall
Geronimo
Joseph, Chief
Massasoit
Osceola
Parker, Ely
Philip, King
Pocahontas
Pontiac
Powhatan
Sacagawea
Samoset
Sequoyah
Sitting Bull
Squanto
Tecumseh
Thorpe, Jim
Watie, Stand
Little Turtle*
Logan*
Manuelito*
McGillivray, Andrew*
Poundmaker*
Qanah*
Red Cloud*
Red Jacket*
Spotted Tail*
Winnemucca, Sarah*
Washakie*

African Americans
Abernathy, Ralph
Anderson, Marian
Attucks, Crispus
Banneker, Benjamin
Bethune, Mary McLeod
Bluford, Guion S., Jr.
Carver, George Washington
Douglass, Frederick
Forten, James
Giovanni, Nikki
Jackson, Jesse
Johnson, Earvin
King, Martin Luther
Marshall, Thurgood
Parks, Rosa Lee
Powell, Colin L.
Truth, Sojourner
Tubman, Harriet
Washington, Booker T.
Wheatley, Phillis
Wilkins, Roy
Williams, Daniel Hale
Love, Nat*
Miller, Dorie*
Moton, Robert Russa*
Paige, Satchel*
Price, Leontyne*
Thomas, Clarence*
Turner, Nat*
Walker, David*
Wells, Ida B.*
Woods, Granville T.*
Young, Andrew*

Women
Addams, Jane
Anthony, Susan B.
Barton, Clara
Blackwell, Antoinette
Blackwell, Elizabeth
Bloomer, Amelia
Bly, Nellie
Dix, Dorothea
Earhart, Amelia
Eddy, Mary Baker
Friedan, Betty
Kirkpatrick, Jeane
Landers, Ann
Montessori, Maria
Mott, Lucretia
Nation, Carry
Nightingale, Florence
Picotte, Susan La Flesche
O'Connor, Sandra Day
Pitcher, Molly
Ride, Sally K.
Roosevelt, Eleanor
Ross, Betsy
Stanton, Elizabeth Cady
Stowe, Harriet Beecher
Tereshkova, Valentina
Thatcher, Margaret
Paul, Alice*
Price, Leontyne*
Stone, Lucy*
Wald, Lillian*
Willard, Emma Hart*
Wright, Frances*
Woodhull, Victoria Claflin*

Name________________________
Date________________________

	Page Numbers
1. Railroads	________
2. Managua	________
3. Century	________
4. Victoria Falls	________
5. Worms	________
6. Eskimos	________
7. Guam	________
8. Addition	________
9. Kampala	________
10. Python	________

Name________________________
Date________________________

	Page Numbers
1. Middle Ages	________
2. Halley's Comet	________
3. Sandstone	________
4. Income Tax	________
5. Yukon River	________
6. Father's Day	________
7. Baltic Sea	________
8. Charlemagne	________
9. Omaha	________
10. Krakatoa	________

Name________________________
Date________________________

	Page	Column
1. Stethoscope		
2. Plato		
3. Mekong River		
4. Amphibians		
5. Soyuz		
6. Tugela Falls		
7. Ostrich		
8. Leap seconds		
9. Dinosaurs		
10. South Pole		

Name________________________
Date________________________

	Page Numbers
1. Oroville Dam	________
2. Interview	________
3. Scandinavia	________
4. Yerevan	________
5. Dynamite	________
6. Bahrain	________
7. Himalayas	________
8. Rocket	________
9. Liberty Bell	________
10. Vesuvius	________

Name________________________
Date________________________

	Page Numbers
1. Osceola	________
2. Kiribati	________
3. Alexandrite	________
4. Etymology	________
5. Hungary	________
6. Timor Sea	________
7. Nicaragua	________
8. Doldrums	________
9. Byars, Betsy	________
10. Leopard	________

Teachers: Lesson plan on p. 2, Answers on p. 8

Name________________________
Date________________________

	Page Numbers
1. X rays	________
2. Rainbow	________
3. Kabul	________
4. Mount Cook	________
5. Anemia	________
6. Saxophone	________
7. Plasma	________
8. Bolivia	________
9. Vitamins	________
10. Cornucopia	________

Name______ **KEY** ______
Date______

		Page Numbers
1.	Railroads	3, 77
2.	Managua	64, 131
3.	Century	2, 12, 74
4.	Victoria Falls	49
5.	Worms	37
6.	Eskimos	110
7.	Guam	101
8.	Addition	202
9.	Kampala	68, 137
10.	Python	39

Name______ **KEY** ______
Date______

		Page Numbers
1.	Middle Ages	74-75
2.	Halley's Comet	17
3.	Sandstone	32
4.	Income Tax	120
5.	Yukon River	50
6.	Father's Day	9, 7
7.	Baltic Sea	49, 138
8.	Charlemagne	79, 74
9.	Omaha	104, 132
10.	Krakatoa	30

Name______ **KEY** ______
Date______

		Page Numbers
1.	Stethoscope	87
2.	Plato	82
3.	Mekong River	50
4.	Amphibians	37, 28
5.	Soyuz	20
6.	Tugela Falls	49
7.	Ostrich	37, 38
8.	Leap seconds	229
9.	Dinosaurs	28, 39
10.	South Pole	142, 11, 14

Name______ **KEY** ______
Date______

		Page Numbers
1.	Oroville Dam	90
2.	Interview	221
3.	Scandinavia	70
4.	Yerevan	53, 139
5.	Dynamite	85, 33
6.	Bahrain	54, 70
7.	Himalayas	52, 28, 30
8.	Rocket	87
9.	Liberty Bell	126
10.	Vesuvius	30

Name______ **KEY** ______
Date______

		Page Numbers
1.	Osceola	82
2.	Kiribati	60, 70, 135
3.	Alexandrite	12
4.	Etymology	152
5.	Hungary	59, 138
6.	Timor Sea	49
7.	Nicaragua	64, 70, 131
8.	Doldrums	26
9.	Byars, Betsy	161
10.	Leopard	39

Teachers: Lesson plan on p. 2, copy master on p. 7

Name______ **KEY** ______
Date______

		Page Numbers
1.	X rays	84
2.	Rainbow	198
3.	Kabul	53, 139
4.	Mount Cook	52
5.	Anemia	44, 45
6.	Saxophone	87
7.	Plasma	229
8.	Bolivia	55, 136
9.	Vitamins	43, 44, 229
10.	Cornucopia	10

Name ______________________________

Across:
1. Number of acres in Lake Clark National Park
3. The year *The Westing Game* won a Newbery award
4. Population of Cleveland, Ohio
6. How many million times a human heart beats in 10 years
8. Zip code of Crater Lake National Park
10. Population density of Comoros
12. The year North Dakota entered the Union
13. Population of Wyoming
15. Length of the Nile River in miles
18. Number of years in a century
19. Population of Tokyo-Yokohama, Japan
21. Height of the Empire State Building in feet
22. Feet in main span of Brooklyn Bridge
23. Area of Virginia in square miles

Down:
1. Speed of the peregrine falcon
2. Number of earth days in a year on Uranus
3. The year Amerigo Vespucci was born
5. Approximate number of skeletal muscles
6. Number of degrees in a circle
7. Length of the equator in miles
9. Elevation of Mount St. Helens
11. Number of people added to world population per day in 1992
12. Speed of light in miles per second
14. Year the compound microscope was invented
16. Year the donkey became a symbol for the Democratic Party
17. Area of Venezuela in square miles
18. Area of Lake Baikal
20. Temperature at which iron will melt
21. The age at which citizens of the U.S. can vote according to the 26th amendment to the Constitution

Crossnumber Puzzle

Teachers: Answers on p. 10

Note: Page numbers are from Facts Plus.

KEY

Across:

1. Number of acres in Lake Clark National Park (p. 108)
3. The year *The Westing Game* won a Newbery award (p. 161)
4. Population of Cleveland, Ohio (p. 103)
6. How many million times a human heart beats in 10 years (p. 41)
8. Zip code of Crater Lake National Park (p. 106)
10. Population density of Comoros (p. 56)
12. The year North Dakota entered the Union (p. 98)
13. Population of Wyoming (p. 101)
15. Length of the Nile River in miles (p. 50)
18. Number of years in a century (p. 2)
19. Population of Tokyo-Yokohama, Japan (p. 105)
21. Height of the Empire State Building in feet (p. 90)
22. Feet in main span of Brooklyn Bridge (p. 88)
23. Area of Virginia in square miles (p. 100)

Down:

1. Speed of the peregrine falcon (p. 38)
2. Number of earth days in a year on Uranus (p. 17)
3. The year Amerigo Vespucci was born (p. 83)
5. Approximate number of skeletal muscles (p. 40)
6. Number of degrees in a circle (p. 209)
7. Length of the equator in miles (p. 11)
9. Elevation of Mount St. Helens (p. 30)
11. Number of people added to world population per day in 1992 (p. 71)
12. Speed of light in miles per second (p. 15)
14. Year the compound microscope was invented (p. 86)
16. Year the donkey became a symbol for the Democratic Party (p. 127)
17. Area of Venezuela in square miles (p. 69)
18. Area of Lake Baikal (p. 48)
20. Temperature at which iron will melt (p. 35)
21. The age at which citizens of the U.S. can vote according to the 26th amendment to the Constitution (p. 122)

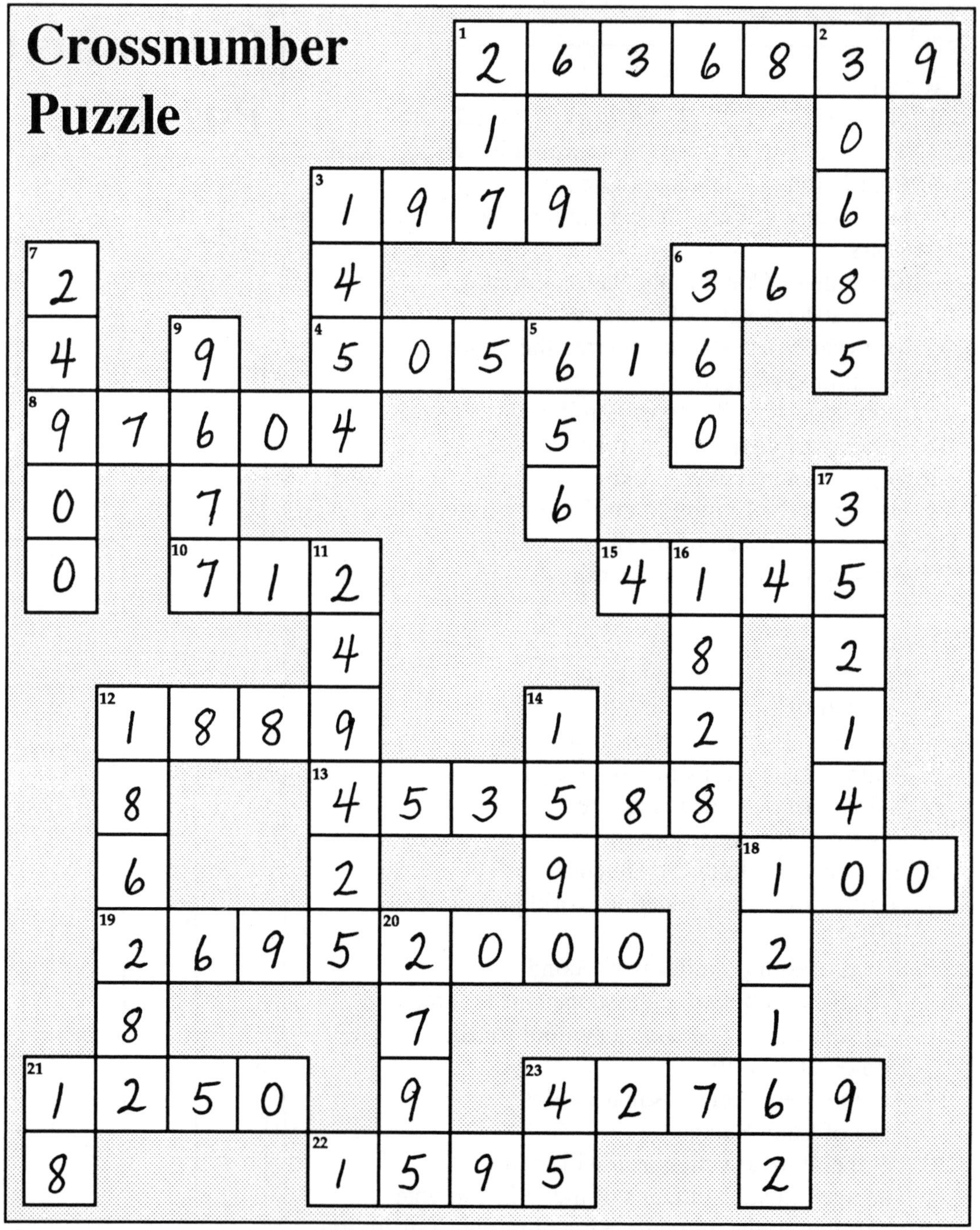

Teachers: Copy master on p. 9

Name______________________________ Date________________________

MOUNTAINS, DESERTS AND ISLANDS

1. Which mountain range has 59 of the 100 tallest peaks in the world? ______________________________
2. What is the tallest peak in the Appalachians? ____________
3. Which mountain range has the tallest mountains in the western hemisphere? ____________
4. How long are the Rocky Mountains? ____________
5. On which continent are the Alps? ____________
6. What is the second highest peak in the world? ____________
7. How much higher is Mt. Everest than the second highest mountain in the world? ____________
8. How high is the highest point in Antarctica? ____________
9. What is the highest active volcano in the world? ____________
10. How much higher is Mt. McKinley than Mt. Logan? ____________
11. What is the height of Mt. Fuji? ____________
12. In which mountain range is Mt. Rainier? ____________
13. What is the highest mountain in New Zealand? ____________
14. How much higher is Aconcagua than Mt. McKinley? ____________
15. What is the highest mountain in Europe? ____________
16. What is the largest desert in the world? ____________
17. How large is the Arabian Desert? ____________
18. Where is the Gobi Desert? ____________
19. What is the largest island in the world? ____________
20. How large is the island of Great Britain? ____________
21. In which ocean is the island of New Guinea? ____________
22. What is the largest island in the Indian Ocean? ____________
23. How much larger is Victoria Island than Ellesmere Island? ____________ ______________________________
24. Arrange in order the mountains in the chart above 20,000 feet.

____

____

____

Teachers: Lesson plan and answers on p. 4

Name________________________________ Date__________________________

Facts Plus SCAVENGER HUNT

Directions: Write an answer *and* the page number(s) where the answer was found.

1. Find the name of a nonprescription analgesic. (p._____) ____________________
2. Find the name of a national park in Utah. (p _____) ____________________
3. Find the date of the next eclipse. (p. _____) ____________________
4. Find the name of an animal with a speed slower than man. (p. _____)____________
5. Find a month which was named after a Roman goddess. (p. _____) ____________
6. Find a state whose lowest point is *below* sea level. (p. _____)____________
7. Find something which was invented in the 1600's. (p. _____)____________
8. Find the name of an element which begins with "c." (p. _____)____________
9. Find a country with an area of less than 500 sq. miles. (p. _____)____________
10. Find the name of an astronaut who was killed. (p. _____) ____________________
11. Find a prefix which means "not." (p. _____) ____________________
12. Find the name of a Supreme Court justice. (p. _____) ____________________
13. Find a planet with a day longer than its year. (p. _____)____________________
14. Find a good source of Vitamin A. (p. _____) ____________________
15. Find the name of a governor whose term will end in 1993. (p. _____)____________
16. Find the name of a river in the U.S.S.R. (p._____) ____________________
17. Find a major U.S. city whose area is less than 50 square miles. (p. _____)________
18. Find the name of a Pueblo Indian tribe. (p. _____)____________________
19. Find the name of a famous tunnel in Japan. (p. _____)____________________
20. Find the name of a star *more than* 400 light years away. (p. _____)____________

Challenge questions

21. Find a planet on which tin would melt. (p. _______) ____________________
22. Find a planet on which oxygen would be frozen. (p. ________) ____________
23. Find a president who died during his term of office. (p. _____)____________
24. Find the name of a person on a United States bill (money) who is *not* a president. (p._______) ________________________________
25. Find a state of the U.S. with an area almost the same as that of Kuwait. (p. ______) ________________________________

Teachers: Lesson plan and answers on p. 4

ACROSS

1. The city with the Liberty Bell
7. A male swan
8. Another name for wind instruments
9. The country where Hinduism began
12. The island in Italy where Mount Etna is located
14. A new country. Kiev is the capital.
15. Stones or minerals used for ornament, such as diamonds
16. Scientific name for stored energy. Opposite of kinetic.
18. Postal abbreviation for Pennsylvania
20. Another name for Vitamin B-1
21. The governor of Pennsylvania's last name
22. First word in the name of the river which forms the border between the U.S. and Mexico
24. Postal abbreviation for Arkansas
25. A homonym which sounds like "2"
28. A Chicago skyscraper with a height of 1,136 ft.
29. One of the states of matter
31. A flat drawing of the earth
32. Postal abbreviation for Maine
34. Author of "Around the World in 80 Days" (last name)

DOWN

1. An element with an atomic number of 78
2. Another name for Lao-Tzu
3. Author of "Charlie & The Chocolate Factory"
4. Texas is nicknamed the _____ Star State.
5. One name used for the drug cannabis
6. A national park in Maine
10. Last name of a famous Iowa Indian
11. The _______ canal is part of the digestive system.
13. One of Jean Foucault's inventions
15. The ______ period of an antelope is 9 months.
17. Abbreviation for "Associated Press"
19. Name for a book of maps
23. Postal abbreviation for Michigan
26. One of the elements in the core of the earth
27. Postal abbreviation for Louisiana
28. A branch of mathematics dealing with points, lines, angles, and figures such as the rhombus and trapezoid
30. Postal abbreviation for California
33. Postal abbreviation for Nevada

CROSSWORD PUZZLE

Name ______________________________

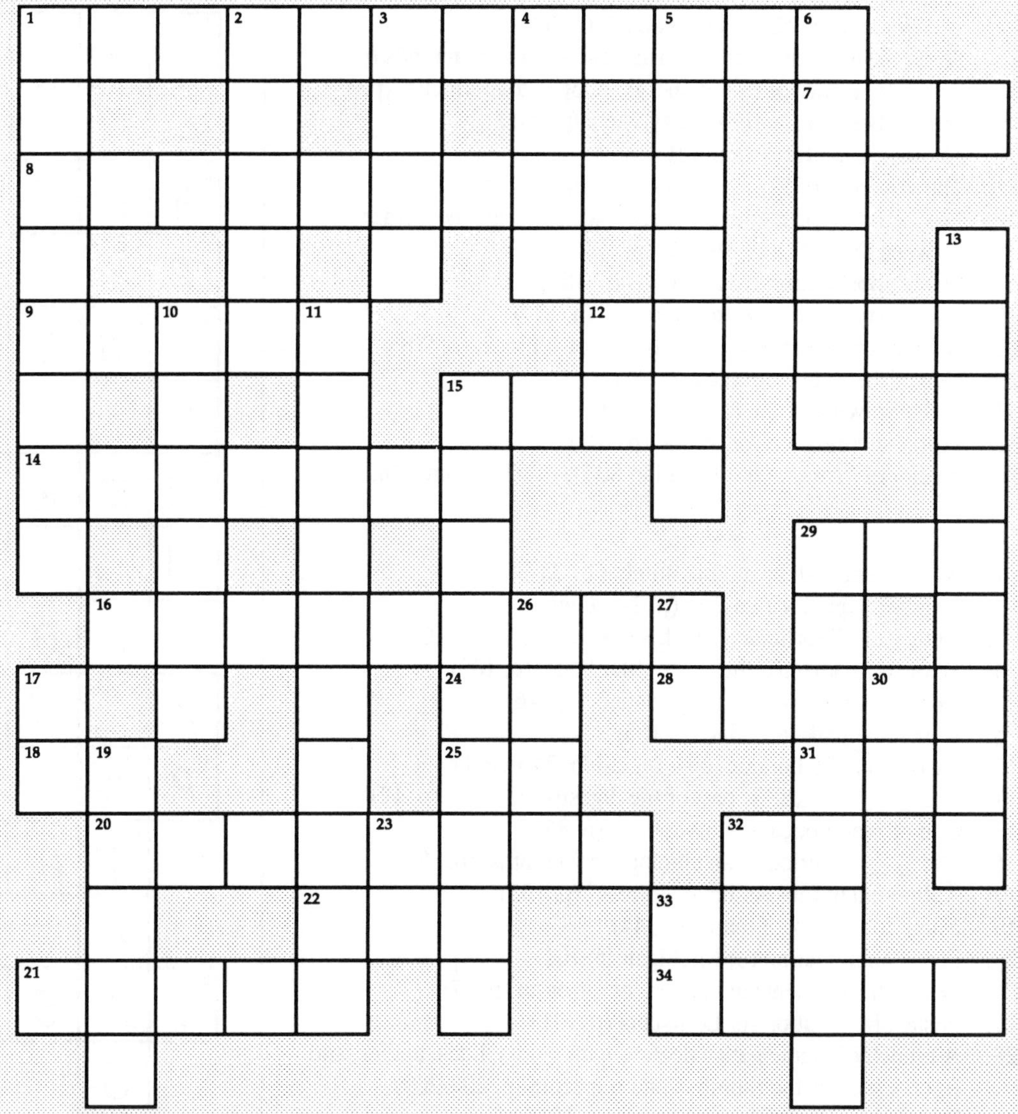

Teachers: Answers on p. 14

Page numbers are from Facts Plus.

KEY

ACROSS

1. The city with the Liberty Bell (p. 126)
7. A male swan (p. 38)
8. Another name for wind instruments (p. 197)
9. The country where Hinduism began (p. 91)
12. The island in Italy where Mount Etna is located (p. 30)
14. A new country. Kiev is the capital. (p. 68)
15. Stones or minerals used for ornament, such as diamonds (p. 32)
16. Scientific name for stored energy. Opposite of kinetic. (p. 33)
18. Postal abbreviation for Pennsylvania (p. 101)
20. Another name for Vitamin B-1 (p. 44)
21. The governor of Pennsylvania's last name (p. 99)
22. First word in the name of the river which forms the border between the U.S. and Mexico (p. 50)
24. Postal abbreviation for Arkansas (p. 101)
25. A homonym which sounds like "2" (p. 174)
28. A Chicago skyscraper with a height of 1,136 ft. (p. 90)
29. One of the states of matter (p. 35)
31. A flat drawing of the earth (p. 143)
32. Postal abbreviation for Maine (p. 101)
34. Author of "Around the World in 80 Days" (last name) (p. 162)

DOWN

1. An element with an atomic number of 78 (p. 34)
2. Another name for Lao-Tzu (p. 241 x-ref)
3. Author of "Charlie & The Chocolate Factory" (p. 162)
4. Texas is nicknamed the _____ Star State. (p. 100)
5. One name used for the drug cannabis (p. 46)
6. A national park in Maine (p. 106)
10. Last name of a famous Iowa Indian (p. 240 x-ref)
11. The _______ canal is part of the digestive system. (p. 42)
13. One of Jean Foucault's inventions (p. 86)
15. The ______ period of an antelope is 9 months. (p. 38)
17. Abbreviation for "Associated Press" (p. 155)
19. Name for a book of maps (p. 144)
23. Postal abbreviation for Michigan (p. 101)
26. One of the elements in the core of the earth (p. 27)
27. Postal abbreviation for Louisiana (p. 101)
28. A branch of mathematics dealing with points, lines, angles, and figures such as the rhombus and trapezoid (p. 208-209)
30. Postal abbreviation for California (p. 101)
33. Postal abbreviation for Nevada (p. 101)

CROSSWORD PUZZLE

Name ______________________________

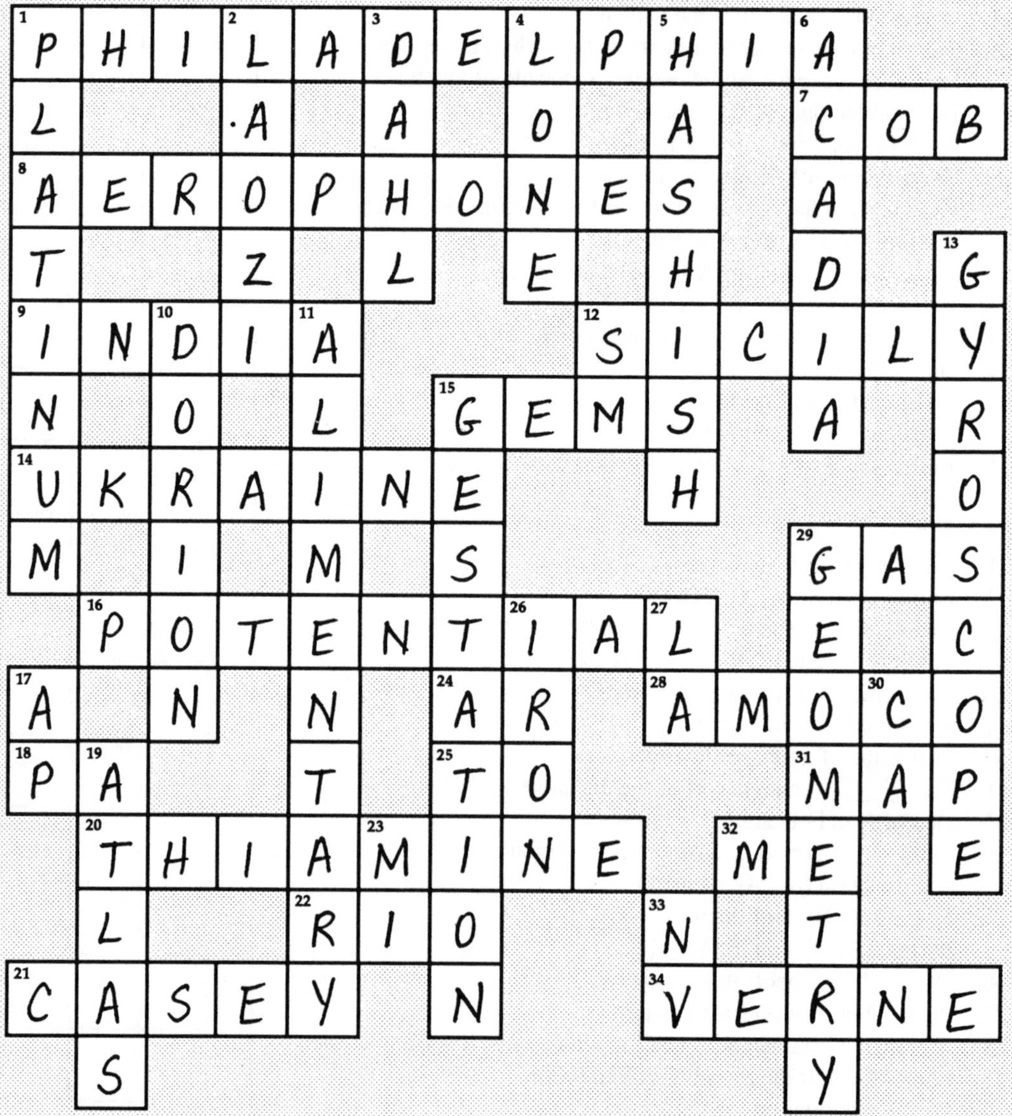

Teachers: Copy master on p. 14

A Tiny Trivia Book

This book belongs to: ______________

The Answers

1. ______________
2. ______________
3. ______________
4. ______________
5. ______________
6. ______________

Teachers: Instructions and answers on p. 5

1

Which country has the most tunnels which are more than ten miles long?

2

Which state has the most national parks?

a. Utah
b. California
c. Alaska

3

What is the most popular state bird?

a. Mockingbird
b. Cardinal
c. Bluebird

4

Which country has two of the three tallest waterfalls in the world?

5

How many months were named after Roman gods and goddesses?

6

On what day of the week were three of the presidents since John F. Kennedy born?

4

3

2

1

5

6

The Answers

1. ____________________

2. ____________________

3. ____________________

4. ____________________

5. ____________________

6. ____________________

Teachers: Instructions on p. 5

My Tiny Trivia Book

By: ________________

THE FACTS GAME

One way to encourage students to learn facts is to make a game of it. The questions in this section are common knowledge for most educated adults and would be good for students to learn "by heart." The question cards may be used for numerous games. I encourage you to make up your own games, or, even better, have *students* make up games using the cards. They can be board games, "game show" games, team games, or active games. The only requirement is that players must answer or look up the answer to questions on the cards as part of the game, and answering from memory should reap a higher reward than looking up the answer. A map, a calendar, the periodic table on Activity Book p. 181, or the floor plan of your school may be the gameboard.

I recommend that students get familiar with the cards before using them in games or competition. One way to do this would be for the teacher to present a few questions each day. Anyone who knows the answer can share it. If no one knows the answer, students can look it up. Review questions the next day and add a few more.

The cards can be used during minutes that might otherwise be unproductive, such as when a class is waiting in line. Again, make a game of it. A little practice in recalling these facts once in a while throughout the school year can make a big difference in long-term retention. Students need not be put under pressure or tested.

Preparing the Materials

The Cards:

1. Duplicate Activity Book p. 18 to 22. If more than one set of cards is needed, use a different color for each set for easy sorting. I recommend three sets per class.
2. Cut on the dotted lines. The bold numbers are the card numbers, which are used when a student monitor checks an answer against the answer sheet (p. 26). The point values may or may not be used in a particular game.
3. Mount each question on the back of a business card (2" x 3½") or on half of a 3" x 5" index card.
4. Laminate cards for repeated use.

The Gameboard:

Duplicate the gameboard, p. 23 and 24 of the Activity Book. Glue it inside a 9" x 12" manila folder. It will look like the small example shown on the right. Students may add color if desired. One gameboard should be made for each 2-3 students who will play at a time.

Folders, Dice, Markers, Almanac:

1. Make a folder for each two or three students who will be playing at a time. Besides the gameboard (glued in), include a copy of the Directions, Activity Book p. 25, the Answer Sheet, Activity Book p. 26, one die, and markers for each player (or players can make their own).
2. Make sure each playing group has a copy of *Facts Plus: An Almanac of Essential Information,* and about 50 question cards. A complete set of cards is not necessary for a game.

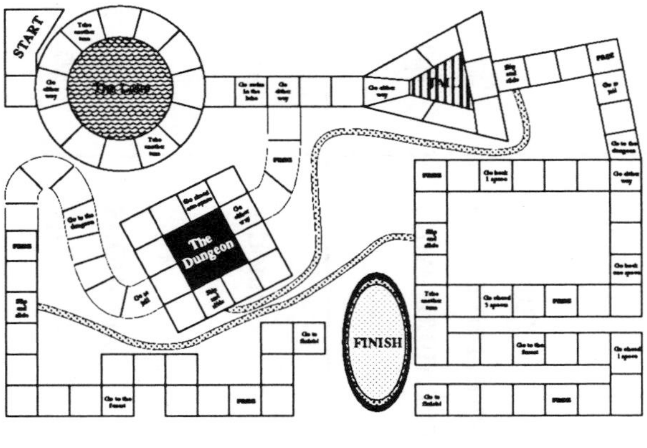

How many days are in a year? 1 point **1**	How many seconds are in a minute? 1 point **2**	How many minutes are in an hour? 1 point **3**	How many hours are in a day? 1 point **4**	How many days are in a week? 1 point **5**
How many months are in a year? 1 point **6**	How many weeks are in a year? 2 points **7**	How many years are in a decade? 1 point **8**	How many years are in a century? 1 point **9**	During what war was Abraham Lincoln president? 1 point **10**
In what year did Columbus first come to America? 1 point **11**	In what month is Election Day? 1 point **12**	Name the days of the week in order. 1 point **13**	Name the months of the year in order. 3 points **14**	Which month is the shortest? 1 point **15**
What is different about Leap Year? 1 point **16**	What does B.C. mean? 1 point **17**	What is the speed of light? 2 points **18**	What travels in orbit between Mars and Jupiter? 2 points **19**	How many planets are in our solar system? 1 point **20**

Teachers: Directions on p. 17, answers on p. 26

Name the planets of the solar system in order. 3 points **21**	How many days does it take for the moon to revolve around the earth? 2 points **22**	Which planet has large rings? 1 point **23**	Who was the first man on the moon? 1 point **24**	What schoolteacher was killed in the explosion of space shuttle *Challenger?* 1 point **25**
What are the four basic types of clouds? 2 points **26**	What is another name for rain, snow, sleet and hail? 1 point **27**	How does water get into the air? 1 point **28**	What are the three layers of the earth? 3 points **29**	What does the Richter Scale measure? 1 point **30**
What are the three types of rocks? 3 points **31**	What are the three primary fossil fuels? 3 points **32**	What kind of energy does the decibel measure? 1 point **33**	What are the three main particles of an atom? 3 points **34**	What are the three states of matter? 3 points **35**
At what temperature Fahrenheit does water freeze? 1 point **36**	At what temperature Fahrenheit does water boil? 1 point **37**	At what temperature Centigrade does water freeze? 1 point **38**	At what temperature Centigrade does water boil? 1 point **39**	Which body system contains the bones? 1 point **40**

Teachers: Directions on p. 17, answers on p. 26

Which body system has to do with the blood? 1 point **41**	Which body system has to do with breathing? 1 point **42**	Which body system has to do with food and eating? 1 point **43**	Which body system contains the brain? 1 point **44**	Name the four oceans. 1 point **45**
What is the longest river in the world? 1 point **46**	Name the seven continents. 1 point **47**	What is the largest continent? 1 point **48**	What is the world's largest desert? 1 point **49**	What is the world's largest island? 1 point **50**
What is the world's highest mountain? 1 point **51**	What is North America's highest mountain? 1 point **52**	What is the major mountain range in South America? 1 point **53**	What is the capital of France? 1 point **54**	What is the capital of Italy? 1 point **55**
What is the capital of Japan? 1 point **56**	What is the capital of Russia? 1 point **57**	What is the capital of the United Kingdom? 1 point **58**	What is the capital of the United States? 1 point **59**	What were kings called in ancient Egypt? 1 point **60**

Teachers: Directions on p. 17, answers on p. 26

What Viking came to America before Columbus? 1 point **61**	Who celebrated the first Thanksgiving? 1 point **62**	Who invented the airplane? 1 point **63**	Who invented the practical incandescent light bulb? 1 point **64**	Who invented the telephone? 1 point **65**
What is the tallest building in the world? 1 point **66**	On what exact date was the Declaration of Independence signed? 1 point **67**	What are the first ten amendments to the Constitution called? 1 point **68**	Who delivered the Gettysburg Address? 1 point **69**	Who delivered the speech, "I Have a Dream"? 1 point **70**
What do the stars stand for in the United States flag? 1 point **71**	What are the two main political parties in the United States? 2 points **72**	What is the national anthem of the United States? 1 point **73**	What are the three branches of the United States government? 3 points **74**	What are the two branches of the United States legislature? 2 points **75**
What imaginary line circles the globe halfway between North & South Poles? 1 point **76**	What continents are in the western hemisphere? 1 point **77**	What is the emergency phone number? 1 point **78**	How many inches are in a foot? 1 point **79**	How many feet are in a yard? 1 point **80**

Teachers: Directions on p. 17, answers on p. 26

How many feet are in a mile? 1 point **81**	How many cups are in a quart? 1 point **82**	How many quarts are in a gallon? 1 point **83**	How many ounces are in a pound? 1 point **84**	How many pounds are in a ton? 1 point **85**
How many degrees are in a right angle? 1 point **86**	What is the largest state of the United States? 1 point **87**	What is the largest city in the United States? 1 point **88**	What is the smallest state in the United States? 1 point **89**	Who is the president of the United States? 1 point **90**
Who is the vice-president of the United States? 1 point **91**	What president said, "Ask not what your country can do for you. . ." 1 point **92**	What are the five types of animals (vertebrates)? 1 point **93**	What kind of writing did the ancient Egyptians use? 1 point **94**	What do the stripes stand for in the United States flag? 1 point **95**
What is the name of the 0° longitude line through Greenwich, England? 1 point **96**	What four countries are united in the United Kingdom? 4 points **97**	In what reference book would you look to find collections of maps? 1 point **98**	In what reference book would you find pronunciations of words? 1 point **99**	In what reference book would you find addresses of companies? 1 point **100**

Teachers: Directions on p. 17, answers on p. 26

The Facts Game

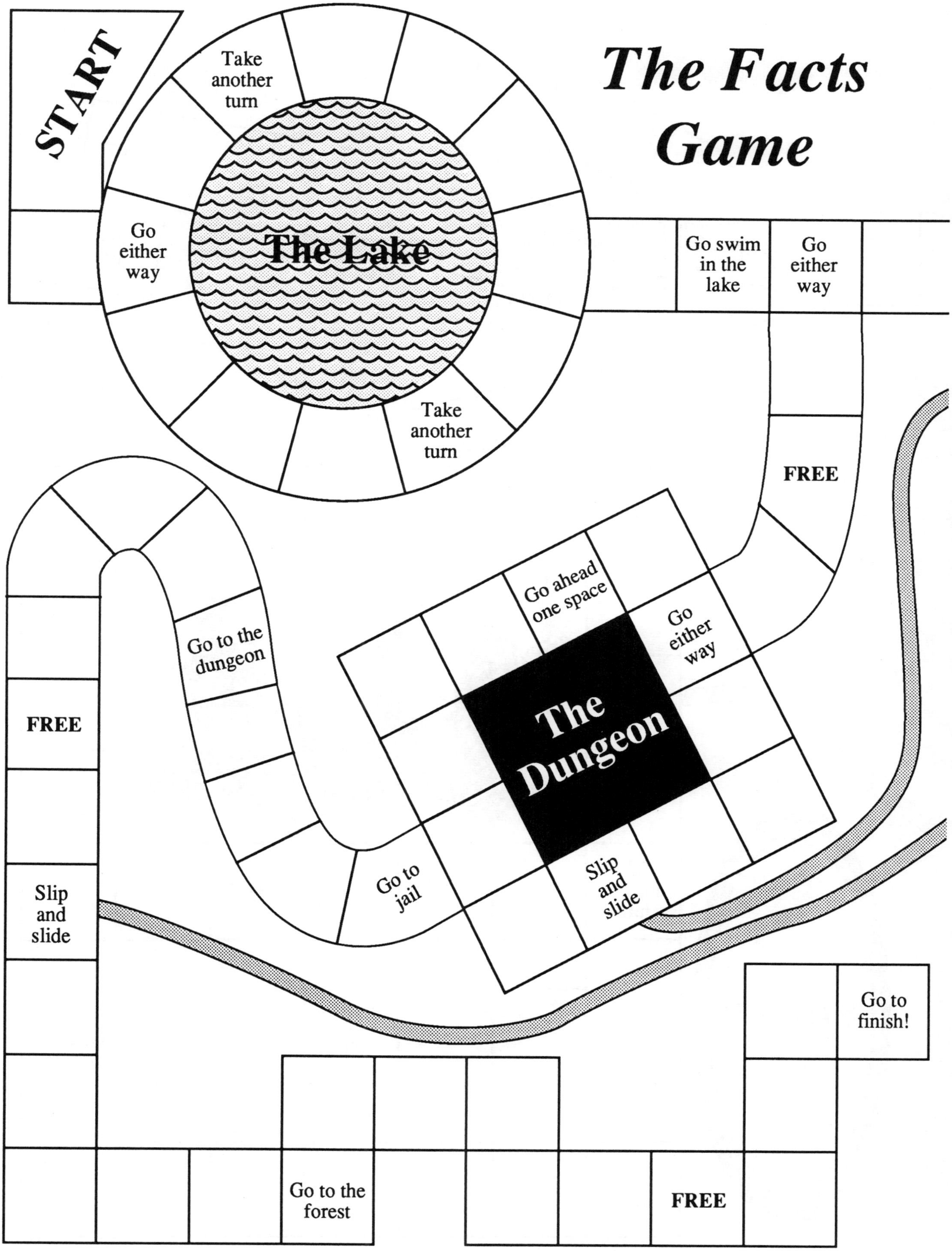

Teachers: Directions on p. 17 and 25

Directions for Playing the Facts Game

Number of Players:
Two or three. If more than two play, the third person can serve as a monitor and check the answers.

Materials:

Facts Plus almanac
Gameboard
One die
Facts cards
A marker for each player
Optional: Answer sheet

Getting Started:
Roll the die. The person with the highest number goes first.

How to Play:
First player picks a card and answers the question. If you are playing with a monitor, give her the number of the card so she can check that the answer is correct.

If the answer is correct, you will move forward either the number of points on the card or the number you roll on the die. Your choice.

If you don't know the answer, you have until your next turn to find the answer in *Facts Plus*. If you find it, take the turn you missed plus your new turn.

If you can't find the answer in time, stay where you are.

If you think you're right but your opponent thinks you're wrong, look up the answer in *Facts Plus*. Whoever was correct gets an extra turn.

If you don't even try to look it up, go back two spaces.

If you land on a FREE space, you don't need to pick a card on your next turn, just roll the die and move.

If you go to the lake, the dungeon, jail, or the forest, continue from there on your next turn. You can choose your way out using any of the spaces touching where you are.

If you land on SLIP AND SLIDE, slide along the path to the other end and continue from there.

Answers to Facts Game

(*Facts Plus* page numbers in parentheses)

1. 365¼ days (365 days acceptable), (2)
2. 60 seconds (2)
3. 60 minutes (2)
4. 24 hours (2)
5. 7 days (2)
6. 12 months (2)
7. 52 weeks (2)
8. 10 years (2)
9. 100 years (2)
10. Civil War (8)
11. 1492 (8)
12. November (10)
13. Sunday, Monday, Tuesday, Wednesday, Thursday, Friday, Saturday (11)
14. January, February, March, April, May, June, July, August, September, October, November, December (12)
15. February (12)
16. February has 29 days (12)
17. before Christ (13)
18. 186,282 miles per second (186,000 mps acceptable), (15)
19. asteroids (16)
20. nine (16)
21. Mercury, Venus, Earth, Mars, Jupiter, Saturn, Uranus, Neptune, Pluto (17)
22. 29½ days (29 days acceptable), (18)
23. Saturn (16)
24. Neil A. Armstrong (20)
25. Christa McAuliffe (20)
26. cirrus, stratus, cumulus, nimbus (22)
27. precipitation (23)
28. evaporation (23)
29. crust, mantle, core (27)
30. earthquakes (31)
31. igneous, sedimentary, metamorphic (32)
32. coal, oil, natural gas (32)
33. sound (34)
34. electron, proton, neutron (34)
35. solid, liquid, gas (35)
36. 32°F (35)
37. 212°F (35)
38. 0°C (35)
39. 100°C (35)
40. skeletal system (40)
41. circulatory system (41)
42. respiratory system (41)
43. digestive system (42)
44. nervous system (42)
45. Pacific, Atlantic, Indian, Arctic (48)
46. Nile (50)
47. North America, South America, Europe, Asia, Africa, Australia, Antarctica (51)
48. Asia (51)
49. Sahara Desert (51)
50. Greenland (51)
51. Mt. Everest (52)
52. Mt. McKinley (52)
53. Andes (52)
54. Paris (58)
55. Rome (60)
56. Tokyo (61)
57. Moscow (67)
58. London (69)
59. Washington, D.C. (69)
60. Pharaoh (72)
61. Leif Ericson (74)
62. Pilgrims/Indians (76)
63. Wright brothers (85)
64. Thomas Edison (86)
65. Alexander Graham Bell (87)
66. Sears Tower (90)
67. July 4, 1776 (112)
68. Bill of Rights (119)
69. Lincoln (125)
70. Martin Luther King, Jr., 125
71. States (126)
72. Democrat, Republican (127)
73. Star-Spangled Banner (126)
74. Legislative, Executive, Judicial (128-9)
75. Senate, House of Representatives (128)
76. equator (142)
77. North and South America (142)
78. 911 (157)
79. 12 inches (206)
80. 3 feet (206)
81. 5,280 feet (206)
82. 4 cups (206)
83. 4 quarts (206)
84. 16 ounces (206)
85. 2000 pounds (206)
86. 90° (208)
87. Alaska (101)
88. New York City (104)
89. Rhode Island (101)
90. Bill Clinton
91. Al Gore
92. John F. Kennedy (124)
93. mammals, birds, reptiles, amphibians, fish (37)
94. hieroglyphics (164)
95. original colonies (126)
96. Prime Meridian (142)
97. England, Scotland, Wales, Northern Ireland (70)
98. atlas (144)
99. dictionary (152)
100. telephone directory (157)

Teachers: Answers are to questions on p. 18-22

CALENDAR CAPERS

Time is one fundamental way to organize information, and calendars are one of the most-used reference tools. Most adults use Day-Timers, Weekly-Minders, or other types of calendars to keep track of plans and appointments. Teachers have plan books, another type of calendar.

The activities in this section are to help students become comfortable with using calendars as a reference tool.

I recommend that teachers at every level check to see if students have memorized the days of the week and the months of the year. There are many 6th graders who don't know these.

Assignment Board

Materials:

36" x 36" sheets of butcher paper marked as shown on Activity Book p. 28

Optional: Individual copies of assignment sheets, Activity Book p. 28

Suggested procedure:

1. Post the large assignment sheets on a permanent bulletin board.
2. Record assignments on the day they are made. Put an X on the date due and a line with an arrow from the assignment date to the date due.
3. Each week, staple a new assignment sheet over the last one, leaving the bottom unstapled so that students who were absent on Friday can check what was assigned or due then.
4. At your option, students may be given their own assignment sheets, completed in advance by you or to be filled in by students as assignments are made.

Make Your Own Calendar

Materials:

1 copy of Activity book p. 29 per child

12 copies of Activity Book p. 30 per child

12 sheets of 12" x 18" construction paper

Suggested procedure:

Follow directions on p. 29 of Activity Book.

Perpetual Calendar Worksheet

Materials:

Facts Plus perpetual calendar, p. 4-5

Copies of Activity Book, p. 31

Answers on p. 32

Background information:

There are 14 possible calendars, 7 for regular years and 7 for leap years, one beginning on each day of the week. A perpetual calendar has all possible calendars, with a chart to show which is used for each year.

Suggested procedure:

1. Have all students use the perpetual calendar to figure out on which day of the week they were born. Challenge them to go home and figure out on which day their parents and family members were born.
2. Do the first worksheet question together.
3. Have students use the index to look up the dates needed to answer the first part of all the questions.
4. Then students refer to the perpetual calendar to find the day of the week on which each event happened.

Holidays of the Future

Have students use p. 8-10 of *Facts Plus* to figure out the holidays for 1996 and 1997. Circle them on the calendars on Activity Book p. 33. *Legal* holidays should be the ones circled if there is a choice.

About My Birthday

Materials:
Activity Book p. 34
Facts Plus pages shown below

Page numbers for answers:
Perpetual calendar, p. 4-5
Heavenly body, p. 11
Diameter/speed, p. 16 or 17
Roman/Norse god, p. 11
Other questions on day, p. 4-5
Months, p. 12-13
Holidays, p. 8-10 and 4-5
Date, consult *The World Book Encyclopedia* under the name of the month
Year, check the library
Notable People, p. 78-83
Inventors, p. 84-87

ASSIGNMENTS

Week of:	MONDAY	TUESDAY	WEDNESDAY	THURSDAY	FRIDAY
READING					
LANGUAGE					
MATH					
SOCIAL STUDIES					
SCIENCE-HEALTH					

Teachers: Directions p. 27

Make Your Own Calendar

Each student needs: 12 copies of the blank calendar on p. 30, one copy of this sheet, scissors, yarn or comb binding
12 pieces of 12"x18" construction paper (choose colors to go with holidays of the month)

Punch holes and tie together with yarn or comb bind.

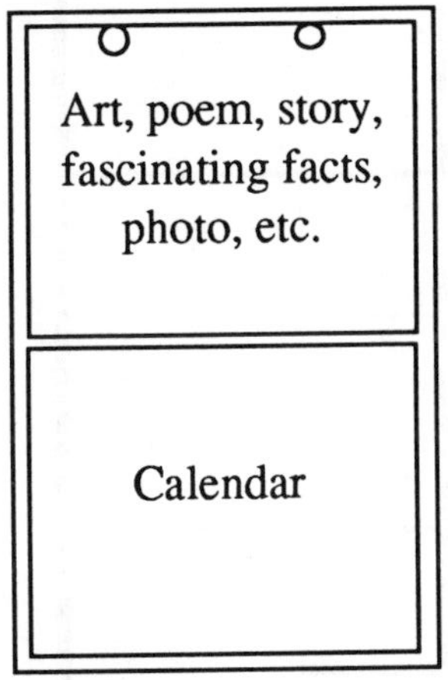

Directions for making the calendar:

1. Cut and glue the name of each month on top of a calendar page.
2. Write in the numbers of dates for the year. See *Facts Plus* p. 4-5.
3. Cut and glue in symbols for holidays. Write in names of holidays which have no symbols and illustrate if you like.
4. Write in family birthdays, vacations, special days.
5. Write in events from the school calendar.
6. Write in eclipses.
7. Illustrate the top part of the calendar with art, stories, poems, fascinating facts, photographs, or whatever looks good.

Using the calendar:

1. Consider giving the calendar to someone for Christmas.
2. Use it to note something you did each day.
3. Give yourself a star for each day you did homework or met some other goal.

JANUARY	**FEBRUARY**	**MARCH**
APRIL	**MAY**	**JUNE**
JULY	**AUGUST**	**SEPTEMBER**
OCTOBER	**NOVEMBER**	**DECEMBER**

Sunday	Monday	Tuesday	Wednesday	Thursday	Friday	Saturday

Name______________________________ Date_______________________

USING THE PERPETUAL CALENDAR

Directions: Use the index and the perpetual calendar on pages 4-5 of *Facts Plus: An Almanac of Essential Information* to answer these questions.

1. On what day of the week was the Declaration of Independence signed?
   Date _____________________ Day of week___________________
2. On what day of the week was the U.S. Constitution signed?
   Date _____________________ Day of week___________________
3. On what day of the week was the flag adopted?
   Date _____________________ Day of week___________________
4. On what day of the week was the great Alaska earthquake?
   Date _____________________ Day of week___________________
5. On what day of the week was Pearl Harbor bombed?
   Date _____________________ Day of week___________________
6. On what day of the week did Hawaii enter the Union?
   Date _____________________ Day of week___________________
7. On what day of the week did Lincoln deliver the Gettysburg Address?
   Date _____________________ Day of week___________________
8. On what day of the week was Yellowstone National Park established?
   Date _____________________ Day of week___________________
9. On what day of the week did the Space Shuttle *Challenger* explode?
   Date _____________________ Day of week___________________
10. On what day of the week did President John F. Kennedy die?
    Date _____________________ Day of week___________________
11. On what day of the week did Mount St. Helens explode?
    Date _____________________ Day of week___________________
12. What day of the week will begin the next century (the year 2000)?
    Date _____________________ Day of week___________________
13. On what day of the week was the Bill of Rights ratified?
    Date _____________________ Day of week___________________
14. On what day of the week did the space age begin?
    Date _____________________ Day of week___________________
15. On what day of the week was President Theodore Roosevelt born?
    Date _____________________ Day of week___________________

Teachers: Lesson plan on p. 27, answers on p. 32

Name **KEY** ______________________ Date ______________________

USING THE PERPETUAL CALENDAR

Directions: Use the index and the perpetual calendar on pages 4-5 of *Facts Plus: An Almanac of Essential Information* to answer these questions.

1. On what day of the week was the Declaration of Independence signed?
   Date.......*July 4, 1776 (p. 112)* Day of week...................*Thursday*
2. On what day of the week was the United States Constitution signed?
   Date....... *Sept. 17, 1787 (114)* Day of week.....................*Monday*
3. On what day of the week was the United States flag adopted?
   Date........*June 14, 1777 (126)* Day of week....................*Saturday*
4. On what day of the week was the great Alaska earthquake?
   Date.......*March 27, 1964 (31)* Day of week.......................*Friday*
5. On what day of the week was Pearl Harbor bombed?
   Date... *December 7, 1941 (77)* Day of week......................*Sunday*
6. On what day of the week did Hawaii enter the Union?
   Date......*August 21, 1959 (95)* Day of week.......................*Friday*
7. On what day of the week did Lincoln deliver the Gettysburg Address?
   Date.......*Nov. 19, 1863 (125)* Day of week..................*Thursday*
8. On what day of the week was Yellowstone National Park established?
   Date.......*March 1, 1872 (106)* Day of week......................*Friday*
9. On what day of the week did the Space Shuttle *Challenger* explode?
   Date.....*January 28, 1986 (20)* Day of week.................... *Tuesday*
10. On what day of the week did President John F. Kennedy die?
    Date.......*Nov. 22, 1963 (130)* Day of week.......................*Friday*
11. On what day of the week did Mount St. Helens explode?
    Date..........*May 18, 1980 (30)* Day of week......................*Sunday*
12. What day of the week will begin the next century (the year 2000)?
    Date.............*January 1, 2000* Day of week....................*Saturday*
13. On what day of the week was the Bill of Rights ratified?
    Date........*Dec. 15, 1791 (119)* Day of week...................*Thursday*
14. On what day of the week did the space age begin?
    Date...........*Oct. 4, 1957 (20)* Day of week.......................*Friday*
15. On what day of the week was President Theodore Roosevelt born?
    Date........ *Oct. 27, 1858 (130)* Day of week............... *Wednesday*

Teachers: Lesson plan on p. 27, copy master on p. 31

1996

January

S	M	T	W	T	F	S
	1	2	3	4	5	6
7	8	9	10	11	12	13
14	15	16	17	18	19	20
21	22	23	24	25	26	27
28	29	30	31			

February

S	M	T	W	T	F	S
				1	2	3
4	5	6	7	8	9	10
11	12	13	14	15	16	17
18	19	20	21	22	23	24
25	26	27	28	29		

March

S	M	T	W	T	F	S
					1	2
3	4	5	6	7	8	9
10	11	12	13	14	15	16
17	18	19	20	21	22	23
24	25	26	27	28	29	30
31						

April

S	M	T	W	T	F	S
	1	2	3	4	5	6
7	8	9	10	11	12	13
14	15	16	17	18	19	20
21	22	23	24	25	26	27
28	29	30				

May

S	M	T	W	T	F	S
			1	2	3	4
5	6	7	8	9	10	11
12	13	14	15	16	17	18
19	20	21	22	23	24	25
26	27	28	29	30	31	

June

S	M	T	W	T	F	S
						1
2	3	4	5	6	7	8
9	10	11	12	13	14	15
16	17	18	19	20	21	22
23	24	25	26	27	28	29
30						

July

S	M	T	W	T	F	S
	1	2	3	4	5	6
7	8	9	10	11	12	13
14	15	16	17	18	19	20
21	22	23	24	25	26	27
28	29	30	31			

August

S	M	T	W	T	F	S
				1	2	3
4	5	6	7	8	9	10
11	12	13	14	15	16	17
18	19	20	21	22	23	24
25	26	27	28	29	30	31

September

S	M	T	W	T	F	S
1	2	3	4	5	6	7
8	9	10	11	12	13	14
15	16	17	18	19	20	21
22	23	24	25	26	27	28
29	30					

October

S	M	T	W	T	F	S
		1	2	3	4	5
6	7	8	9	10	11	12
13	14	15	16	17	18	19
20	21	22	23	24	25	26
27	28	29	30	31		

November

S	M	T	W	T	F	S
					1	2
3	4	5	6	7	8	9
10	11	12	13	14	15	16
17	18	19	20	21	22	23
24	25	26	27	28	29	30

December

S	M	T	W	T	F	S
1	2	3	4	5	6	7
8	9	10	11	12	13	14
15	16	17	18	19	20	21
22	23	24	25	26	27	28
29	30	31				

1997

January

S	M	T	W	T	F	S
			1	2	3	4
5	6	7	8	9	10	11
12	13	14	15	16	17	18
19	20	21	22	23	24	25
26	27	28	29	30	31	

February

S	M	T	W	T	F	S
						1
2	3	4	5	6	7	8
9	10	11	12	13	14	15
16	17	18	19	20	21	22
23	24	25	26	27	28	

March

S	M	T	W	T	F	S
						1
2	3	4	5	6	7	8
9	10	11	12	13	14	15
16	17	18	19	20	21	22
23	24	25	26	27	28	29
30	31					

April

S	M	T	W	T	F	S
		1	2	3	4	5
6	7	8	9	10	11	12
13	14	15	16	17	18	19
20	21	22	23	24	25	26
27	28	29	30			

May

S	M	T	W	T	F	S
				1	2	3
4	5	6	7	8	9	10
11	12	13	14	15	16	17
18	19	20	21	22	23	24
25	26	27	28	29	30	31

June

S	M	T	W	T	F	S
1	2	3	4	5	6	7
8	9	10	11	12	13	14
15	16	17	18	19	20	21
22	23	24	25	26	27	28
29	30					

July

S	M	T	W	T	F	S
		1	2	3	4	5
6	7	8	9	10	11	12
13	14	15	16	17	18	19
20	21	22	23	24	25	26
27	28	29	30	31		

August

S	M	T	W	T	F	S
					1	2
3	4	5	6	7	8	9
10	11	12	13	14	15	16
17	18	19	20	21	22	23
24	25	26	27	28	29	30
31						

September

S	M	T	W	T	F	S
	1	2	3	4	5	6
7	8	9	10	11	12	13
14	15	16	17	18	19	20
21	22	23	24	25	26	27
28	29	30				

October

S	M	T	W	T	F	S
			1	2	3	4
5	6	7	8	9	10	11
12	13	14	15	16	17	18
19	20	21	22	23	24	25
26	27	28	29	30	31	

November

S	M	T	W	T	F	S
						1
2	3	4	5	6	7	8
9	10	11	12	13	14	15
16	17	18	19	20	21	22
23	24	25	26	27	28	29
30						

December

S	M	T	W	T	F	S
	1	2	3	4	5	6
7	8	9	10	11	12	13
14	15	16	17	18	19	20
21	22	23	24	25	26	27
28	29	30	31			

Teachers: Lesson plan on p. 27 - Holidays of the Future

ABOUT MY BIRTHDAY

Name________________________

DAY

Use the perpetual calendar to find the day on which you were born and fill it in above.

What heavenly body is your day named after?

____

Find more information on that heavenly body.
Diameter______________
Speed________________

What Roman and/or Norse god is your day named after?

____

On what day of the week will your next birthday be?

____

On what day of the week will your 50th birthday be?

____

On what day of the week will your birthday be in 2000 A.D.?

____

How old will you be in the year 2000 A.D.? __________

MONTH

Birthstone ______________

Flower________________

Meaning of the month's name.

Number of days in the month.

Are there any holidays which fall on your birthday between now and 2000 A.D.?

DATE

What important events happened on this date in history?*

Were any famous people born on this date?*

Did any famous people die on this date?*

*Not in *Facts Plus*. Check *The World Book Encyclopedia*.

YEAR

What important events happened the year you were born?*

Look through the sections on Notable People and Inventors in *Facts Plus*. Are there any famous people with your first or last name?

*Not in *Facts Plus*. Check the library.

Teachers: Directions on p. 28

ON THIS DAY IN HISTORY

On the following pages are questions for each day of the year relating to an event that happened on that day in history. Answers to all questions may be found in *Facts Plus: An Almanac of Essential Information,* 1992 edition. Italicized questions at the end of each month may require comparison, calculation, or thinking beyond that needed for the basic questions. An answer key is provided. Some answers may vary if reference sources other than the 1992 edition of *Facts Plus* are used.

Preparing Materials for Use

Reproduce Activity Book pages needed from p. 37-84. Cut on the dotted lines. For repeated use, mount on a 3x5 index cards and laminate. Possibly color-code by month.

The Calendar Game

Materials:

Question cards for one month from p. 37-84. Groups can play with different months. Answers on p. 85-88 of Activity Book

A page from a calendar for the month corresponding to the questions. Use an old calendar or Activity Book p. 30.

A duplicated answer sheet for each student or team of students, Activity Book p. 36.

A copy of *Facts Plus* for each student or team.

How to Play:

Two or more students can play at a time. If four or more students play, divide into two or three cooperative teams.

This game is similar to BINGO. The object is to be the first to fill in 4 spaces in a row, vertically, horizontally, or diagonally.

Place the calendar page in the center of the playing area, with the question cards face down near it. Each player takes one card, keeping it face down. At the same time, everyone reads their question and searches for its answer in *Facts Plus*. When the answer is found, the player writes it next to the correct date on his answer sheet and puts his mark or initial on the appropriate square on the calendar page. He then draws another card and continues.

If a player or team cannot find the answer to a question after searching, he may "give up." In this case, the opposing team is entitled to erase any one of his marks earned so far.

If a player draws a card printed in *italics,* he may find or figure the answer and place his mark in the square for the date shown *or* in any undated square on the calendar (before the first or after the last day of the month). Or, he may choose to pass and draw another card.

To Win:

A player with four marks in a row calls for his/her answers to be checked. If all are correct, he wins. If not, the game continues.

General Suggestions

1. Have students find the answer to the question of the day for extra credit points or some other classroom reward.
2. Use selected events of the day to stimulate student interest. Encourage students to find "the rest of the story" in the library. Recommend literature.
3. While planning, read through the events of the month and consider tying units of study, read-alouds, recommended literature or special activities to something which happened in history that month.
4. Substitute teachers may use *Facts Plus* and the question of the day to provide a special challenge or introduce an interesting mini-lesson in history.

Answer Sheet

Name ______________________________

Month ______________________________

1. ______________________________
2. ______________________________
3. ______________________________
4. ______________________________
5. ______________________________
6. ______________________________
7. ______________________________
8. ______________________________
9. ______________________________
10. ______________________________
11. ______________________________
12. ______________________________
13. ______________________________
14. ______________________________
15. ______________________________
16. ______________________________
17. ______________________________
18. ______________________________
19. ______________________________
20. ______________________________
21. ______________________________
22. ______________________________
23. ______________________________
24. ______________________________
25. ______________________________
26. ______________________________
27. ______________________________
28. ______________________________
29. ______________________________
30. ______________________________
31. ______________________________

Record answers to questions in italics below:

___ ______________________________

___ ______________________________

___ ______________________________

___ ______________________________

___ ______________________________

___ ______________________________

Teachers: Directions on p. 35, answers on p. 85-88

Answer Sheet

Name ______________________________

Month ______________________________

1. ______________________________
2. ______________________________
3. ______________________________
4. ______________________________
5. ______________________________
6. ______________________________
7. ______________________________
8. ______________________________
9. ______________________________
10. ______________________________
11. ______________________________
12. ______________________________
13. ______________________________
14. ______________________________
15. ______________________________
16. ______________________________
17. ______________________________
18. ______________________________
19. ______________________________
20. ______________________________
21. ______________________________
22. ______________________________
23. ______________________________
24. ______________________________
25. ______________________________
26. ______________________________
27. ______________________________
28. ______________________________
29. ______________________________
30. ______________________________
31. ______________________________

Record answers to questions in italics below:

___ ______________________________

___ ______________________________

___ ______________________________

___ ______________________________

___ ______________________________

___ ______________________________

January 1

What Roman emperor made January the first month of the year?

January 2

On this day in 1870, construction began on the Brooklyn Bridge. In what year did the Brooklyn Bridge open?

January 3

On this day, Alaska became the 49th state. What was the year?

January 4

On this day in 1958, Sputnik I, the first earth-orbiting satellite, reentered the earth's atmosphere. When had it been launched?

January 5

On this day in 1925, Mrs. Nellie Taylor Ross of Wyoming was sworn in as America's first woman governor. Who is the governor of Wyoming now?

January 6

On this day in 1838, the telegraph was first demonstrated. What code was used to transmit telegraph messages?

January 7

On this day in 1610, Galileo discovered the four largest moons of Jupiter. What is the name of Jupiter's largest moon?

January 8

On this day in 1923, it was 90°F in Los Angeles, California. About how many degrees is that on the Celsius scale?

January 9

On this day in 1861, Mississippi became the second state to secede (withdraw) from the United States and join the Confederate States of America. How many states seceded altogether?

January 10

William Frederick Cody died on this day in 1917. What is the name he was usually called?

January 11

On this day in 1964, the Surgeon General of the United States named cigarettes a "health hazard." What drug is in cigarettes?

January 12

On this day in 1839, anthracite coal was first used to smelt iron. "Smelting" is melting it to separate the impurities. What is the melting point of iron?

January 13

On this day in 1733, Georgia was established as the last of the original 13 American colonies to be settled. Name the first.

January 14

On this day in 1914, Henry Ford introduced an "assembly line" which could produce one Model T Ford every 90 minutes. In what year was Henry Ford born?

January 15

On this day in 1870, Thomas Nast used the donkey as a symbol in a famous political cartoon. What does it symbolize?

January 16

The 18th Amendment of the Constitution was ratified on this day, making alcoholic beverages illegal and beginning the era of "Prohibition." What was the year?

January 17

U.S. President Rutherford B. Hayes died on this day in 1893. Where had he been born?

January 18

On this day in 1966, Indira Gandhi became the prime minister of India. In what year was she assassinated?

January 19

Antarctica was first sighted by Lt. Charles Wilkes on this day in 1840. What is the area of Antarctica?

January 20

On this day in 1892, the first officially recognized basketball game was played in Springfield, Massachusetts. Who invented basketball?

January 21

V. I. Lenin, the leader of the 1917 Communist Revolution in Russia, died on this day. Lenin's Tomb in Moscow was one of the Soviet Union's most honored monuments during the Communist era. In what year did he die?

January 22

Lyndon Baines Johnson died on this day in 1973. What assassinated president had he replaced?

January 23

Pluto crossed inside the orbit of Neptune on this day in 1979. In what year will it cross back outside to become the most distant planet from the sun?

January 24

On this day in 1908, the first Boy Scout troup was organized. Who founded (started) the Boy Scouts?

January 25

On this day in 1890, Nellie Bly completed the fastest trip ever taken around the world. It took her 72 days, 6 hours and 11 minutes. What was her occupation (job)?

January 26

David R. Atchison died on this day in 1866. He was president of the United States for just one day, March 4, 1849, before the elected president was sworn in. Who was the next president?

January 27

A deadly fire broke out on an Apollo spacecraft on this day in 1967. How many people died in that fire?

January 28

The space shuttle *Challenger* exploded 73 seconds after takeoff on this day in 1986. What American schoolteacher died in that accident?

January 29

A patent was issued on this day for the "motorwagen," an automobile with a gasoline engine invented in 1885. In what country was it invented?

January 30

The first attempt to assassinate a United States president occurred on this day in 1835. Who was the president at that time?

January 31

A. A. Milne died on this day in 1956. What famous storybook character did he create?

January 20

This has been Inauguration Day for Presidents since 1937. In the oath of office taken on that day, what does a president promise to preserve, protect and defend?

January 23

In 1849, Elizabeth Blackwell graduated from college and became the first woman in her profession in United States history. What was her profession?

January 5

George Washington Carver died on this day in 1943. He is famous for finding more than 100 uses for the peanut. How old was he when he died?

January 22

The temperature went from 4° to 45° F. in just two minutes in Spearfish, South Dakota on this day in 1943. About how hot would it have been in five minutes if it had kept warming at this rate?

January 24

Photos from Voyager 2 showed 10 previously unknown moons of Uranus on this day in 1986. How many known moons are in the entire solar system?

February 1

On this day in 1792, the U.S. Supreme Court met for the first time. How many justices are on the Supreme Court?

February 2

Today is Ground Hog Day. According to folklore, is it better for today to be sunny or cloudy if you're anxious for summer to come?

February 3

What kind of tax was established on this day in 1913 by the 16th Amendment to the Constitution?

February 4

The Confederate States of America was organized on this day in 1861. Which war did this lead to?

February 5

This is Hank Aaron's birthday. In what year was he born?

February 6

In 1964 on this day, Britain and France announced that they would build a railroad tunnel under the English Channel. How long will the tunnel be?

February 7

Charles Dickens, author of *A Christmas Carol,* was born on this day in 1812. In which country was he born?

February 8

On this day in 1974, three *Skylab* astronauts returned to earth after 84 days in space. On what date was *Skylab* launched?

February 9

In 1825 on this day, John Quincy Adams was elected president by the House of Representatives. Why was his father famous?

February 10

In 1846 on this day, the Mormons began their westward migration to Utah. This was two years after the death of the founder of the church, Joseph Smith. Who led the migration?

February 11

Thomas A. Edison was born in 1849 on this day. What are two things he invented besides the incandescent light bulb?

February 12

Abraham Lincoln was born on this day in 1809. In what year did the U.S. begin observing his birthday as a holiday?

February 13

Jesse James robbed his first bank on this day in 1866. In what year was he born?

February 14

Today is Valentine's Day. Use the perpetual calendar to see on what day of the week Valentine's Day will be in the year 2000.

February 15

Susan B. Anthony was born on this day in 1820. What is on the *other* side of the Susan B. Anthony dollar?

February 16

King Tutankhamen's tomb was opened on this day in 1923. Where had he been king during his lifetime?

February 17

The first ship passed through the Suez Canal on this date. In what year did the canal open?

February 18

The planet Pluto was discovered on this day in 1930. What is Pluto's average distance from the sun?

February 19

Charles Blondin died on this day in 1897. He was the first person to walk across Niagara Falls on a tightrope. What is the height of Niagara Falls?

February 20

On this date in 1943, a volcano was born in a Mexican cornfield. What is the name of the volcano?

February 21

On this date in 1878, the first telephone directory was published. What are the three colors of pages in modern phone books?

February 22

George Washington was born on this day in 1732. When is the legal holiday celebrated?

February 23

On this day in 1886, Charles M. Hall discovered the process for manufacturing something that is quite common today. What is it?

February 24

On this day in 1582, Pope Gregory XIII corrected the Julian calendar. What was the new calendar called?

February 25

On this day in 1868, the United States president was impeached (charged with a crime). Who was the president?

February 26

How many national parks were established on this day?

February 27

The 22nd Amendment to the Constitution was ratified on this day in 1951. It said that no one could be elected president more than how many times?

February 28

On this day in 1849, the first hopeful gold seekers arrived, beginning a gold rush in what state?

February 29

This is Leap Year Day. How often do we have Leap Years?

February 13

How old was Jesse James when he robbed his first bank in 1866?

February 2

Ben Hogan, famous golf pro, was in a terrible auto accident on this day in 1949. How old was he?

February 22

In 1639 on this day, the Indians introduced the Pilgrims to popcorn. How long had the Pilgrims been in America by then?

February 1

Alexander Selkirk was rescued on this day in 1709. His story is the basis for Robinson Crusoe. Who wrote Robinson Crusoe?

February 2

Dogsled teams reached Nome, Alaska from Anchorage on this day in 1925 with serum for the diptheria epidemic. How many years ago was that?

February 6

The game of Monopoly was invented on this day in 1935. How many years ago was that?

February 16

In 1918 on this day, Lithuania declared its independence. It was later occupied by the Soviet Union. Name the other two "Baltic States."

Teachers: Directions on p. 35, answers on p. 85

March 1

Yellowstone National Park was established on this day as the very first national park. This began a worldwide national park movement. What was the year?

March 2

This day in 1933 brought one of the largest earthquakes ever recorded—8.9 on the Richter Scale. What country was it near?

March 3

The Star-Spangled Banner became the national anthem of the United States on this day in 1931. During which war was it written?

March 4

On this day in 1933, President Franklin D. Roosevelt said, "The only thing we have to fear is ______________." What is the rest of the quote?

March 5

In 1770 on this day there was a major event leading to the American Revolutionary War. Five people were killed. What was the event?

March 6

On this day in 1947, Dick Pope, Jr. became the first person to water ski barefoot. In what year were water skis invented?

March 7

Alexander Graham Bell patented the telephone on this day. What was the year?

March 8

Two presidents died on this day. Who were they?

March 9

An Italian navigator named Amerigo Vespucci was born on this day in 1454. What was named after him?

March 10

The first paper money in the U.S. was issued on this day in 1862. Before then, people used gold and silver coins. What is the largest bill still produced in the U.S.?

March 11

On this day in 1985, Mikhail Gorbachev was named the leader of what country?

March 12

On this day in 1912, the first Girl Scout troop was formed in Savannah, Georgia. Who was the founder of the Girl Scouts?

March 13

On this day in 1781, Sir William Herschel discovered the seventh planet from the sun. What is it?

March 14

In 1681 on this day, William Penn was granted land which later became a state. What is the area of that state?

March 15

Columbus returned to Spain after his first voyage to the New World on this day in 1493. He brought the first tobacco Europeans had ever seen. Is tobacco a stimulant or a depressant?

March 16

The greatest 24-hour rainfall on earth ended on this day in 1952. How much rain fell?

March 17

This is Saint Patrick's Day. What is the capital of the country which especially honors Saint Patrick?

March 18

In 1965, a Russian cosmonaut took the first space walk. What was his name?

March 19

In 721 B.C. on this day, Ptolemy was the first to record a lunar eclipse. What causes the moon to darken during a lunar eclipse?

March 20

Today is the vernal equinox, which means that spring begins. The sun shines directly over the ____________ on this day.

March 21

Henry Morton Stanley started searching for David Livingstone on this day in 1871. What important African river did Stanley later explore?

March 22

The Grand Coulee Dam began producing electricity on this day in 1941. What is the height of the dam?

March 23

On this day in 1775, Patrick Henry said, "As for me, give me liberty or give me death." What did he want the American colonies to do?

March 24

In 1788 on this day, voters in Rhode Island rejected the U.S. Constitution. Why didn't Rhode Island want the Constitution?

March 25

In 1655 on this day, Christiaan Huygens discovered the largest moon in the solar system. Around which planet does it revolve?

March 26

The Salk vaccine was announced on this day in 1953. What disease does it prevent?

March 27

The Alaska earthquake occured on this day in 1964. How many people were killed?

March 28

In 1984 on this day, there were 36 tornadoes in North and South Carolina. How fast can winds blow in a tornado?

March 29

On this day in 1973, the last U.S. troups left Vietnam. In what year did the war in Vietnam finally end?

March 30

In 1867 on this day, the U.S. purchased Alaska from Russia for $7.2 million. What does the word "Alaska" mean?

March 31

In 1918 on this day, Daylight Saving Time first went into operation. In what year was Daylight Saving proclaimed for the whole country?

March 2

The first school for educating the blind was founded in New England on this day in 1829. How many years earlier had a system been invented by which blind people can read by touch?

March 3

Factory workers under the age of 12 were restricted to a 10-hour workday in Massachusetts on this day in 1842. How many hours a week was that if they had the weekend off?

March 15

Julius Caesar was assassinated on this day in 44 B.C. Who was the queen of Egypt at that time?

March 14

Eli Whitney patented his most famous invention on this day. What year was it?

March 25

The British Parliament abolished the slave trade on this day in 1807. How many years later was slavery legally abolished in the United States?

April 1

Bubonic plague hit London on this day in 1665. How many people died each day in Rome when the plague hit there in 262 A.D.?

April 2

Florida was discovered and named on this day in 1513 by Juan Ponce de Leon. What does the name "Florida" mean?

April 3

The first pony express run began on this day in 1860, carrying mail from St. Joseph, Missouri to Sacramento, California. How fast can a horse run?

April 4

In 1818 on this day, Congress decided to have a flag with only 13 stripes and a star for each state. Before then, there was a stripe for each state. What do the stripes stand for now?

April 5

In 1887, Anne Sullivan taught Helen Keller the meaning of the following word using the manual alphabet. What is the word?

April 6

Admiral Robert E. Peary and Matthew Henson became the first known explorers to reach the North Pole on this day in 1909. What is the latitude of the North Pole?

April 7

The first successful demonstration of television took place on this day in 1927. Who are two of the inventors given credit for making TV possible?

April 8

The moon Io was found to have active volcanoes in 1979. Around which planet does it revolve?

April 9

Robert E. Lee surrendered to Ulysses S. Grant at 1:30 p.m. on this day, ending the Civil War. What was the year?

April 10

The first Arbor Day was held on April 10, 1872 in Nebraska. A million trees were planted. How old is the oldest living tree?

April 11

Jackie Robinson became the first black man to play in a major game in his sport on April 11, 1947. What was his sport?

April 12

A man first orbited the earth on this day in 1961. What was his name?

April 13

On this day in 1987, the world population was reported to have reached 5 billion. In what year is the population expected to reach 6 billion?

April 14

President Abraham Lincoln was assassinated on this day in 1865. Who shot him?

April 15

Income taxes are due on this day. When was the constitutional amendment ratified which allowed Congress to collect income tax?

April 16

Today is Wilbur Wright's birthday. He was born in 1867. What was his brother's name?

April 17

Canada gained complete independence from Britain in 1982. What is the name of Canada's tallest mountain?

April 18

The term "Third World" was first used on this day in 1955. About how many countries are now considered part of the "Third World."

April 19

The American Revolution began on this day in Lexington, Massachusetts in 1775. Who made the famous ride announcing, "The British are coming!"?

April 20

Marie and Pierre Curie isolated the radioactive element of radium on this day in 1902. What is the atomic number of radium?

April 21

Benjamin Franklin's funeral was held on this day in 1790. 20,000 people attended. His picture is on a U.S. bill today. Which bill?

April 22

The first Earth Day took place on this day in 1970. What is one endangered large animal?

April 23

The first public showing of a motion picture took place in New York City on this day in 1896. Who invented motion pictures?

April 24

The Library of Congress was established on April 24, 1800. About how many items are in that library now?

April 25

Forty-six countries gathered in San Francisco to organize the United Nations on this day in 1945. How many countries are in the U.N. now?

April 26

John Wilkes Booth was shot by federal troops in Bowling Green, Virginia on this day in 1865. For what crime was he wanted?

April 27

Ferdinand Magellan was killed on this day in the Philippines in the year 1521. In what year did his ship finish its trip around the globe?

April 28

Maryland became the 7th state on this date. What was the year?

April 29

Emperor Hirohito was born on this day in 1901. What country did he rule?

April 30

The Louisiana Territory was purchased from France on this day in 1803. How many square miles were added to the U.S. by this purchase?

April 30

How many more square miles were in the original Louisiana Purchase than in the state of Louisiana today?

April 10

The United States patent system was established on this day in 1790. Why do inventors get patents?

April 15

The Titanic sank on this day in 1912. Who was the president of the United States at that time?

April 30

TV was broadcast to the public for the first time from the Empire State Building on this day in 1939. How many years ago was that?

April 6

On this day in 1896, the first modern Olympic games were formally opened in the capital of Greece. What is the name of that city?

April 12

The fastest winds not in a tornado were recorded on this day in 1934. How fast did they blow?

May 1

The Empire State Building was dedicated on May 1, 1931. It was the world's tallest building until 1972. How many buildings are taller than the Empire State Building today?

May 2

Lou Gehrig missed his first game after 2,130 consecutive starts in 1939. What kind of game did he miss?

May 3

Margaret Thatcher became the first female prime minister of a major European nation in 1979. What is her nationality?

May 4

The dictator of Yugoslavia died on this day in 1980. What was his name?

May 5

The Cinco de Mayo is celebrated in Mexico, to remember the defeat of French invaders at Puebla. What is the population of Mexico?

May 6

Josef Stalin became the leader of the Soviet government in 1941. What kind of a leader was he?

May 7

Germany surrendered, ending World War II in Europe. What was the year?

May 8

Hernando de Soto discovered the Mississippi River on this day in 1541. How long is the Mississippi?

May 9

Mother's Day was proclaimed a public holiday on this day in 1914. When was it first observed?

May 10

The first railroad connecting the east and west coast of North America was completed on this day in 1869. A golden spike was driven in Utah. In what year did a railroad first carry passengers?

May 11

The country of Siam changed its name on this day in 1949. What was its new name?

May 12

A man named Samuel Wilson was named as the original "Uncle Sam" by a New York paper in 1830. During which war was the name "Uncle Sam" first used?

May 13

A farmer was killed by hail on this day in 1930. How much did the largest hailstone on record weigh?

May 14

On this day in 1796, Edward Jenner gave the first vaccination against a disease which had killed hundreds of millions of people. The disease was completely eliminated by 1978. What was the disease?

May 15

The first regular airmail service began in the U.S. on this day in 1918. How much does it cost to send a postcard airmail to Canada?

May 16

On this day in 1969, the Soviet spacecraft *Venus 5* landed on Venus. What was the temperature there?

May 17

John Cabell Breckinridge died on this day in 1875. He was vice-president under the 15th president. When did his term begin and end?

May 18

Mount St. Helens erupted on this day in 1980. How many people died because of that eruption?

May 19

The Simplon I tunnel was opened on this day in 1906. What two contries does it connect?

May 20

The International Bureau of Weights and Measures was founded in Paris on this day in 1875. Its function is to make sure measurements are the same all around the world. What are the two major systems of measurement?

May 21

The first Democratic National Convention was held on this day in 1832. What is the symbol for this political party?

May 22

Crater Lake National Park was established on this day in 1902. In what state is it?

May 23

Captain William Kidd was hanged in 1701 on May 23. Why was he hanged?

May 24

The first telegraph message was sent in 1844, using Morse Code. Decode it. // is between words, / between letters.
.-- / .... /.- / - // .... / .- / - / .... // --. / --- /
-.. // .-- / .-. / --- / ..- / --. / .... / - //
..--..

May 25

The Constitutional Convention opened on this day in 1787. When was it *supposed* to begin?

May 26

British Guiana became an independent nation on this day in 1966. On which continent is it located?

May 27

The Golden Gate Bridge was opened on this day in 1937. It was the longest single span suspension bridge in the world until what year?

May 28

Greece became the tenth member of the European Common Market in 1979. How many members are there now?

May 29

In 1953, Sir Edmund Percival and Tenzing Norkay became the first climbers to reach the peak of Mount Everest. In what mountain range is Mount Everest located?

May 30

The first Memorial Day was observed in 1866. What is another name for Memorial Day?

May 31

The U.S. copyright law was passed on this day in 1790. What is the name of the crime of copying words written by someone else and representing them as your own?

May 29

How much higher is Mount Everest than Mount McKinley, the tallest peak in North America?

May 1

The United Kingdom was formed on this day in 1707. What countries were united?

May 6

The Hindenburg airship burned on this day in 1937. Who was the president then?

May 14

Meriwether Lewis and his partner began exploring the Missouri River on this day in 1804. Who was his partner?

May 30

Joan of Arc was burned at the stake on this day in 1431. What was her country?

June 1

The fifteenth and sixteenth states entered the Union on this day in 1792 and 1796. What were the states?

June 2

In 1835, Phineas T. Barnum entered show business. What kind of show did he become famous for?

June 3

On this day in 1972, the first female rabbi in the U.S., Sally Preisand, was ordained in Cincinnati, Ohio. What was her religion?

June 4

Roquefort cheese was discovered on this day in 1070, according to legend. Name one vitamin and one mineral that can be found in cheese.

June 5

On this day in 1783, the first public demonstration of a hot air balloon took place in the country of the inventors. What was the country?

June 6

Land was granted on June 6, 1639 for the first gunpowder mill in the American colonies. Where was gunpowder invented?

June 7

Danville, Vermont had 20" of snow on this day in 1816. What is the most snow that *ever* fell in 24 hours in the U.S.?

June 8

Thomas Paine died on this day in 1809. What is his most famous quotation?

June 9

The United Kingdom leased Hong Kong from China for 99 years on this day in 1898. How many people per square mile live in Hong Kong?

June 10

The first U.S. mint for producing coins was opened on this day in Boston in 1652. Give the 1990 population of Boston.

June 11

Kamehameha Day is celebrated on this day in one of the states. Which state?

June 12

Anne Frank was born on this day in 1929. In what year was her famous diary published?

June 13

Thurgood Marshall became the first black many to be nominated for the Supreme Court on this day in 1967. Is he still on the Supreme Court?

June 14

Today is Flag Day. The Stars & Stripes became the U.S. flag on this day in 1777. What are two other names for the flag?

June 15

Benjamin Franklin flew a kite in a thunderstorm on this day in 1752 to prove that lightning is electricity. What invention was the result of this experiment?

June 16

Russia sent the first woman into space on this day in 1963. What was her name?

June 17

Iceland became independent from Denmark on this day in 1944. Which country is larger, Denmark or Iceland?

June 18

Napoleon Bonaparte, who had conquered most of Europe for France, was defeated by the Duke of Wellington on this day in 1815. Where did the battle take place?

June 19

Father's Day was first celebrated on this day in 1910. On what date will it be celebrated this year?

June 20

Two of the U.S. symbols were adopted on this day in 1782. Which symbols were they?

June 21

The summer solstice (first day of summer) occurs on this day in most years. It is the longest day of the year in which hemisphere?

June 22

Galileo Galilei was sentenced by the Inquisition on this day in 1633 for believing that the earth moved around the sun. What country was he from?

June 23

The Congress of the independent Republic of Texas agreed to become part of the U.S. on this day in 1845. On what date did Texas actually become a state?

June 24

Mary McLeod Bethune became the first black woman to be appointed to a major federal office. What was her profession?

June 25

General George Armstrong Custer was killed in a battle with Indians on this day in 1876. What is the battle often called?

June 26

The Saint Lawrence Seaway was dedicated by President Eisenhower and Queen Elizabeth II on this day in 1959. How many miles long is it?

June 27

Afar & Issas became independent from France in 1977. What is its new name and on what continent is it located?

June 28

On this day in 1968, Monday was established as the date for most legal holidays. How many major U.S. legal holidays are listed in *Facts Plus?*

June 29

The United States first bombed Hanoi in 1966. In what country is Hanoi?

June 30

June 30 is Official Calendar Day. Leap seconds are added on this day. How many leap seconds have been added so far?

June 9

The United Kingdom leased Hong Kong from China for 99 years on June 9, 1898. When will Hong Kong go back to Chinese rule?

June 24

The first reports of flying saucers were received on this day in 1942. How many years ago is that?

June 4

Henry Ford completed his first car on this day in 1896. The car was wider than the door! How old was Henry Ford at that time?

June 5

The gold standard was abolished on this day in 1933. Before then, U.S. bills could be exchanged for gold. Who had just become president?

June 10

The first personal computer, the Apple II, was shipped on this day in 1977. How many years ago was that?

June 12

A cat named Dusty gave birth to her 420th kitten on this day in 1952. What is the special name for a group of cats?

July 1

The first postage stamps in the U.S. were issued on this day in 1847. Five-digit zip codes were first used July 1, 1963. When were nine-digit zip codes first used?

July 2

The last president to be born in a log cabin, and the second to be assassinated was shot on this day in 1881. He died that September. What was his name?

July 3

The Confederate army under General Robert E. Lee lost the Battle of Gettysburg on this day in 1863. About 38,000 people were killed in that battle. What war was being fought?

July 4

Today is Independence Day! The Declaration of Independence was signed in 1776 and the Statue of Liberty was given to the U.S. in 1884. How many presidents died on July 4?

July 5

July 5 is Independence Day in Venezuela. What is the main language spoken in Venezuela?

July 6

The first Republican Convention was held on this day in 1854. Who was the first Republican president?

July 7

A woman was nominated to the Supreme Court on this day in 1981. She is still a Supreme Court justice. What is her name?

July 8

The Liberty Bell cracked on this day in 1835. Where is it located?

July 9

Daniel Hale Williams performed the first successful surgical closure of a heart wound in Chicago in 1893. In what year was he born?

July 10

Telstar I relayed the first satellite TV between the U.S. and Europe. What was the year?

July 11

Skylab fell to earth on this day in 1979. When had it been launched?

July 12

The minimum wage for workers was set at 40¢ an hour on this day in 1933. A full time worker would have made only $832.00 a year at that wage. What is the average per capita GNP now in the United States?

July 13

The source of the Mississippi River was discovered by Henry R. Schoolcraft on this day in 1832. What is the second longest river in the U.S.?

July 14

The Bastille prison in Paris was stormed by French peasants on this day in 1789, beginning the French Revolution. In what year did that revolution end?

July 15

The U.S. *Apollo* and Soviet *Soyuz* spacecraft were launched on this day in 1975. What was their mission?

July 16

Congress designated the District of Columbia as the capital of the United States on this day in 1790. What is the area of Washington, D.C.?

July 17

Spain turned Florida over to the U.S. in 1821. What is Florida's nickname?

July 18

Disneyland opened on this day in 1955. In what year did Walt Disney die?

July 19

NASA selected Christa McAuliffe to be the first schoolteacher in space on this day in 1985. What was the name of the *first* American woman in space?

July 20

Neil Armstrong and Buzz Aldrin, Jr. were the first men to walk on the moon on this day in 1969. What were Neil Armstrong's first words?

July 21

Belgium became independent from the Netherlands on this day in 1831. Which country is the larger?

July 22

Gangster John Dillinger, then Public Enemy #1, was killed on this day. What was the year?

July 23

The first ice cream cone was introduced in Saint Louis in 1904. In which state is Saint Louis?

July 24

Brigham Young and his followers reached the Great Salt Lake Basin on this day in 1847. Who were his followers?

July 25

The greatest 24-hour rainfall in the United States took place on this day in 1979. How much rain fell?

July 26

New York became the 11th state on this day in 1788. Who is the governor of New York now?

July 27

The Korean War ended on this day in 1953. In what year had it begun?

July 28

The deadliest earthquake in modern times occurred in China on this day in 1976. About how many people were killed?

July 29

Vincent Van Gogh died on this day in 1890. Why is he famous?

July 30

The U.S. motto was officially adopted on this day in 1956. Where is the motto printed?

July 31

Oxygen was discovered on this day in 1774. What percentage of the air is oxygen?

July 11

Skylab fell to earth in 1979. How many years was it in space?

July 12

The minimum wage was increased on this day in 1933. Full time workers then earned no more than $832.00 a year. How much less is that than the average per capita income in your state?

July 2

Amelia Earhart disappeared on this day in 1937 as she attempted to be the first woman to fly across the Pacific Ocean. How old was she at the time?

July 16

San Diego was established as the first Catholic mission in California. How many people live in San Diego now?

July 21

The lowest known temperature on earth was recorded on this day in 1983 in Antarctica. How could this season be so cold?

August 1

Colorado became the 38th state on this day in 1876. What is Colorado's nickname?

August 2

Iraq invaded Kuwait on this day in 1990. What war resulted from that invasion?

August 3

Christopher Columbus left Spain on his first voyage to the New World in 1492. How many generations has it been since Columbus first came to America?

August 4

Upper Volta changed its name on this day in 1984. What is the new name for that country and where is it located?

August 5

It was 118°F. in Ice Harbor, Washington on this day in 1961. What is the highest recorded temperature ever in the United States?

August 6

The United States dropped the first atomic bomb in 1945. About 80,000 people were killed by that bomb. On what city was it dropped?

August 7

The first photograph of the earth from space was taken on this day in 1959. What continent shows on the photo of the world on the cover of *Facts Plus?*

August 8

The first official visit by a U.S. president to America Indians of the West took place on this day in 1883. Who was the president?

August 9

Track star Jesse Owens won his 4th gold medal in the 1936 Olympic games. Adolf Hitler was watching these games, held in the capital city of his country. What was the city?

August 10

Missouri became a state on this day in 1821. More than 10,000 of the people living there at the time were slaves. Which war led to a constitutional amendment legally abolishing slavery in the U.S.?

August 11

Franklin D. Roosevelt contracted (got) polio on this day in 1921. Despite this crippling illness, what did he become?

August 12

King Philip was killed on this day at Mt. Hope, Rhode Island, ending a war between American Indians and white settlers. What was the year?

August 13

Hernando Cortés conquered Mexico City on this day in 1521. What group of people did he conquer?

August 14

This is V-J Day, marking the surrender of Japan which ended World War II in 1945. Who became president that same year?

August 15

The Panama Canal was officially opened in 1914. In what region of the world is Panama?

August 16

Rock singer Elvis Presley died on August 16. What was the year?

August 17

Gold was discovered in the Klondike on this day in 1896. What river became famous in the gold rush that followed?

August 18

A 4-month old kitten, following a climbing party, made it to the top of the Matterhorn in 1950. What is the height of the Matterhorn?

August 19

Philo T. Farnsworth was born on this day in 1906. For what did he become famous?

August 20

Voyager 2 was launched on this day in 1977. What was its mission?

August 21

The Mona Lisa, painted by Leonardo da Vinci, was stolen from the Louvre in Paris on this day in 1911. What important river flows through Paris?

August 22

The first local chapter of the American Red Cross was formed in 1881. Who was the founder?

August 23

The first human-powered flight took place on this day in 1977. In what year did the first machine-powered flight take place (first airplane)?

August 24

Mt. Vesuvius erupted on this day in 79 A.D. What is one of the cities that was buried under its cinders and ash?

August 25

The City of New Orleans was founded on this day in 1718. What is the lowest altitude in New Orleans?

August 26

An major volcanic eruption began on this day in 1883. It blew a 2,640 foot mountain into bits and caused a tsunami which killed 36,000 people. What was the volcano?

August 27

The first successful oil well was drilled in Pennsylvania on this day in 1859. About what percentage of our energy comes from petroleum now?

August 28

Dr. Martin Luther King, Jr. gave his "I Have a Dream" speech during a civil rights rally in Washington, D.C. on this day in 1963 About how many people were there?

August 29

Francisco Pizarro strangled the last of the Inca emperors on this day in 1533, despite the fact that his people had filled a room with gold and another room twice with silver in ransom. What was the emperor's name?

August 30

The hot line from the capital of the United States to the capital of Russia (then Soviet Union) was installed on this day in 1963. What cities were connected?

August 31

A Packard became the first automobile to cross the U.S. under its own power on this day in 1903. It took 52 days. In what year was the automobile invented?

August 24

Hurricane Andrew hit the Florida coast on this day in 1992, causing one of the worst disasters in U.S. history. How many miles in diameter can hurricanes be?

August 4

Alexander Graham Bell's funeral was held on this day in 1922. 13 million phones were silent for one minute in his honor. How many years after the telephone was invented did he die?

August 18

On this day in 1587, Virginia Dare became the first English child to be born in the New World. How many years was this after Columbus first came to America?

August 22

On this day in 565, St. Columba reported seeing a monster in Loch Ness. Loch Ness is in Scotland. What country is Scotland now a part of?

August 5

In 1825 on August 5, Uruguay declared its independence from the country just to its north. What is that country?

September 1

The passenger pigeon became extinct on this day in 1914. What is a word meaning "in danger of becoming extinct?"

September 2

The Gregorian calendar was first adopted in 1752. September 3 became September 14. Who drew up the calendar which had been used until then?

September 3

Labor Day was first observed as a legal holiday on this day. Who first sponsored its celebration in New York?

September 4

The city of Los Angeles was founded on this day in 1781. In what way is Los Angeles larger than New York City?

September 5

The longest motor vehicle tunnel in the world was opened on this day in 1980. How long is it?

September 6

The groundbreaking for the world's first nuclear power plant took place in Shippingport, Pennsylvania on this day in 1954. What percentage of our energy currently comes from nuclear power?

September 7

Boulder Dam first went into use on this day in 1936. What is it called now?

September 8

A hurricane and tsunami hit Galveston, Texas on this day in 1900, killing 10,000 people. Which way do hurricanes rotate in the northern hemisphere?

September 9

California became the 31st state on this day in 1850. How many representatives does California have in the House of Representatives?

September 10

A patent was granted to Elias Howe for the sewing machine on this day in 1846. What happened to the man who *really* invented the sewing machine?

September 11

Henry Hudson discovered Manhattan Island on this day in 1609. On a later expedition, he discovered Hudson Bay. What kind of clothing did the Indians wear around Hudson Bay?

September 12

Peter Mark Roget, author of the thesaurus, died on this day in 1869. What kind of words are found in a thesaurus?

September 13

The hottest known day on earth was September 13, 1922, in the Sahara Desert in Libya. How hot was it?

September 14

The Star-Spangled Banner, the U.S. national anthem, was written on this day in 1814. Near which state was the author when he wrote it?

September 15

All Central American countries except Belize and Panama gained their independence from Spain on this day in 1821. How many countries was that?

September 16

The Pilgrims left Plymouth, England for America on this day in 1620. What was the name of their ship?

September 17

The U.S. Constitution was signed on this day in 1787. In which city was it signed?

September 18

The first issue of the New York Times was published on this day in 1851. What can be used to find articles published in the Times?

September 19

The Mesabi iron range was discovered near Lake Superior on this day in 1844. What combines with iron to make rust?

September 20

The inventor of the safety elevator demonstrated it on this day in 1854 by cutting the lifting rope while standing in the elevator. Who was the inventor?

September 21

The tiny island of Malta became independent on this day in 1964. Where is Malta located?

September 22

Nathan Hale, a Revolutionary War hero, was hanged for spying on this day in 1776. What did he say just before he was hanged?

September 23

A time capsule was buried at the site of the New York World's Fair on this day in 1938, to be opened in the year 6939. Check the time line of history to see what was happening between 1929 and 1942.

September 24

Augustus Caesar, the first Roman emperor, was born on this day in 63 B.C. What was his real name?

September 25

Vasco de Balboa sighted the Pacific Ocean on this day in 1513 after crossing the isthmus of Panama. What ocean trench is the deepest part of the Pacific Ocean?

September 26

Fidel Castro gave the longest speech in United Nations history on this day in 1960. He spoke for 4 hours and 29 minutes. Who is Fidel Castro?

September 27

On this day in 1825, the first passengers were transported by railroad. In what country did this happen?

September 28

Indonesia joined the United Nations on this day in 1950. What is the capital of Indonesia?

September 29

Which space shuttle blasted off on this day in 1988?

September 30

The Orion Nebula was first photographed on this day in 1880. What are nebulae?

September 1

In 1977 on this day, it became illegal to put lead in paint. What is the scientific symbol for lead?

September 2

The Great Fire of London began on this day in 1666. 13,000 homes burned in just 4 days. About how many people live in London now?

September 18

On this day in 1983, George Meegan finished a 6-year walk from the southern tip of Chile to the Arctic Ocean. What 2 continents did he cross during his 19,021 mile walk?

September 24

In 1986 on this day, the rose was adopted as the U.S. national flower. What is the national bird?

September 26

The Spanish Inquisition began on this day in 1480. People were brought to trial and punished because of their religious beliefs. How long did the entire Inquisition last?

September 26

John Chapman was born on this day in 1774. What name is he best known by?

October 1

Mao Tse-tung set up a Communist government in China in 1949. The U.S. has a capitalist system where individual people and private businesses own most of the country's factories and land. Who controls these things in a Communist system?

October 2

Aristotle, an ancient Greek pholosopher and scientist, died on this day in 322 B.C. What does the abbreviation B.C. mean?

October 3

Germany was officially reunified on this day in 1990. What is the area of unified Germany?

October 4

The first earth-orbiting satellite was launched on this day in 1957. What country launched it?

October 5

Charlie Smith, the oldest known American, died on this day at the age of 137 in 1979. What is the average life expectancy in the U.S.?

October 6

Antioch College in Ohio became the first public school for both boys and girls in 1853. What is Ohio's state motto?

October 7

Mother Teresa was awarded the Nobel Peace Prize on this day in 1979. Who won the Nobel Peace Prize in 1964?

October 8

Eddie Rickenbacker was born on this day. He became the leading U.S. air ace in World War II. He shot down 22 enemy planes and 4 ballons. In what year was he born?

October 9

A Viking became the first known European to discover North America in about 1002. What was his name?

October 10

The words "under God" were added to the Pledge of Allegiance on this day in 1954. When was the pledge first said by public school children?

October 11

A. A. Milne's book *The House at Pooh Corner* was published on this day in 1928. In what year was his other famous book published?

October 12

Columbus landed in the Bahamas on this day after his first trip across the Atlantic Ocean to the Americas. What was the year?

October 13

The cornerstone for the White House was laid on this day in 1792. Who lives in the White House?

October 14

Pilot Chuck Yeager was the first person to fly an airplane faster than the speed of sound on October 14, 1946. How many miles per hour does sound travel?

October 15

The first photographic evidence of planets in a solar system outside our own was presented on this day in 1984. Name the nearest star other than our sun.

October 16

Noah Webster, American author of the dictionary, was born on this day in 1758. How many words are estimated to be in the English language?

October 17

The British surrendered to the Americans at Saratoga in 1777. Where did George Washington and his troops spend the rest of that winter?

October 18

The first U.S. labor organization was formed on this day in 1648. Who is a modern-day labor union leader in Poland?

October 19

The barometer measured only 28.86" on this day in 1844 during a storm in Toronto, Canada. What is the standard barometric pressure at 59°F at sea level?

October 20

On this day in 1944, General Douglas MacArthur returned as promised. To what country did he return?

October 21

Alfred Nobel, founder of the Nobel Peace Prize, was born on this day in 1833. What did he invent?

October 22

The Chinese were the first to record a solar eclipse on this day in 2137 B.C. How many solar eclipses will occur in 1995?

October 23

241 U.S. Marines and 58 French soldiers were killed in Lebanon on this day in 1983. In what region of the world is Lebanon?

October 24

The first telegram was sent across the United States on this day in 1861. This meant the end of the pony express. When had the telegraph been invented?

October 25

The first postcard in the U.S. was sent on this day in 1870. How much does it cost to send a postcard to Brazil?

October 26

The Erie Canal, the first man-made waterway in the U.S., opened on this day in 1825. What canal system is it now a part of?

October 27

DuPont Company announced an invention by Wallace H. Carothers on this day in 1938. What was that invention?

October 28

The Statue of Liberty was dedicated on this day in 1886. How many steps could people climb inside of it?

October 29

The Stock Market crashed on this day in 1929, leading to the Great Depression. What were the years of the Great Depression?

October 30

The first Methodist Church in America was dedicated on this day in 1768. Name a Protestant church other than Methodist.

October 31

Halloween is the eve of what other special day?

October 1

John Philip Sousa became the conductor of the U.S. Marine Corps band on this day in 1880. About how old was he when he died?

October 10

A dam burst in northern Italy on this day in 1963. About 3000 people were killed. Where in the world is the dam with the largest capacity?

October 16

The first Ann Landers column was published on this day in 1955. How many years have Americans been reading her advice?

October 21

A coal waste slide buried the village of Aberfan in Wales on this day in 1966, killing more than 140 people. What percentage of our energy comes from coal?

October 29

In 1947 on October 29, dry ice was first used to seed clouds and produce rain. Dry ice is frozen carbon dioxide. What is the chemical symbol for carbon dioxide?

November 1

The National Weather Service was founded on this day in 1870. What device to they use to measure wind speed?

November 2

In 1917 on this day, Arthur Balfour proposed establishing a Jewish homeland in Palestine. His dream came true in 1948. What is the name of that homeland?

November 3

Stephen Austin, colonizer of Texas, was born on this day in 1793. In what year did he die?

November 4

The presidential election was first held on "Election Day" in 1945. On what day of the week is election day?

November 5

Susan B. Anthony was thrown into jail for voting in the presidential election of 1872 on this day. In what year were women given the right to vote?

November 6

The first hydrogen bomb was exploded on this day in 1952. How many electrons are in a hydrogen atom?

November 7

Franklin D. Roosevelt was re-elected for his 4th term as president on this day in 1944. In 1951, Congress amended the Constitution to limit the number of times a person may be elected president. What is the limit?

November 8

Halley's Comet was spotted on this day in 1985. Edmond Halley, for whom the comet was named, was born on this day in 1656. How often does the comet appear?

November 9

The Berlin Wall was opened on this day in 1989. About how many people live in Berlin?

November 10

Henry Morton Stanley found David Livingstone on this day in 1871. What continent was explored during his search?

November 11

The Armistice was signed on this day in 1918, ending World War I. Many people thought this would be "the war to end all wars." What do we now call the holiday celebrating this event?

November 12

Arches National Park was established on this day in 1971. In what state is it located?

November 13

The Holland Tunnel in New York City was opened on this day in 1927. It was the first underwater tunnel for vehicles. What is the *longest* tunnel for motor vehicles in the U.S.?

November 14

Newspaper reporter Nellie Bly set off around the world in 1889, attempting to make it in less time than the hero of Jules Verne's 1873 novel. How many days would *equal* his time?

November 15

Pikes Peak was first sighted by Zebulon Pike on this day in 1806. What became the slogan for the Colorado gold rush?

November 16

Oklahoma entered the Union on this day in 1907. What is Oklahoma's state flower?

November 17

46,000 meteorids fell over Arizona in 20 minutes on this day in 1966. What often collides and breaks into meteroids?

November 18

The United States adopted standard time zones on this day in 1883. Who first divided the U.S. into these zones?

November 19

President Abraham Lincoln delivered his most famous speech on this day in 1863. What is it called?

November 20

The whaling ship Essex of Nantucket was sunk by a sperm whale on this day in 1820. How long can the largest whales get?

November 21

The Mayflower Compact was signed on this day in 1620, setting up self-government in Plymouth Colony. What group of people colonized Plymouth?

November 22

President John F. Kennedy was assassinated on this day. What was the year?

November 23

One of the United States presidents was born on this day. What is his name?

November 24

Hershey Company sold the last nickel chocolate bar on this day in 1969. What drug does chocolate contain?

November 25

Johann Strauss, Jr., wrote “On the Beautiful Blue Danube” on this day in 1867. What kind of music was it?

November 26

George Washington proclaimed the first national Thanksgiving Day on this day in 1789. How did the custom of eating turkey get started?

November 27

The friction match was invented on this day in 1826. When had the first match been patented?

November 28

Mauritania became an independent country on this day in 1960. What languages are spoken there?

November 29

On this day in 1929, Richard Byrd and his crew flew over the South Pole. What is the imaginary line running from the North Pole to the South Pole through Greenwich, England called?

November 30

Yemen was divided into North and South Yemen in 1967. In what year were the two countries reunited?

November 2

Howard Hughes took the Spruce Goose on its only flight in 1947. It was as large as a ship and could fly just above the water so submarines could not detect it by radar. About how old was Hughes at the time?

November 3

Eddie Rickenbacker was rescued along with others after 23 days on a life raft on this day in 1942. Why was he famous?

November 26

Alice in Wonderland was published on this day in 1865. Who was the author?

November 11

In 1095 on this day, Pope Urban II made the first mention of the Crusades. They began in 1096. How many years did they last?

November 26

France became the third country to launch its own satellite on this day in 1965. What were the first and second countries?

November 28

Washington Irving, the author of Rip Van Winkle, died on this day in 1859. About how old was he?

December 1

The White House got its first telephone on this day in 1878. Who was president then?

December 2

How many national parks were established in Alaska on this day in 1980?

December 3

The first successful human heart transplant was performed on this day in 1967. About how many times does a human heart beat in 10 years?

December 4

East Pakistan became the Republic of Bangladesh on this day in 1971. What is the per capita GNP in Bangladesh?

December 5

Amendment 21 to the Constitution repealed Prohibition on this day in 1933. What had been prohibited?

December 6

Amendment 13 to the Constitution was ratified on this day in 1865. What did it make illegal?

December 7

Some 2,400 people were killed when Pearl Harbor was bombed on this day in 1941. Who did the bombing?

December 8

The government of Taiwan was set up by Chinese fleeing the Communists in 1949. What is a major religion of Taiwan?

December 9

Petrified Forest National Park was established on this day in 1962. The trees there grew about 225 million years ago. What geologic period began then?

December 10

The metric system was established in France on this day in 1799. What temperature scale is part of the metric system?

December 11

Indiana became a state on this day in 1816. What is Indiana's state tree?

December 12

The first radio signal was sent across the Atlantic Ocean from England to Newfoundland on this day in 1901. It was received by the inventor of the radio. What was his name?

December 13

The first music store in America opened on this day in 1759. How many basic types of musical instruments are there?

December 14

Roald Amundsen reached the South Pole on this day in 1911. What is the coldest temperature ever recorded in Antarctica?

December 15

Sitting Bull died on this day in 1890. Of what American Indian tribe was he the chief?

December 16

Thirty to sixty American patriots threw 342 chests of tea into the sea on this day in 1773. They were protesting the tax on tea in an event leading to the American Revolutionary War. Where did this "tea party" take place?

December 17

History's first successful airplane flight took place on this day at Kitty Hawk, North Carolina. What was the year?

December 18

New Jersey ratified the Constitution on this day in 1787. In what year did New Jersey become a colony?

December 19

George Washington's army made camp at Valley Forge for the winter. What was the year?

December 20

South Carolina voted to secede from the Union on this day in 1860. What group of states did South Carolina join after that?

December 21

The first crossword puzzle appeared in a U.S. newspaper on this day in 1913. Into which of the four major categories of information in the newspaper do crossword puzzles fit?

December 22

A living coelacanth, thought to have been extinct for millions of years, was caught off the coast of South Africa on this day in 1938. Coelacanths appeared in the fossil record during the Devonian Period. How many million years ago did the Devonian Period begin?

December 23

The Federal Reserve Banking System went into effect on this day in 1913. Nearly all paper money in the U.S. is issued by Federal Reserve Banks. What is the dollar amount of the largest U.S. bill ever issued?

December 24

The first solar heating system was demonstrated on this day in 1948. Solar energy is renewable, but fossil fuels are not. Name three fossil fuels.

December 25

Today is Christmas. This holiday celebrates the birth of Jesus Christ. In what year do historians think Christ was born?

December 26

President Harry Truman died on this day in 1972. What did the sign on his desk say?

December 27

The Soviet Union invaded Afghanistan on this day in 1979. What is the capital of Afghanistan?

December 28

Iowa became the 29th state on this day in 1846. Which president was from Iowa?

December 29

The large buffalo herds on the Great Plains disappeared about the time that a key battle was lost by the Sioux Indians on this day in 1890. What was the battle?

December 30

The United States paid $10 million to Mexico in 1853 for land which is now Arizona and New Mexico. When did the Spanish establish the first permanent settlement in what is now New Mexico?

December 31

Britain's Queen Victoria named Ottawa the capital of what country on this day in 1857?

December 3

On this day in 1818, tin cans were introduced to the U.S. When was the process for canning food invented?

December 6

The United States Congress moved its meeting place from New York City to Philadelphia on this day in 1790. In what city does Congress now meet?

December 6

The Republic of Ireland was proclaimed on this day in 1922. What country is Northern Ireland still a part of?

December 19

Vinson Massif was climbed for the first time on this day in 1966. On which continent is Vinson Massif?

December 24

Astronauts orbited the moon 10 times on this day in 1968. How many months later did the first man land on the moon?

ANSWERS (Index entry, page number)

Note: Answers may be found through more than one index entry. Only one is shown.

January 1. Julius Caesar (Months, p. 13)
January 2. 1883 (Brooklyn Bridge, p. 88)
January 3. 1959 (Alaska, p. 94)
January 4. October 4, 1957 (Sputnik I, p. 20)
January 5. Michael J. Sullivan (Wyoming, p. 101)
January 6. International Morse Code (Telegraph, p. 165)
January 7. Ganymede (Jupiter, p. 19)
January 8. 32° C. (Celsius scale, p. 207)
January 9. 11 (Confederate States, p. 101)
January 10. Buffalo Bill (Cody, p. 79)
January 11. Nicotine (Cigarettes, p. 46)
January 12. 2795°F (Iron, p. 35)
January 13. Virginia (Colonies, p. 76)
January 14. 1863 (Ford, p. 80)
January 15. Democratic Party (Donkey, p. 127)
January 16. 1919 (Prohibition, p. 121)
January 17. Ohio (Hayes, p. 130)
January 18. 1984 (Gandhi, p. 80)
January 19. 5,400,000 sq. mi. (Antarctica, p. 51)
January 20. James Naismith (Basketball, p. 85)
January 21. 1924 (Lenin, p. 81)
January 22. John F. Kennedy (Johnson, p. 130)
January 23. 1999 (Pluto, p. 17)
January 24. Robert S. Baden-Powell (Boy Scouts, p. 78)
January 25. Newspaperwoman (Bly, p. 78)
January 26. Zachary Taylor (Presidents, p. 130)
January 27. Three (Apollo, p. 20)
January 28. Christa McAuliffe (Challenger, p. 20)
January 29. Germany (Automobile, p. 85)
January 30. Andrew Jackson (Presidents, p. 130)
January 31. Winnie the Pooh (Milne, p. 159 or 162)
January 20. *The Constitution of the U.S. (Presidents, 117)*
January 23. *Doctor (Blackwell, p. 78)*
January 5. *79 years old (Carver, p. 79—1943-1864)*
January 22. *105°F (no reference, increasing 20° per minute)*
January 24. *61 (Solar System, p. 17, add all moons)*

February 1. Nine (Supreme Court, p. 129)
February 2. Cloudy (Ground Hog Day, p. 8)
February 3. Income tax (Constitution, p. 120)
February 4. Civil War (Confederate States, p. 101)
February 5. 1934 (Aaron, p. 78)
February 6. 30.6 miles (Tunnel, p. 89)
February 7. England (Dickens, p. 79)
February 8. May 25, 1973 (Skylab, p. 20)
February 9. Second U.S. president (Adams, p. 151)
February 10. Brigham Young (Mormons, x-ref to p. 83)
February 11. Phonograph, Motion pictures (Edison, p 86)
February 12. 1866 (Lincoln, p. 8)
February 13. 1847 (James, p. 81)
February 14. Monday (Perpetual calendar, p. 5)
February 15. Eagle (Anthony, p. 210)
February 16. Egypt (Tutankhamen, p. 72)
February 17. 1869 (Suez Canal, p. 88)
February 18. 3,666 million miles (Pluto, p. 17)
February 19. 167 ft. (Niagara Falls, p. 49)
February 20. Paricutin (Volcanoes, p. 30)
February 21. White, yellow, blue (Telephone, p. 157)
February 22. Third Monday in February (Washington, George, p. 8)
February 23. Aluminum (Hall, Charles, p. 85)
February 24. Gregorian calendar (Julian calendar, p. 12)
February 25. Andrew Johnson (Presidents, p. 130)
February 26. Four (National parks, p. 106-109)
February 27. Two (Amendments, p. 121)
February 28. California (Gold rush, p. 77)
February 29. Four (Leap Year, p. 8)
February 13. *19 years old (James, p. 81, 1866-1847)*
February 2. *37 years old (Hogan, Ben, p. 80, 1949-1912)*
February 22. *19 years (Pilgrims, p. 76, 1639-1620)*
February 1. *Daniel DeFoe (Robinson Crusoe, p. 162)*
February 2. *68 years before 1993 (no reference, answers vary with year)*
February 6. *58 years before 1993 (no reference, answers vary with year)*
February 16. *Latvia, Estonia (Lithuania, p. 70)*

March 1. 1872 (Yellowstone, p. 106)
March 2. Japan (Earthquake, p. 31)
March 3. War of 1812 (Star-Spangled Banner, p. 126)
March 4. fear itself (Roosevelt, p. 124)
March 5. Boston Massacre (American Revolutionary War, p. 145)
March 6. 1922 (Water skis, p. 87)
March 7. 1876 (Telephone, p. 87)
March 8. Millard Fillmore, William H. Taft (Presidents, p. 130)
March 9. American continents (Vespucci, p. 83)
March 10. $100.00 bill (Money, p. 210)
March 11. Soviet Union (Gorbachev, p. 80)
March 12. Juliette Gordon Low (Girl Scouts, x-ref to p. 81)
March 13. Uranus (Planet, p. 17)
March 14. 46,058 sq. mi. (Penn, p. 82, then Pennsylvania, p. 99)
March 15. Stimulant (Tobacco, p. 46)
March 16. 74 inches (Rain, p. 25)
March 17. Dublin (Saint Patrick's Day, p. 8, then Ireland, p. 60)
March 18. Alexei A. Leonov (Cosmonaut, p. 20)
March 19. Earth's shadow (Lunar eclipse, p. 19)
March 20. Equator (Vernal equinox, p. 14)
March 21. Congo or Zaire (Stanley, p. 50)
March 22. 551 feet (Grand Coulee Dam, p. 90)
March 23. Revolt against England (Henry, p. 124)
March 24. They didn't want a national government interfering with state's affairs (Rhode Island, p. 122)
March 25. Saturn (Moon, p. 19)
March 26. Polio (Salk, p. 83)
March 27. 131 (Earthquake, p. 31)
March 28. 280 miles per hour (Tornado, p. 24)
March 29. 1975 (Vietnam War, p. 77)
March 30. Great land (Alaska, p. 94)
March 31. 1967 (Daylight Saving, p. 9)
March 2. *Five (Blind x-ref to Braille, p. 165, 1829-1824)*
March 3. *50 hours (no reference, 10 x 5)*
March 15. *Cleopatra (Egypt, p. 73)*
March 14. *1793 (Whitney, p. 85)*
March 25. *58 years (Slavery, p. 121, 1865-1807)*

April 1. 5,000 (Plague, p. 74)
April 2. Feast of flowers (Florida, p. 95)
April 3. 45 mph (Horse, p. 38)
April 4. Original 13 colonies (Flag, p. 126)
April 5. W a t e r (Manual alphabet, p. 165)
April 6. 90° north latitude (North Pole, p. 142)
April 7. John Baird, Philo T. Farnsworth (Television, p. 87)
April 8. Jupiter (Moon, p. 19)
April 9. 1865 (Civil War, p. 77)
April 10. 4,700 years old (Trees, p. 38)
April 11. Baseball (Robinson, Jackie, p. 82)
April 12. Yuri A. Gagarin (Orbit, p. 20)
April 13. 1998 (Population, p. 71)
April 14. John Wilkes Booth (Lincoln, x-ref to Booth, p. 78)
April 15. February 3, 1913 (Income tax, p. 120)
April 16. Orville (Wright, p. 85)
April 17. Mt. Logan (Mountains, p. 52)
April 18. 120 (Third World, p. 70)
April 19. Paul Revere (American Revolutionary War, p. 145)
April 20. 88 (Radium, p. 34)
April 21. $100.00 bill (Bills, p. 210)
April 22. Answers vary (Endangered animals, p. 39)
April 23. Thomas Edison (Motion pictures, p. 86)
April 24. Over 97 million items (Library of Congress, p. 146)
April 25. 179 countries (United Nations, p. 70)
April 26. He assassinated Lincoln (Booth, p. 78)
April 27. 1522 (Magellan, p. 76)
April 28. 1788 (Maryland, p. 96)
April 29. Japan (Hirohito, p. 80)
April 30. 827,987 sq. mi. (Louisiana Territory, p. 77)
April 30. *776,144 sq. mi. (Louisiana, p. 96, Louisiana Territory, p. 77, 827,987-51,843)*
April 10. *To keep others from copying the idea (Patent, p. 84)*
April 15. *William H. Taft (Presidents, p. 130)*
April 30. *54 years before 1993 (no reference, current year - 1939)*
April 6. *Athens (Greece, p. 58)*
April 12. *231 mph (Wind, p. 229)*

May 1. Two (Empire State Building, p. 90)
May 2. Baseball (Gehrig, p. 80)
May 3. British (Thatcher, p. 83)
May 4. Josip Broz Tito (Yugoslavia, x-ref to Tito, p. 83)
May 5. 87,715,000 (Mexico, p. 63)
May 6. Dictator (Stalin, p. 123)
May 7. 1945 (World War II, p. 77)
May 8. 2,340 miles (Mississippi River, p. 50)
May 9. 1907 (Mother's Day, p. 9)
May 10. 1825 (Railroad, p. 77)
May 11. Thailand (x-ref, p. 247)
May 12. War of 1812 (Uncle Sam, p. 127)
May 13. 1⅔ pounds (Hail, p. 25)
May 14. Smallpox (Jenner, p. 87)
May 15. 30¢ (Postcard, p. 191)
May 16. 864°F (Venus, p. 17)
May 17. 1857-1861 (Presidents, p. 130)
May 18. 60 (Mount St. Helens, p. 30)
May 19. Italy & Switzerland (Simplon I, p. 89)
May 20. Metric & English (Measurement, p. 206)
May 21. Donkey (Democratic Party, p. 127)
May 22. Oregon (Crater Lake, p. 106)
May 23. Pirate (Kidd, p. 81)
May 24. What hath God wrought? (Morse Code, p. 165)
May 25. May 14, 1787 (Constitutional Convention, p. 122)
May 26. South America (British Guiana x-ref to Guyana, p. 59)
May 27. 1964 (Golden Gate Bridge, p. 89)
May 28. Twelve (European Common Market, p. 70)
May 29. Himalayas (Mount Everest, p. 52)
May 30. Decoration Day (Memorial Day, p. 9)
May 31. Plagiarism (Copyright, p. 226)
May 29. *8,708 feet (Mount McKinley, p. 52, 29,028 - 20,320)*
May 1. *England, Scotland, Wales, Northern Ireland (United Kingdom, p. 70)*
May 6. *Franklin D. Roosevelt (Presidents, p. 130)*
May 14. *William Clark (Lewis, x-ref to Lewis & Clark, x-ref to Clark, William)*
May 30. *France (Joan of Arc, p. 81)*

June 1. Kentucky, Tennessee (States of U.S., scan for answers, p. 96, 99)
June 2. Circus (Barnum, p. 78)
June 3. Jewish (Rabbi, p. 91)
June 4. Vitamin B-12, phosphorus (Cheese, p. 44, 45)
June 5. France (Balloon, hot air, p. 85)
June 6. China (Gunpowder, p. 72)
June 7. 76 inches (Snow, p. 25)
June 8. These are the times that try men's souls. (Paine, p. 124)
June 9. 247,004 (Hong Kong, p. 231)
June 10. 574,283 (Boston, p. 103)
June 11. Hawaii (Kamehameha, p. 81)
June 12. 1947 (Frank, Anne, p. 162)
June 13. No (Supreme Court, p. 129)
June 14. Star-Spangled Banner, Old Glory (Flag, U.S., p. 126)
June 15. Lightning rod (Franklin, p. 86)
June 16. Valentina V. Tereshkova (Space, p. 20)
June 17. Iceland (Denmark, p. 57, Iceland, p. 59, compare)
June 18. Waterloo (Bonaparte, p. 77)
June 19. June 20 in 1993 (Father's Day, p. 7)
June 20. Great Seal and Bald Eagle (Symbols, U.S., p. 127)
June 21. Northern (Summer, p. 9)
June 22. Italy (Galileo, p. 80)
June 23. December 29, 1845 (Texas, p. 100)
June 24. Educator (Bethune, p. 78)
June 25. Custer's Last Stand (Custer, p. 77)
June 26. 182 miles (Saint Lawrence Seaway, p. 88)
June 27. Djibouti, Africa (x-ref to Djibouti, p. 57)
June 28. 4 (Legal holiday, p. 7)
June 29. Vietnam (Hanoi, p. 69)
June 30. 16 (Leap seconds, p. 229)
June 9. *1997 (no reference, calculate 1898 + 99)*
June 24. *51 years before 1993 (no reference, calculate current year - 1942)*
June 4. *33 years old (Ford, Henry, p. 80, calculate 1896 - 1863)*
June 5. *Franklin D. Roosevelt (Presidents, p. 130)*
June 10. *16 years before 1993 (no reference, calculate current year - 1977)*
June 12. *Clowder (Cat, p. 38)*

July 1. 1981 (Zip codes, p. 193)
July 2. James A. Garfield (Presidents, p. 130)
July 3. Civil War (Gettysburg Address, p. 125)
July 4. Three (Presidents, p. 130)
July 5. Spanish (Venezuela, p. 69)
July 6. Abraham Lincoln (Republican, p. 127)
July 7. Sandra Day O'Connor (Supreme Court, p. 129)
July 8. Philadelphia, Pennsylvania (Liberty Bell, p. 127)
July 9. 1856 (Williams, Daniel Hale, p. 83)
July 10. 1962 (Telstar I, p. 20)
July 11. May 25, 1973 (Skylab, p. 20)
July 12. $21,700 (Per capita GNP, 68)
July 13. Missouri River (Rivers, p. 50)
July 14. 1799 (French Revolution, p. 77)
July 15. U.S. Soviet linkup (Apollo, p. 20)
July 16. 61.4 sq. mi. (Washington, D.C., p. 105)
July 17. Sunshine State (Florida, p. 95)
July 18. 1966 (Disney, p. 79)
July 19. Sally K. Ride (Space, p. 20)
July 20. "That's one small step for man, one giant leap for mankind." (Armstrong, p. 18)
July 21. The Netherlands (Belgium, p. 54, Netherlands, p. 63, compare areas)
July 22. 1934 (Dillinger, p. 79)
July 23. Missouri (Saint Louis, p. 105)
July 24. Mormons (Young, Brigham, p. 83)
July 25. 19 inches (Rain, p. 25)
July 26. Mario M. Cuomo (New York, p. 98)
July 27. 1950 (Korean War, p. 77)
July 28. 242,000 (Earthquake, p. 31)
July 29. Painter (Van Gogh, p. 83)
July 30. On money (Motto of U.S., p. 126)
July 31. 21% (Oxygen, p. 22)
July 11. *6 years (Skylab, p. 20, calculate 1979 - 1973)*
July 12. *Answers vary (State per capita income, pg. 94-101, calculate by subtracting $832.00)*
July 2. *40 years old (Earhart, p. 79, calculate 1937 - 1897)*
July 16. *1,110,549 (San Diego, p. 105)*
July 21. *It is summer in the southern hemisphere. (Seasons, p. 14)*

August 1. Centennial State (Colorado, p. 94)
August 2. Persian Gulf War (Iraq, p. 77)
August 3. 17 (Columbus, p. 71)
August 4. Burkina Faso, Western Africa (x-ref to Burkina Faso, p. 55)
August 5. 134°F (Temperature, p. 25)
August 6. Hiroshima (Atoms, atomic bomb, p. 77)
August 7. Africa (Cover and inside maps)
August 8. Chester A. Arthur (Presidents, p. 130)
August 9. Berlin (Hitler, p. 80, then Germany, p. 58)
August 10. Civil War (Slavery, p. 77)
August 11. President (Roosevelt, Franklin, p. 130)
August 12. 1676 (Philip, King, p. 82)
August 13. Aztecs (Cortés, Hernando, p. 79)
August 14. Harry S. Truman (Presidents, p. 130)
August 15. Central America (Panama, p. 70)
August 16. 1977 (Presley, Elvis, p. 82)
August 17. Yukon River (Klondike Gold Rush, p. 50)
August 18. 14,692 feet (Matterhorn, p. 52)
August 19. Inventing television camera (Farnsworth, Philo T., p. 87)
August 20. To photograph planets in the outer solar system (Voyager spacecraft, p. 20)
August 21. Seine (Paris, p. 50)
August 22. Clara Barton (Red Cross x-ref to Barton, Clara, p. 78)
August 23. 1903 (Airplane, p. 77)
August 24. Pompeii (Vesuvius, p. 30)
August 25. 4 feet below sea level (New Orleans, p. 104)
August 26. Krakatoa (Volcanoes, p. 30)
August 27. 43% (Petroleum, p. 33)
August 28. More than 200,000 (King, Martin Luther, p. 125)
August 29. Atahualpa (Inca, x-ref to Atahualpa, p. 78)
August 30. Washington, D.C. and Moscow (United States, p. 68, Russia, p. 65)
August 31. 1885 (Automobile, p. 85)
August 24. *200 to 300 miles (Hurricanes, p. 24)*
August 4. *46 years (Telephone, p. 87, calculate 1922 - 1876)*
August 18. *95 years (Columbus, p. 75, calculate 1587 - 1492)*
August 22. *United Kingdom of Great Britain (Scotland, p. 70)*
August 5. *Brazil (Uruguay, p. 136)*

September 1. Endangered (Extinct, p. 39)
September 2. Julius Caesar (Gregorian, p. 12)
September 3. Central Labor Union (Labor Day, p. 10)
September 4. Larger area (Los Angeles *or* New York City, p. 104, compare)
September 5. 10.1 miles (Tunnels, p. 89)
September 6. 6% (Nuclear energy, p. 33)
September 7. Hoover Dam (In index as x-ref)
September 8. Counterclockwise (Hurricanes, p. 24)
September 9. 52 (House of Representatives, p. 128)
September 10. Angry tailors destroyed his shop (Sewing machine, p. 84)
September 11. Caribou or moose skin (Hudson Bay, p. 110)
September 12. Synonyms and antonyms (Thesaurus, p. 153)
September 13. 136°F (Libya, p. 25)
September 14. Maryland (Star-Spangled Banner, p. 126)
September 15. Five (Central America, p. 70)
September 16. Mayflower (Pilgrims, p. 76)
September 17. Philadelphia (Constitution, p. 114)
September 18. New York Times Index (New York Times, p. 154)
September 19. Water and oxygen (Rust, p. 35)
September 20. Elisha Otis (Elevator, p. 85)
September 21. Mediterranean Sea (Malta, p. 62)
September 22. "I only regret that I have but one life to lose for my country." (Hale, Nathan, p. 124)
September 23. Great Depression (Time line, p. 77)
September 24. Octavian (Caesar, Augustus, p. 79)
September 25. Mariana Trench (Pacific Ocean, p. 48)
September 26. Cuban dictator (Castro, Fidel, p. 79)
September 27. England (Railroad, p. 77)
September 28. Jakarta (Indonesia, p. 59)
September 29. Discovery (Space shuttle, p. 20)
September 30. Clouds of dust and gas (Nebulae, p. 15)
September 1. *Pb (Lead, p. 34)*
September 2. *9,170,000 (London, p. 68)*
September 18. *South America and North America (Chile, Arctic Ocean, p. 134)*
September 24. *Bald eagle (Birds, p. 127)*
September 26. *603 years (Inquisition, p. 75-77, calculate 1834 - 1231)*
September 26. *Johnny Appleseed (x-ref)*

October 1. The government. (Communism, p. 123)
October 2. Before Christ (Abbreviations, p. 167)
October 3. 137,800 sq. mi. (Germany, p. 58)
October 4. Russia (Satellites, p. 20)
October 5. 76 years (Life expectancy, p. 68)
October 6. "With God, all things are possible." (Ohio, p. 98)
October 7. Martin Luther King, Jr. (Nobel Peace Prize, p. 125)
October 8. 1890 (Rickenbacker, Eddie, p. 82)
October 9. Leif Ericson (Viking, p. 74)
October 10. 1892 (Pledge of Allegiance, p. 126)
October 11. 1926 (Milne, A. A., p. 159, then 162)
October 12. 1492 (Columbus, p. 75)
October 13. The President (White House, p. 129)
October 14. 761 mph (Sound, p. 24)
October 15. Proxima Centauri (Stars, p. 15)
October 16. 600,000 words (English language, p. 152)
October 17. Valley Forge (Washington, George, p. 145)
October 18. Lech Walesa (Labor union x-ref to Lech Walesa)
October 19. 29.92 (Barometer, p. 25)
October 20. Philippines (MacArthur, Douglas, p. 124)
October 21. Dynamite (Nobel, Alfred, p. 85)
October 22. Two (Solar eclipse, p. 19)
October 23. Middle East or Western Asia (Lebanon, p. 61 or 70)
October 24. 1837 (Telegraph, p. 87)
October 25. 40¢ (Postcard, p. 191)
October 26. New York State Barge System (Erie Canal, p. 88)
October 27. Nylon (Carothers, Wallace H., p. 86)
October 28. 142 steps (Statue of Liberty, p. 126)
October 29. 1929-1942 (Great Depression, p. 77)
October 30. Congregationalist, Episcopal, Baptist, Lutheran, or Presbyterian (Protestant, p. 92)
October 31. All Saint's Day (Halloween, p. 10)
October 1. *78 years old (Sousa, John, p. 83, calculate 1932 - 1854)*
October 10. *Uganda (Dams, p. 90)*
October 16. *38 years in 1993 (no reference, calculate 1993 - 1955)*
October 21. *24% (Coal, p. 33)*
October 29. *CO_2 (Carbon dioxide, p. 35)*

November 1. Anemometers (Wind, p. 25)
November 2. Israel (Palestine, x-ref to Israel)
November 3. 1836 (Austin, Stephen, p. 78)
November 4. Tuesday (Election Day, p. 10)
November 5. 1920 (Women, right to vote, p. 121)
November 6. 1 (Hydrogen, p. 34, read that atomic # equals number of electrons)
November 7. Twice (Constitution, p. 121)
November 8. 76 to 79 years (Halley's Comet, p. 17)
November 9. 3,022,000 (Berlin, p. 58)
November 10. Africa (Stanley, p. 83)
November 11. Veterans Day (Armistice Day, x-ref to Veterans Day)
November 12. Utah (Arches National Park, p. 106)
November 13. Lincoln Tunnel (Tunnels, p. 89)
November 14. 80 days (Verne, Jules, p. 162)
November 15. Pikes Peak or Bust (Pikes Peak, p. 52)
November 16. Mistletoe (Oklahoma, p. 99)
November 17. Asteroids (Meteorids, p. 16)
November 18. Railroad companies (Time Zones, p. 3)
November 19. The Gettysburg Address (Lincoln, Abraham, p. 125)
November 20. 110 feet long (Whale, p. 38)
November 21. Pilgrims (Plymoth, p. 10)
November 22. 1963 (Kennedy, p. 130)
November 23. Franklin Pierce (Presidents, p. 130)
November 24. Caffeine (Chocolate, p. 46)
November 25. Waltz (Strauss, Johann, p. 83)
November 26. Indians brought wild turkeys (Thanksgiving, p. 10)
November 27. 1816 (Match, p. 86)
November 28. Arabic, French (Mauritania, p. 62)
November 29. Prime meridian (Greenwich, p. 142)
November 30. 1990 (Yemen, p. 230)
November 2. *42 years old (Hughes, p. 81, calculate 1947 - 1905)*
November 3. *Aviator (Rickenbacker, Eddie, p. 82)*
November 26. *Lewis Carroll (Alice in Wonderland, p. 162)*
November 11. *195 years (Crusades, p. 75, calculate 1291 - 1096)*
November 26. *Soviet Union or Russia and the United States (Satellites, p. 20)*
November 28. *76 years old (Irving, Washington, p. 81, calculate 1859-1783)*

December 1. Rutherford B. Hayes (Presidents, p. 130)
December 2. Seven (National Parks, p. 106-109, scan and count)
December 3. 368 million times (Heart, p. 41)
December 4. $200 (Bangladesh, p. 54)
December 5. Intoxicating liquors (Amendments, p. 121, Amendment 21 to Amendment 18)
December 6. Slavery (Amendments, p. 120)
December 7. Japanese (Pearl Harbor, p. 77)
December 8. Confucianism (Taiwan, p. 92)
December 9. Triassic (Petrified Forest, p. 28)
December 10. Celsius or Centigrade (Temperature, p. 207)
December 11. Tulip Poplar (Indiana, p. 95)
December 12. Guglielmo Marconi (Radio, p. 86)
December 13. Five (Music, p. 197)
December 14. -129°F (Antarctica, p. 25)
December 15. Sioux Indians (Sitting Bull, p. 83)
December 16. Boston (American Revolutionary War, p. 145)
December 17. 1903 (Airplane, p. 77)
December 18. 1660 (Colonies, p. 76)
December 19. 1777-78 (Valley Forge, p. 145)
December 20. Confederate States of America (South Carolina, p. 101)
December 21. Features (Newspapers, p. 155)
December 22. 400 million years ago (Devonian, p. 28)
December 23. $100,000 (Money, p. 210)
December 24. Coal, oil, natural gas (Fossil fuels, p. 32)
December 25. 4 B.C. (Christ, p. 74)
December 26. "The buck stops here." (Truman, p. 124)
December 27. Kabul (Afghanistan, p. 53)
December 28. Herbert C. Hoover (Iowa, p. 130)
December 29. Battle of Wounded Knee (Buffalo, p. 231)
December 30. 1598 (New Mexico, p. 76)
December 31. Canada (Ottawa, p. 55)
December 3. *1810 (Canned food, p. 85)*
December 6. *Washington, D.C. (Congress, p. 128)*
December 6. *United Kingdom of Great Britain (Northern Ireland, p 70)*
December 19. *Antarctica (Vinson Massif, p. 51)*
December 24. *Seven months (Astronauts, p. 20, calculate December to July)*

OUR PLACE IN TIME

As we go through day-to-day life, we seldom think about the amazing amount of time and history which preceded our individual lives on earth. Children, especially, assume that things they've grown used to, such as television and the automobile, have always existed and will always exist. Without an understanding of what has gone before, leading to this point in time, it may be difficult for citizens and leaders of the future to plan what is to come. The activities in this section are intended to give students an appreciation of this moment in history and an internalized outline of major eras and events in western history. Although western history is not the only history or necessarily the most important one, it is the one which has most influenced dominant American culture and thought. It will serve to provide a structure or schematic framework of the past from which the histories of all peoples and cultures can proceed.

I did the activities in this section and the next, "Our Place in Space," during the first 3-4 weeks of every school year to set the stage for all future learning.

Time Line of the Earth

Materials:

2" x 16" piece of paper or 16" piece of adding machine tape for each student

Students need pencil, crayons or markers, and meter sticks or metric rulers

Facts Plus p. 27-32

Optional: fossils, especially of trilobites and/ or dinosaur bones

Background information:

Have students read p. 27-28 of *Facts Plus* for background information. You may wish to tell students that although this geological time line is generally accepted in the scientific community, it is not the only theory. Scientific theories change as new evidence is discovered. At one time, everyone agreed that the earth was flat. As contrary evidence accumulated, ideas long held to be true had to change. The theory of plate tectonics, once known as "continental drift," and the "Big Bang Theory" of the origin of the universe were scorned by scientists at one time, but as more evidence was discovered, they came to be generally accepted.

Scientists formed the theory of geological time by observing and measuring processes that occur today, such as erosion and deposition, and assuming that the same processes have occurred throughout history at a relatively uniform rate. They collect evidence from rocks, such as fossils, which show what kinds of animals and plants existed at various times and places. They deduce what the climate must have been and form theories which seem to explain the evidence.

Suggested procedure:

1. Using metric rulers, students draw a line extending the length of their strip of paper. The left edge of the strip will represent the formation of the earth and the right edge will represent today. Have students guess where along that line dinosaurs and cave men came along.
2. Each centimeter will stand for 100 million years. Each millimeter will stand for 10 million years. Students will use the time line on p. 28 of *Facts Plus* to outline geologic eras.
   Precambrian - 40 cm from right
   Paleozoic (trilobites) - 6 cm from right
   Mesozoic (dinosaurs) - 2.5 cm from right
   Cenezoic - 6.5 mm from right
   First man - .2 mm from right (just a speck)
3. Have students color each era shown on the time line and label or make a key. Discuss. Could cave men have had pet dinosaurs? How long were dinosaurs on the earth?

Geological History in a Year

Information:
One way to help students get a "feel" for geological time is to compress the history of the earth into one year. January 1 represents the beginning of the earth and midnight December 31 represents today. Have students recall where they were a year ago and think about what's happened since then so they remember what a year is like.

If we divide 4 billion years into 12 months, 365 days, etc. this is what each period of time represents:

1 year =	4,000,000,000 years
1 month =	333,333,333 years
1 day =	10,958,904 years
1 hour =	456,621 years
1 minute =	7,610 years
1 second =	127 years

Using this scale, Precambrian time extends from January 1 through winter, spring, summer and into fall. Not until November 6 does the Cambrian Era begin. Trilobites and sea animals appear in the fossil record. The first land plants and air-breathing animals come along about November 22. Forests cover the earth and coal is formed around the end of November and early December. Small dinosaurs show up at the beginning of the Mesozoic Era, December 11, and Pangaea begins to split, forming the continents. Dinosaurs rule the earth for millions of years, but die out completely by Christmas. The Cenezoic Era begins, the Age of Mammals. Not until after 7:00 p.m. on December 31, the last day of the year, does the first creature called "man" appear. Recorded, or written, history doesn't begin until about 5000 years ago, less than 40 seconds before midnight on this time scale. Columbus came to America about 4 seconds before midnight. The U.S. began about 1¾ seconds before midnight. In the *second* before midnight, people invented cars, airplanes, televisions, computers, even electric lights and zippers. Fossil fuels were mined and exploited, soil was plowed and opened to rapid erosion. Only within the last ½ second were synthetic chemicals and plastics invented, the first materials not naturally "recycled." Pesticides, atomic weapons and ozone-destroying chemicals are *very* recent innovations.

One second after midnight will be the year 2127 A.D. Five seconds after midnight will be 2635, and January 2 will be 10,960,904 A.D!

Geological Time Line Questions

Materials:
Copies of Geological Periods and Events questions, Activity Book p. 93
Answers on Activity Book p. 94
Facts Plus p. 28

Time Line of Man

Materials:
2½" x 14" strips of paper
Pencils, metric rulers

Background:
On the time line done previously, the section for man is very small. Students will now stretch that section to display more detail.

Suggested procedure:
1. Have students draw a 30 cm line to represent 3 million years. Although scientists do not all agree when the first manlike creatures lived, this will serve.
2. 1 cm = 100,000 years
   1 mm = 10,000 years
   Measure back from the right edge:
   Ice ages began – 15 cm from the right
   Man learned to control fire – 5 cm
   Neanderthal Man – 3 cm
   Cro-Magnon Man – 3.5 mm
   Cave paintings – 3 mm
   People crossed Bering Strait – 2.5 mm
   Last ice retreat – 2 mm
   Recorded history began – .5 mm

Time Line of Recorded History

Materials:

Large wall time line hung in the classroom (see Activity Book p. iv for details)

Copies of Time Line of World History, Activity Book p. 97

Facts Plus p. 72-77, 12-13

Background information:

About 5,000 years ago, things began to change quickly. The wheel was invented and writing began. People had by then domesticated plants and animals and had begun to farm and live in groups. What is called "civilization" had begun. This activity will give a brief overview of western history. Point out that there were people living throughout the world in ancient times.

Suggested procedure:

1. Using the large wall time line, talk about the way years are numbered. We use the Gregorian calendar, but there are others. Have students use the index of *Facts Plus* to find out about them. Christ was not actually born in 1 A.D. but in about 4 B.C. The makers of the calendar goofed! The years are numbered forward from Christ's birth and backwards before Christ's birth. A.D. means *anno Domini* (in the year of our Lord), and B.C. means "before Christ." We say "nineteen ninety-two" not "one thousand, one hundred ninety-two." Written 1992 not 1,992.
2. Pass out copies of Time Line of World History (AB p. 97). Every tic mark on this time line stands for 100 years. Students should write the date every 500 years, using B.C. and A.D. Then label the eras and events as the directions specify.
3. Briefly talk about ancient Egypt, perhaps showing photos or a film, or reading and introducing literature.
4. Introduce each subsequent era or event in the same way.

I tested kids week after week with this worksheet until they knew it. The large time line was left on the classroom wall all year.

Time Line Questions

Materials:

Copies of Time Line Questions, Activity Book p. 95

Answers on Activity Book p. 96

Facts Plus class set

Suggested procedure:

Students use the index to do the worksheet.

Time Line of U.S. History

Background information:

Those who teach American history may want to post a large wall time line of the past 500 years. As the school year progresses, refer to the time line and perhaps even place labels or pictures to show eras and events as they are studied. A minimum number of the following key events should be placed on it at the beginning, as was the case with the Time Line of World History. Again, these key events are only to give students reference points.

October 12, 1492 - Columbus & crew sighted land in the Bahamas

December 26, 1620 - Pilgrims landed at Plymouth, Massachusetts

1775-1781 - American Revolutionary War

1804 - Lewis & Clark Expedition

1861-1865 - Civil War

1914-1918 - World War I

1929-1942 - Great Depression

1939-1949 - World War II

Suggested procedure:

1. Either post the time line or have students make their own on long strips of paper as in previous activities.
2. Give an overview by briefly explaining key events and eras in American history. These are the first underpinnings of a schematic framework in students' minds which will be filled as study of American history continues throughout the school year. Pictures and events can be added to the time line as they're studied.

Invention Time Lines

Materials:

Copies of Activity Book p. 103-104 and p. 98-101 cut in half and taped together to make a long time line 1600 to 2000

Facts Plus p. 84-87

Background information:

Have students read *Facts Plus* p. 84 for background information on inventions, then skim p. 84-87 and make observations.

Most of the man-made things that surround us have been invented since the Industrial Revolution began. Students may use the index to find in what year that was (1769). Before then, people lived simpler lives, without the technology which makes our lives easier (though perhaps more complicated). Most homes were heated with wood, but matches weren't invented until 1816. There were no cars, bikes or airplanes. People walked or rode horses, and few traveled far from home. There was no electricity and hence nothing powered by electricity (TVs, refrigerators, radios, lights, etc.). Only a few very rich people had indoor plumbing. There are still many people alive who remember those days.

Have students try to imagine the classroom without all of the things invented since 1769. If possible, invite an old-timer to share his/her memories of "life in the olden days" with students.

Suggested procedure:

1. Choose a topic such as transportation from Activity Book p. 103 or 104 for students to put on a time line. Reproduce one copy of the list for each student or write it on the board. Different groups of students could do different time lines which could be hung side by side for a display.
2. Students use *Facts Plus* p. 84-87 to record the year of discovery or invention.
3. Cut and glue, or write each item and the year it was invented on the time line.
4. Look for patterns. Which inventions necessarily came before others?

Other Time Line Ideas

Suggested procedure:

To do any of the following time lines, have students first list events, then put them in time order, then figure the earliest date needed and the latest date needed. Work out the increments that will be best for the particular time line (5 years, 1 year, 1 month, etc.), label the blank time line (Activity Book p. 102) and write in the events and dates. Always look for patterns and cause/effect relationships.

Time line of student birthdays – January to December

Time line of students' family histories – births and deaths of family members and ancestors, major events in family history such as moves, vacations, accidents, etc.

Time line of students' lives – students brainstorm at least one event for each year of their lives and place the events on a time line. One possibility is to have students find a penny for each year they've been alive and use the pennies instead of writing dates. Share their "magnifi-cent" memories with the class.

Time line of states entering the U.S. (*Facts Plus* p. 94-101)

Time line of eclipses (*Facts Plus* p. 19)

Time line of the Space Age (*Facts Plus* p. 20)

Time line of weather & temperature records (*Facts Plus* p. 25)

Time line of the original colonies (*Facts Plus* p. 77)

Time line of various groups of notable people (*Facts Plus* p. 78-83 and Activity Book p. 6)

Time line of important canals, bridges, tunnels or dams, year opened (*Facts Plus* p. 88-90)

Time line of national parks, date established (*Facts Plus* p. 106-109)

Time line of constitutional amendments, date ratified (*Facts Plus* p. 119-122)

Time line of presidents, (*Facts Plus* p. 130)

Time line of long-time favorite books (*Facts Plus* p. 162)

Name ________________________ Date________________________

GEOLOGICAL PERIODS AND EVENTS

Answer the following questions according to the chart on page 28 of *Facts Plus*. Be sure to write "million years" if necessary.

1. How many million years ago was the earth formed? ______________
2. Name the four major eras of geological history.________________
   ____
3. How many periods were in the Paleozoic Era? ________________
4. How many periods were in the Mesozoic Era? ________________
5. How long did the Cambrian Period last? ____________________
6. How long did the Permian Period last? _____________________
7. Which period lasted the longest? __________________________
8. When did the Cretaceous Period begin? _____________________
9. When did the Paleocene Period begin? ______________________
10. In what era are we living now? ___________________________
11. In what period are we living now?__________________________
12. What is the scientific name for the "Age of Fishes"? ____________
13. How long ago were the Himalaya Mountains formed? ____________
14. How long ago were the Appalachians formed? ________________
15. How long ago were the Rocky Mountains formed? _____________
16. Which of these mountain ranges is the oldest?________________
17. In what period did the first air-breathing mammals appear?
    ____
18. In what period did the first birds appear? __________________
19. During what period was there extensive formation of coal?
    ____
20. In what period were the first forests? ______________________
21. In what period was South America cut from Africa? ____________
22. During which period did trilobites appear? __________________
23. During which period were there many large insects? ____________
24. In what period was most of North America underwater?___________
25. During which period did giant sea turtles appear? _____________

Teachers: Answers on p. 94

Name **KEY** ____________ Date ____________

GEOLOGICAL PERIODS AND EVENTS

Answer the following questions according to the chart on page 28 of *Facts Plus*. Be sure to write "million years" if necessary.

1. How many million years ago was the earth formed? ________ *4,000*
2. Name the four major eras of geological history. ________ *Precambrian, Paleozoic, Mesozoic, Cenezoic*
3. How many periods were in the Paleozoic Era? ________ *Seven*
4. How many periods were in the Mesozoic Era? ________ *Three*
5. How long did the Cambrian Period last? ________ *100 million years*
6. How long did the Permian Period last? ________ *55 million years*
7. Which period lasted the longest? ________ *Cambrian*
8. When did the Cretaceous Period begin? ________ *135 million years ago*
9. When did the Paleocene Period begin? ________ *65 million years ago*
10. In what era are we living now? ________ *Cenezoic*
11. In what period are we living now? ________ *Quaternary (or Holocene)*
12. What is the scientific name for the "Age of Fishes"? ________ *Paleozoic*
13. How long ago were the Himalaya Mountains formed? *25 million years*
14. How long ago were the Appalachians formed? *280 million years ago*
15. How long ago were the Rocky Mountains formed? *54 million yrs. ago*
16. Which of these mountain ranges is the oldest? ________ *Appalachians*
17. In what period did the first air-breathing mammals appear? ________ *Silurian*
18. In what period did the first birds appear? ________ *Jurassic*
19. During what period was there extensive formation of coal? ________ *Pennsylvanian*
20. In what period were the first forests? ________ *Devonian*
21. In what period was South America cut from Africa? ________ *Cretaceous*
22. During which period did trilobites appear? ________ *Cambrian*
23. During which period were there many large insects? ________ *Pennsylvanian*
24. In what period was most of North America underwater? ________ *Ordovician*
25. During which period did giant sea turtles appear? ________ *Cretaceous*

Teachers: Copy master on p. 93

Name______________________________ Date______________________

TIME LINE QUESTIONS

1. When did King Tutankhamen rule in Egypt? ____________________
2. When were the first recorded Olympic games held? ______________
3. When was the Golden Age of Athens? _________________________
4. When was the Roman Empire most powerful? __________________
5. What year will begin the 21st century? _______________________
6. About when did Leif Ericson discover North America? ___________
7. When did the Crusades begin? ______________________________
8. When did the Crusades end? _______________________________
9. Subtract to see how long the Crusades lasted. ____________________
10. When did the Inquisition begin? ______________________________
11. When did the Inquisition end? _______________________________
12. Subtract to see how long the Inquisition lasted. __________________
13. About how many of Europe's people were killed during the Black Death of 1347-1351 A.D.? ____
14. When did Columbus first come to America? _____________________
15. Who conquered the Aztecs in Mexico? _________________________
16. What was the first permanent settlement established by Europeans in present-day Florida? ____
17. What gold rush occurred in 1849 A.D.? ________________________
18. Which wars took place in 1689-1763 A.D.? _____________________
19. When did the Great Depression take place? _____________________
20. When did the Vietnam War end? ______________________________

The following questions are based on information on page 71.

21. About how many years ago did recorded history begin? ___________
22. How many generations have there been since slavery was outlawed in the United States? ____
23. How much is the world population increasing each month? _________
24. When is the world population expected to reach 7 billion? _________
25. Subtract to see how many years it took for world population to grow from 4 billion to 5 billion? ______________________________

Teachers: Answers on p. 96

Name **KEY** ______________________ Date ______________________

TIME LINE QUESTIONS

1. When did King Tutankhamen rule in Egypt? ______ *1347-1339 B.C.*
2. When were the first recorded Olympic games held? _______ *776 B.C.*
3. When was the Golden Age of Athens? ______________ *477-431 B.C.*
4. When was the Roman Empire most powerful? ___ *27 B.C. to 180 A.D.*
5. What year will begin the 21st century? __________________ *2000*
6. About when did Leif Ericson discover North America? ___ *1002 A.D.*
7. When did the Crusades begin? _______________________ *1096 A.D.*
8. When did the Crusades end? __________________________ *1291 A.D.*
9. Subtract to see how long the Crusades lasted. ___________ *195 years*
10. When did the Inquisition begin? _____________________ *1231 A.D.*
11. When did the Inquisition end? _______________________ *1834 A.D.*
12. Subtract to see how long the Inquisition lasted. __________ *603 years*
13. About how many of Europe's people were killed during the Black Death of 1347-1351 A.D.? _________________________ *About one-fourth*
14. When did Columbus first come to America? ____________ *1492 A.D.*
15. Who conquered the Aztecs in Mexico? __________ *Hernando Cortés*
16. What was the first permanent settlement established by Europeans in present-day Florida? _____________________ *St. Augustine, Florida*
17. What gold rush occurred in 1849 A.D.? ______ *California Gold Rush*
18. Which wars took place in 1689-1763 A.D.? __ *French & Indian Wars*
19. When did the Great Depression take place? ________ *1929-1942 A.D.*
20. When did the Vietnam War end? ____________________ *1975 A.D.*

The following questions are based on information on page 71.

21. About how many years ago did recorded history begin? *5000 years ago*
22. How many generations have there been since slavery was outlawed in the United States? ____ *4*
23. How much is the world population increasing each month? _ *7,586,664*
24. When is the world population expected to reach 7 billion? _____ *2008*
25. Subtract to see how many years it took for world population to grow from 4 billion to 5 billion? _____________________________ *12 years*

Teachers: Copy master on p. 95

Time Line of World History

Name ____________________

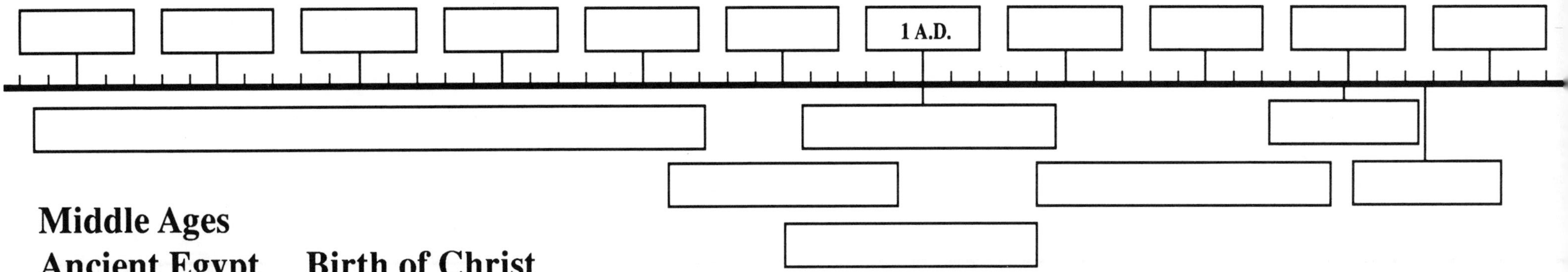

Middle Ages
Ancient Egypt
Ancient Rome
Columbus
Birth of Christ
U.S.A. began
Ancient Greece

Teachers: Lesson ideas on p. 91

Directions: Fill in the blank spaces above the time line with dates in 500 year increments. Include B.C. and A.D. Fill in the blank spaces below with one of the labels from the left.

Time Line of World History

Name ____________________

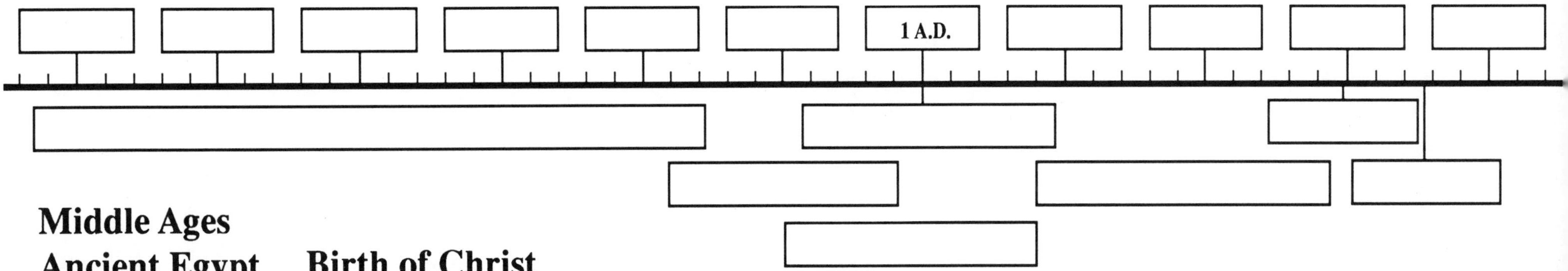

Middle Ages
Ancient Egypt
Ancient Rome
Columbus
Birth of Christ
U.S.A. began
Ancient Greece

Teachers: Lesson ideas on p. 91

Directions: Fill in the blank spaces above the time line with dates in 500 year increments. Include B.C. and A.D. Fill in the blank spaces below with one of the labels from the left.

© 1993 Susan C. Anthony - Reproducible for classroom use

1600

1605

1610

1615

1620

1625

1630

1635

1640

1645

1650

1655

1660

1665

1670

1675

1680

1685

1690

1695

1700

1705

1710

1715

1720

1725

1730

1735

1740

1745

1750

1755

1760

1765

1770

1775

1780

1785

1790

1795

1800

1805

1810

1815

1820

1825

1830

1835

1840

1845

1850

1855

1860

1865

1870

1875

1880

1885

1890

1895

1900

1905

1910

1915

1920

1925

1930

1935

1940

1945

1950

1955

1960

1965

1970

1975

1980

1985

1990

1995

Name ____________________

TRANSPORTATION

Airplane ____________________
Automobile with Gasoline Engine ________
Hot Air Balloon ____________________
Bicycle ____________________
Air Brake ____________________
Magnetic Compass ____________________
Elevator with Brake ____________________
Diesel Engine ____________________
4-cycle Gasoline Engine ____________________
Helicopter ____________________
Jet Engine ____________________
Steam Locomotive ____________________
Outboard Motor ____________________
Motorcycle ____________________
Parachute ____________________
Propeller ____________________
Rocket ____________________
Vulcanized Rubber ____________________
Modern Steam Engine ____________________
Steamship ____________________
Submarine ____________________
Pneumatic Tire ____________________
Tractor ____________________

Teachers: Directions on p. 92, answers on p. 104

Name ____________________

SCIENCE and MEDICINE

Anesthetic (on man) ____________________
Antiseptic for Surgery ____________________
Aspirin ____________________
Barometer ____________________
Electric Battery ____________________
Bifocal Eyeglasses ____________________
Electric Generator ____________________
Laser ____________________
Compound Microscope ____________________
Nuclear Reactor ____________________
Polio Vaccine ____________________
Smallpox Vaccine ____________________
Stethoscope ____________________
Telescope ____________________
Thermometer (Fahrenheit) ____________________
Thermometer (Celsius) ____________________
Bacteria Discovered ____________________
Discovery that Blood Circulates ________
Gravity Discovered ____________________
Laws of Heridity Discovered ____________________
Penicillin Discovered ____________________
Theory of Relativity ____________________
X-rays Discovered ____________________

Name ____________________

FOOD & HOME

Aluminum Manufacture ____________________
Electric Battery ____________________
Corn Flakes Cereal ____________________
Grape Nuts Cereal ____________________
Canned Food ____________________
Quick Frozen Food ____________________
Chewing Gum ____________________
Lawn Mower ____________________
Incandescent Light Bulb ____________________
Fluorescent Light ____________________
Match ____________________
Paper ____________________
Ball-Point Pen ____________________
Wooden Pencil ____________________
Phonograph ____________________
Safety Pin ____________________
Potato Chips ____________________
Pressure Cooker ____________________
Radio ____________________
Rubber Bands ____________________
Drinking Straws ____________________
Telephone ____________________
Television ____________________
Toothbrush ____________________
Home Vacuum Cleaner ____________________

Name ____________________

COMMUNICATION

Adding Machine ____________
Braille ____________
Cash Register ____________
Hand-held Camera ____________
Electronic Digital Computer ____________
Analog Computer ____________
Motion Pictures ____________
Daguerreotype Photography ____________
Printing, Movable Type ____________
Radio ____________
Magnetic Tape Recorder ____________
Telegraph ____________
Telephone ____________
Television ____________
Television Camera ____________
Typewriter ____________
Xerography (copy machine) ____________

Name ____________________

ENTERTAINMENT

Accordion ____________
Basketball ____________
Ferris Wheel ____________
Frisbee ____________
Jigsaw Puzzle ____________
Motion Pictures ____________
Piano ____________
Radio ____________
Roller Skate ____________
Saxophone ____________
Scuba Gear ____________
Synthesizer ____________
Television ____________
Modern Trampoline ____________
Water Skis ____________

Name ____________________

CLOTHING

Cotton Gin ____________
Denim Jeans ____________
Chemical Dyes ____________
Earmuffs ____________
Power Loom ____________
Nylon ____________
Sewing Machine ____________
Flying Shuttle ____________
Spinning Jenny ____________
Spinning Mule ____________
Spinning Wheel ____________
Modern Steam Engine ____________
Velcro ____________
Zipper ____________

COMMUNICATION Answers

1885	1893	1876
1829	1837	1925
1879	1456	1927
1888	1895	1867
1946	1898	1938
1930	1837	

ENTERTAINMENT Answers

1829	1709	1925
1891	1895	1936
1893	1863	1922
1948	1840	
1767	1943	
1893	1964	

CLOTHING Answers

1793	1846	1956
1873	1733	1893
1856	1764	
1873	1779	
1785	c.500 B.C.	
1935	1769	

TRANSPORTATION Answers

1903	1866	1926
1885	1939	1839
1783	1930	1769
1790	1804	1783
1868	1905	1891
c.1088	1885	1845
1854	1783	1892
1892	1836	

Answers: SCIENCE & MEDICINE

1842	1590	1674
1865	1942	1628
1853	1953	1665
1643	1796	1865
c.1800	1816	1928
1784	1608	1905
1832	1714	1895
1960	1742	

FOOD & HOME Answers

		1853
1886	1879	1679
c.1800	1867	1895
1894	1816	1821
1897	105	1888
1810	1888	1876
1925	1683	1925
1870	1877	1770
1830	1849	1908

Teachers: Directions on p. 92

OUR PLACE IN SPACE

Perhaps even more amazing than the expanse of time which preceded our arrival on earth is the expanse of space which surrounds us at this very moment. In my own classes, I begin each year with a unit on time and then space, beginning with the universe, then the galaxy, solar system, the moon and our own earth. The purpose is to set a broad time/space context for everything we see, do and learn in class and in life.

Brainstorm & Read

Materials:

Large sheet of butcher paper to be posted
Facts Plus class set

Suggested procedure:

1. Ask students to brainstorm things they know about space and questions they have. Record responses on the butcher paper.
2. Keep the questions posted in the classroom throughout the unit. Check off the questions as they're answered. Add new questions to the list as they come up. Challenge students to use spare time to research answers and to bring in resources from home.
3. Have students read *Facts Plus* p. 15-16. Also skim p. 11 and 14 and check out books and resources from the library.
   How many ways is the earth moving? How fast?
   Rotating on axis: 1,038 mph on equator
   Revolving around sun: 66,600 mph
   Traveling around Milky Way with the sun: 561,600 mph
   Total: as much as 628,638 mph, or 175 miles per second.
   Name a place about 175 miles away. That's more than three hours drive at 55 miles per hour.
4. When finalizing the unit, check the list to see if all questions have been answered. If not, a student may write to:
   NASA
   600 Independence Avenue
   Washington, DC 20546

Space Questions

Materials:

Space Questions, Activity Book p. 111
Answers on p. 112
Overhead transparency of chart on p. 17 of *Facts Plus* (permission to copy granted)
Calculators

Suggested procedure:

1. Practice reading the Planet Chart on p. 17 of *Facts Plus*. Use a transparency if needed (permission to copy granted for this).
2. Give the students time to find answers to the first 15 questions and brainstorm how to solve the last 10 questions.
3. Check the first 15 questions and work through the last 10 questions with students.
4. Have students make up their own questions and challenge each other to find answers.

Make Your Own Solar System

Materials:

Copies of planet outlines, Activity Book p. 109-110
Long sheets of black paper, 12" x 5'
12" x 3" rectangles of light colored construction paper for Saturn's rings
12" x 5" rectangles of yellow paper for suns
Reference books or photos showing the color of the planets as photographed from space

Suggested procedure:

1. Have students follow directions on Activity Book p. 109.
2. Explain that on this scale the sun would be six *feet* in diameter. Measure six feet.

Cards for Personal Solar Systems

Materials:

Copies of paragraph to be filled in, Activity Book p. 107. This can be written on the board instead of duplicated.

4 x 6 ruled index cards

Planets chart from *Facts Plus* p. 17

Solar systems from earlier activity

Suggested procedure:

1. Demonstrate filling in the paragraph for one of the planets.
2. Students will fill in the blank paragraph on p. 107 for an assigned planet.
3. Check paragraphs as they're completed and have students recopy them in their best handwriting on an index card.
4. Display at least one student's solar system from the previous activity with a card beneath each planet.

Putting the Planets in Order

Materials:

Planets chart from *Facts Plus* p. 17

Suggested procedure:

1. Have students list the planets in order of size, largest to smallest. *Jupiter, Saturn, Uranus, Neptune, Earth, Venus, Mars, Mercury, Pluto.*
2. List planets in order of length of day, long to short. *Venus, Mercury, Pluto, Mars, Earth, Uranus, Neptune, Saturn, Jupiter.*
3. Have students list the planets in order of number of moons, most to least. *Saturn, Jupiter, Uranus, Neptune, Mars, Earth/ Pluto. Venus and Mercury have none.*
4. Have students list the planets in order of temperature, highest to lowest. *Venus, Mercury, Earth, Mars, Jupiter, Saturn, Uranus, Pluto, Neptune.*
5. Are there any patterns?
6. Using the chart of Melting and Boiling Points, *Facts Plus* p. 35, determine on which planets oxygen would be frozen. *Neptune and possibly Pluto.*

Solar System Worksheet

Materials:

Solar System worksheet, Activity Bk. p. 108

Suggested procedure:

1. Follow directions on the worksheet.
2. Have students memorize planets in order. Mnemonic: **M**y **v**ery **e**xcellent **m**other **j**ust **s**erved **u**s **n**ine **p**izzas.
3. Use the worksheet for assessment.

Pacing Out Space

Materials:

10 cards with names of each planet and sun

Suggested procedure:

1. The teacher may wish to pace off these distances in advance on the playground.
2. Assign a child to represent each planet and the sun and pass out the respective cards.
3. Explain that space is so vast that it is hard to comprehend the distances between planets and stars. Students' solar systems show things much too close together. To illustrate this, the sun, six feet in diameter on the scale used for the students' solar systems, is "shrunk" to 1/8" in diameter. How small would Earth be on that scale?
4. On the playground, teacher or another adult paces off the distance between planets and places children representing "planets" in their places.

Sun to Mercury	3/4 pace
Mercury to Venus	1 long pace (1.1)
Venus to Earth	1 1/3 pace
Earth to Mars	1 1/4 pace
Mars to Jupiter	14 paces
Jupiter to Saturn	16 paces
Saturn to Uranus	35 paces
Uranus to Neptune	41 paces
Neptune to Pluto	34 paces

5. On this scale, the nearest star would be 13 *miles* away. Name a place about 13 miles away. There is a lot of *space* in space.

Note: Pluto is currently closer to the sun than Neptune. See *Facts Plus* p. 17.

Measuring Space Between Planets

Materials:

Strips of paper or adding machine tape 15 feet long
Rulers and pencils
Chart below reproduced or on the board

Note to the teacher:

This activity is an alternative to the previous activity, "Pacing Out Space."

Suggested procedure:

1. Explain to students that the solar systems they made show the planets far too close together. In this activity, they'll measure the distance from the sun to each planet. On this scale, the sun would be too small to see. Tiny labeled dots will show the sun and planets, but the dots will be *much* larger than planets would be on this scale.
2. Have students place a small dot for the sun near the left side of the long paper. Measure the distances to each planet *from the sun* (not from the last planet):

Sun to Mercury	2 inches
Sun to Venus	3 inches
Sun to Earth	4 inches
Sun to Mars	6 inches
Sun to Jupiter	1 foot 9 inches
Sun to Saturn	3 feet 2 inches
Sun to Uranus	6 feet 5 inches
Sun to Neptune	10 feet 1 inch
Sun to Pluto	13 feet 3 inches

Weigh Away

Materials and prerequisites:

Calculators or ability to multiply decimals
Interplanetary weight chart on board. Copy from the "weight" column below. This is surface gravity compared to earth if earth = 1.0.

Suggested procedure:

1. Discuss how gravity determines what we call "weight."
2. Have students multiply their weight on earth by the figures in the chart to see how much they would "weigh" elsewhere.
3. Make up math problems based on this. For example, "How much more would I weigh on Jupiter than on Earth?"
4. You may also wish to discuss "density" (hardness or compactness) and the gas planets. Which planets are dense enough for landing a spaceship?

	Weight (Earth = 1)	**Density** (Water = 1)
Sun	28.00	1.4
Mercury	.16	3.8
Venus	.28	5.1
Earth	1.00	5.5
Earth's moon	.17	3.3
Mars	.38	4.0
Jupiter	2.6	1.3
Saturn	1.2	0.7
Uranus	1.1	1.3
Neptune	1.4	2.2
Pluto	?	1.0

_______________ is the _______________ planet from the
(name of planet) (first, second, third, etc.)

sun. It is about _____________ million miles from the sun and it travels about _____________ miles per second in its orbit. _______________'s year is _________ earth days long, and its day is _______________________ long in earth time. ___________ has __________ moons and the temperature there is around _______° Fahrenheit.

____
(student name)

Teachers: Lesson p. 106

THE SOLAR SYSTEM

Name________________________________

Use these words to label the planets:

Jupiter	Uranus
Asteroids	Neptune
Venus	Mercury
Earth	Pluto
Saturn	
Mars	
Sun	

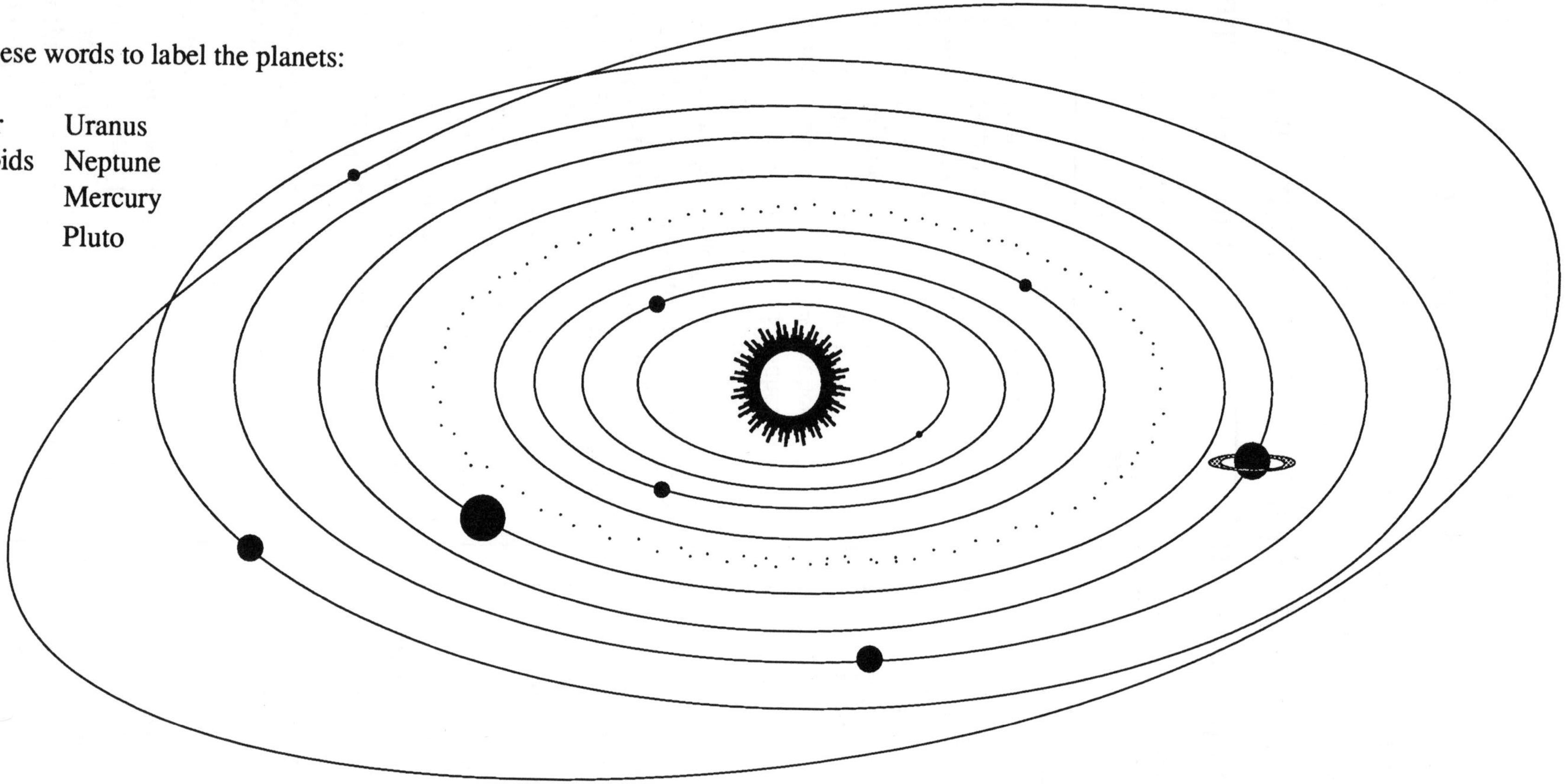

How many planets are there?__________

Directions: Write the name of the planet or the word that best fits in the blanks to the right. The words you will need are listed below:

Jupiter	Mars	Sun
Asteroids	Mercury	Pluto
Venus	Uranus	Saturn
Earth	Neptune	

Teachers: Lesson on p. 106

____________________ The biggest object in the solar system.

____________________ The morning and evening star. It is covered with clouds.

____________________ A planet with rings that can be seen through a telescope.

____________________ Our own home.

____________________ The planet usually furthest from the sun.

____________________ A planet that rotates end over end, beyond Jupiter.

____________________ The biggest planet. It has a big red spot.

____________________ The red planet. Viking I landed there.

____________________ The next to last planet. The last planet until 1999.

Name: ______________________

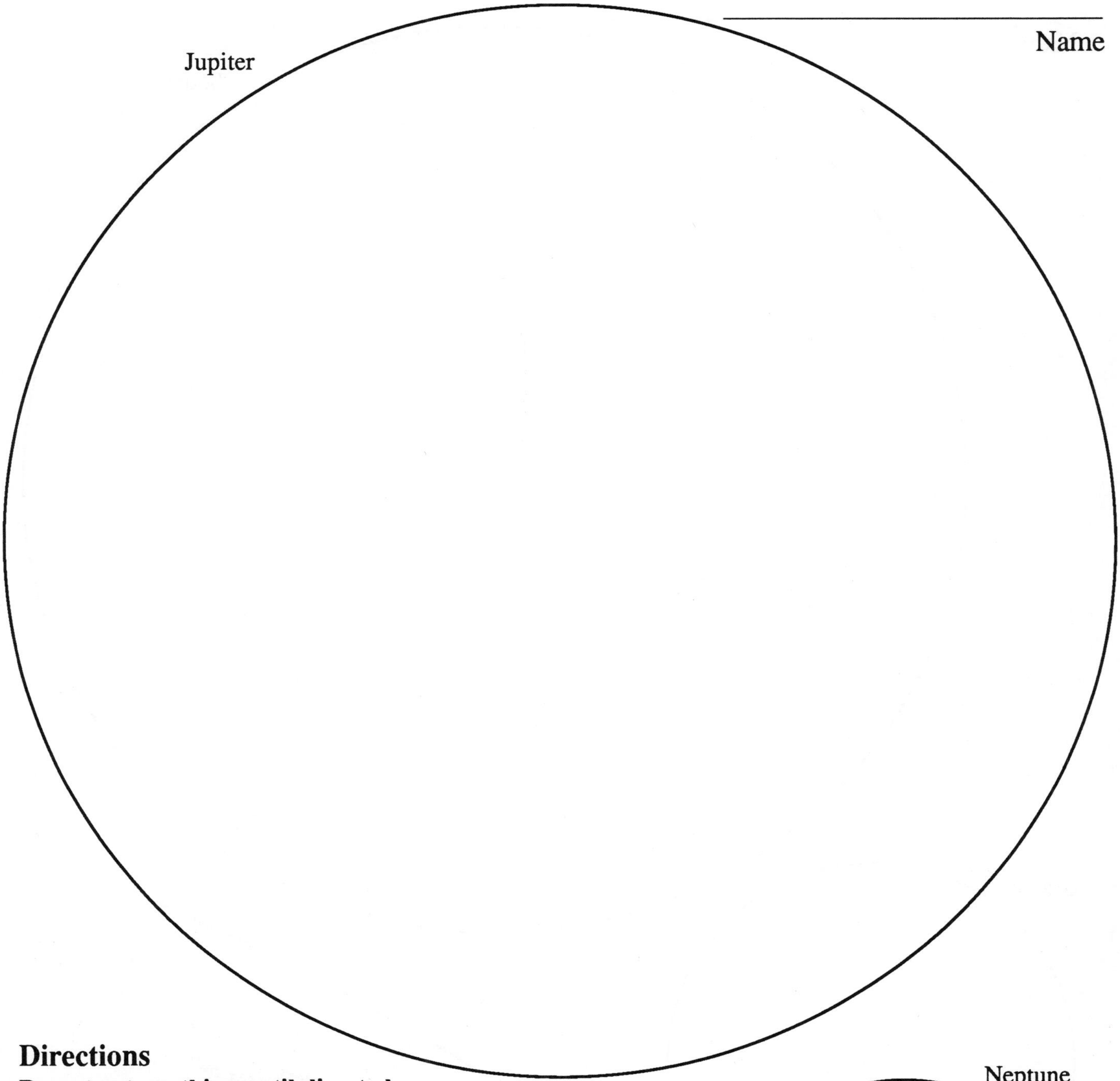

Directions

Do not cut anything until directed.

1. Color the planets. Use reference sources for correct colors. Don't forget Jupiter's red spot in the southern hemisphere.
2. Cut rings for Saturn and put them on.
3. Get a piece of long black paper.
4. Get yellow paper. Make a part of the sun to put on black paper at one end.
5. Cut each planet in order from the sun and glue it down. Spread out the planets so that all fit on the black paper.

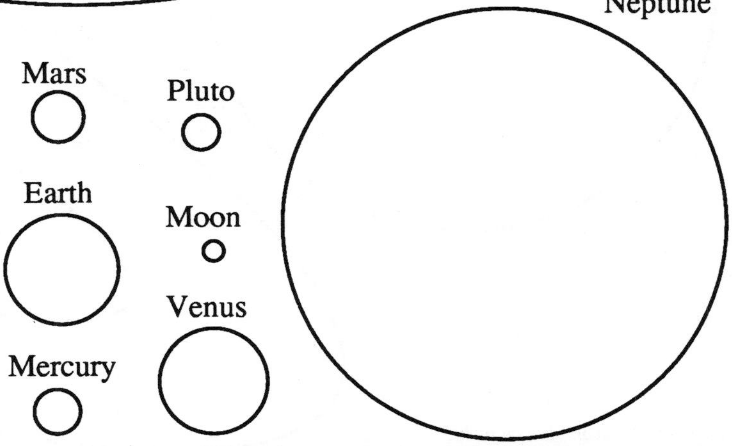

Teachers: Lesson plan on p. 105

____
Name

Saturn

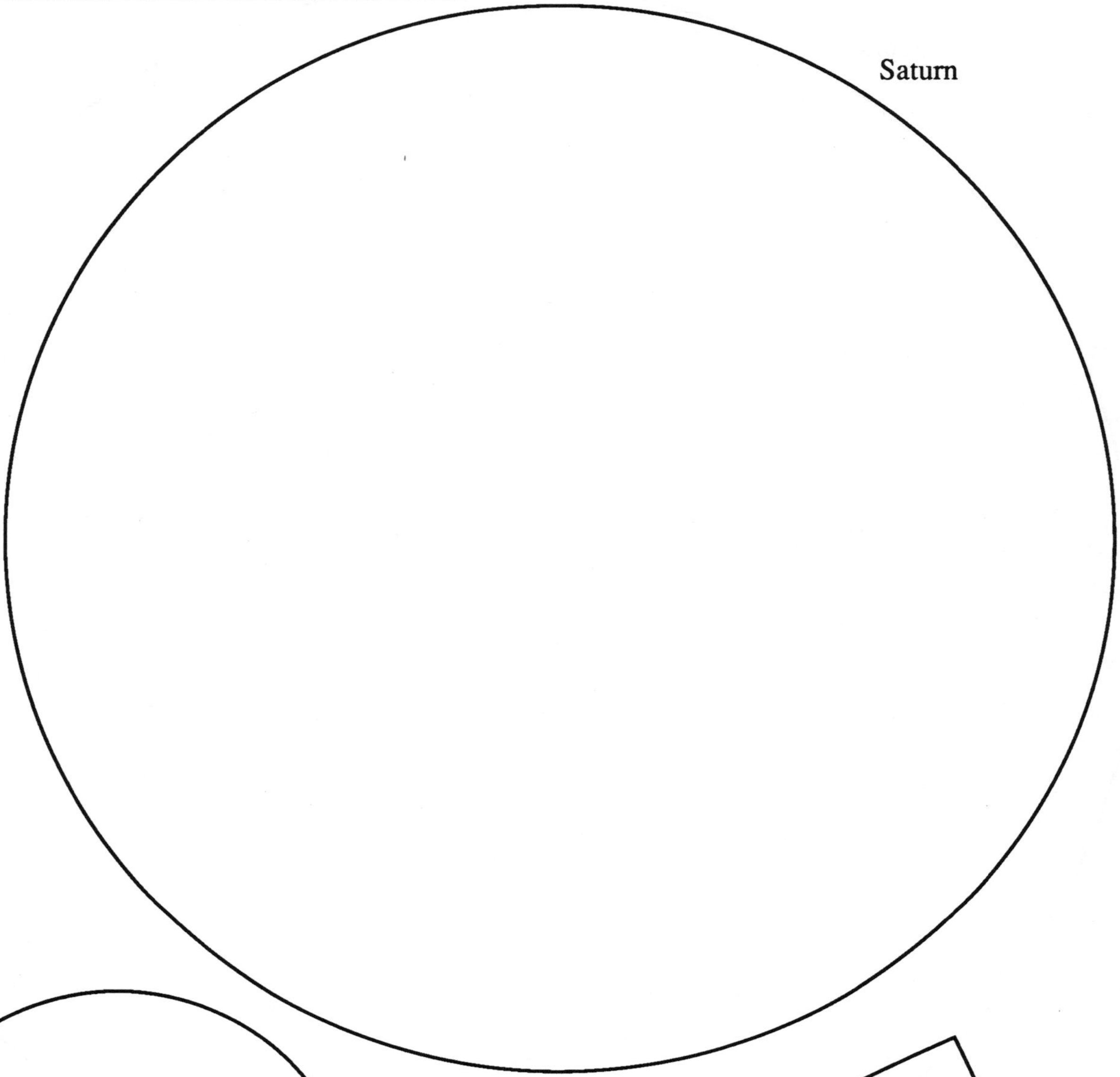

Uranus

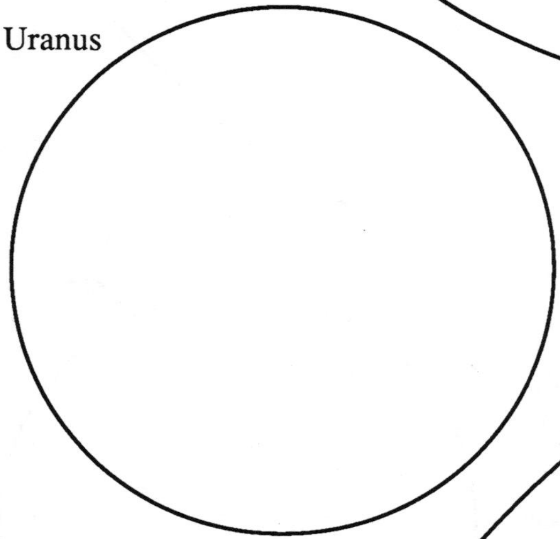

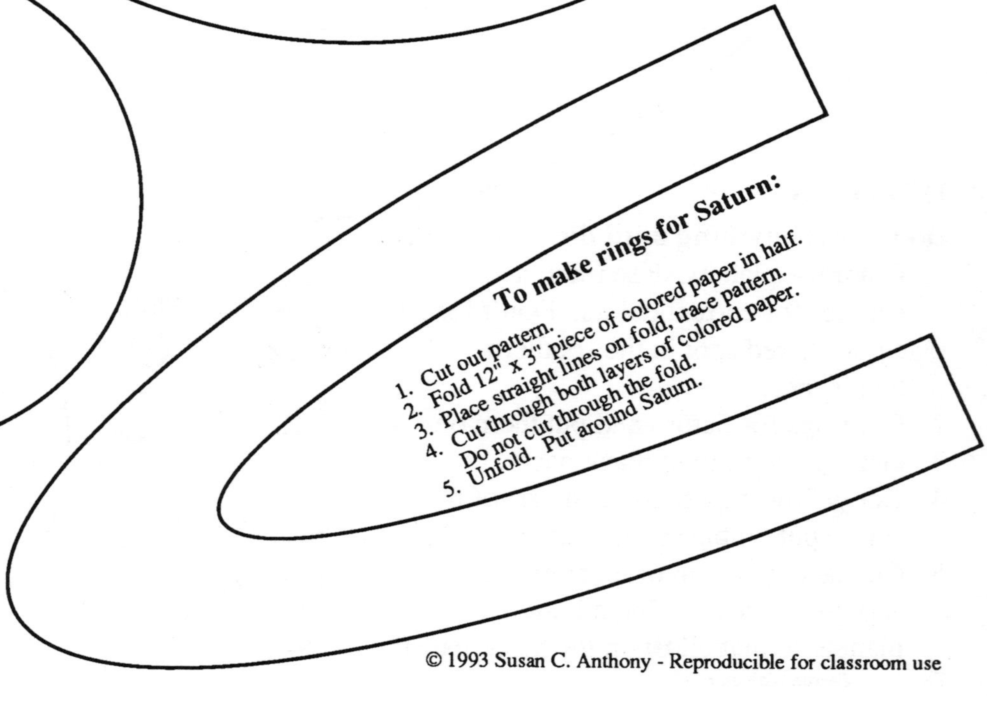

Teachers: Lesson plan on p. 105

Name______________________________ **Date**______________________

SPACE QUESTIONS

1. How far is Earth from the sun? ______________________________
2. Which planet has the greatest diameter? ________________________
3. Which is the smallest planet? ______________________________
4. Which planet is the fastest in its orbit? _______________________
5. Which planets are the slowest in orbit? _______________________
6. What is a pattern concerning speeds in orbit? __________________
   ____
7. How long is a year on Mercury? ____________________________
8. How long is a year on Pluto? ______________________________
9. What is a pattern concerning the lengths of the years? ___________
   ____
10. Which planet has the shortest day? ___________________________
11. Which planet has the longest day? ___________________________
12. Which planet is hottest? _________________________________
13. Which planet is coldest? _________________________________
14. Which planet has the most moons? ___________________________
15. Which planet has 8 moons?__________________________________
16. Which two planets are closest in diameter (only about 400 miles difference)? _________________________________
17. Is Earth's orbit closer to Venus or to Mars? ____________________
18. How much longer is Venus' day than Venus' year in Earth days? ____
    ____
19. How many moons are in the solar system altogether? ____________
20. How much larger in diameter is Jupiter than Saturn? ____________
21. How much faster is Mercury than Earth? _______________________
22. How much longer is a year on Neptune than on Uranus in Earth days?
    ____
23. How much longer is a day on Mars than on Earth?_______________
24. How much further from the sun is Pluto than Neptune on average?
    ____
25. Which planet is furthest from the sun right now? _______________

Teachers: Lesson on p. 105, answers on p. 112

Name **KEY** ________________ Date________________

SPACE QUESTIONS

1. How far is Earth from the sun? ________ *93 million miles*
2. Which planet has the greatest diameter? ________ *Jupiter*
3. Which is the smallest planet? ________ *Pluto*
4. Which planet is the fastest in its orbit? ________ *Mercury*
5. Which planets are the slowest in orbit? ________ *Neptune and Pluto*
6. What is a pattern concerning speeds in orbit? __ *The closer to the sun a planet is, the faster its speed in orbit and vice versa.*
7. How long is a year on Mercury? ________ *88 earth days*
8. How long is a year on Pluto? ________ *90,800 earth days*
9. What is a pattern concerning the lengths of the years? ____ *The closer to the sun a planet is, the shorter its year and vice versa.*
10. Which planet has the shortest day? ________ *Jupiter*
11. Which planet has the longest day? ________ *Venus*
12. Which planet is hottest? ________ *Venus*
13. Which planet is coldest? ________ *Pluto*
14. Which planet has the most moons? ________ *Saturn*
15. Which planet has 8 moons? ________ *Neptune*
16. Which two planets are closest in diameter (only about 400 miles difference)? ________ *Venus and Earth*
17. Is the orbit of Earth closer to Venus or to Mars? ________ *Venus*
18. How much longer is Venus' day than Venus' year in Earth days? ________ *18 Earth days*
19. How many moons are in the solar system altogether? ________ *61*
20. How much larger in diameter is Jupiter than Saturn? ___ *13,948 miles*
21. How much faster is Mercury than Earth? ________ *11 miles per second*
22. How much longer is a year on Neptune than on Uranus in Earth days? ________ *29,505 Earth days*
23. How much longer is a day on Mars than on Earth?________ *37 minutes*
24. How much further from the sun is Pluto than Neptune on average? ________ *867 million miles*
25. Which planet is furthest from the sun right now? ________ *Neptune*

Teachers: Lesson on p. 105, copy master on p. 111

UNITED STATES MAPS, CHARTS AND GRAPHS

The activities here may be used before or during a study of the regions of the United States, or as as a lead-up to individual state reports. First show a world map or globe with the correct size and placement of Alaska and Hawaii. Mapmakers use insets for those states so that they can fit more information on a rectangular piece of paper. The scale of miles for inset maps is often different.

Census Region Maps

Materials:

Maps of a region, Activity Book p. 116, 118, 120, or 122, with names of states and/or capitals from p. 114 taped on if desired.

Suggested activities:

1. Have students fill in a copy of a census region map with state names and capitals. Color it if desired and use it for study.
2. Use blank maps with names of states and capitals taped onto the master for testing.
3. Have students use the base maps to create product maps, physical maps, etc.

Census Region Charts and Graphs

Materials:

Chart for a region, Activity Book p. 115, 117, 119, or 121. Answers on p. 123

Copies of graph pages for population density, Activity Book p. 151 to 154, and per capita income, Activity Book p. 155 through 156. Change *GNP* to *Income*.

Suggested procedure:

1. Make sure students understand the meaning of the terms on the chart. See *Facts Plus* p. 231. Distinguish between "per capita GNP" and "per capita income."
2. Have students guess which state in a region has the most/least people, the highest/lowest population density, the largest/smallest area, etc. Fill in the chart to confirm if guesses were correct.
3. Graph population densities and per capita incomes. Compare results from all regions. What could account for the differences?

Outline Map of the U.S.

Materials:

Activity Book p. 124, with state names from p. 114 taped on to the master if desired.

Suggested activities:

1. Have students fill in state names or place capitals or major cities on the blank map. They may use pages 132-133 of *Facts Plus* or an atlas. Color.
2. Have students use an atlas to find the natural features responsible for "wiggly" state lines (generally rivers).
3. After students have learned state names by region, use the U.S. map for review and testing, with state names from p. 114 of the Activity Book taped on.

U.S. Population Growth

Materials:

U.S. Population Chart, Activity Book p. 125

U.S. Population Graph, Activity Bk., p. 126

Calculators

Suggested activities:

1. Have students divide all populations by all areas for population density.
2. Students subtract census of the year minus previous census for increase.
3. Use the line graph to plot U.S. population growth since 1790.

Answers to p. 125: (1790) 4; (1800) 6 –1,379,269; (1810) 4 - 1,931,398; (1820) 5 – 2,399,572; (1830) 7 – 3,226,567; (1840) 10 – 4,203,433; (1850) 8 – 6,122,423; (1860) 10 – 8,251,445; (1870) 13 – 8,375,128; (1880) 17 – 10,337,334; (1890) 21 – 12,791,931; (1900) 25 – 13,046,861; (1910) 30 – 15,977,691; (1920) 13,738,354; (1930) 17,064,426; (1940) 8,894,229; (1950) 19,028,086; (1960) 28,625,814; (1970) 23,978,856; (1980) 23,243,774; (1990) 22,476,978

Alabama
Alaska
Arizona
Arkansas
California
Colorado
Connecticut
Delaware
Florida
Georgia
Hawaii
Idaho
Illinois
Indiana
Iowa
Kansas
Kentucky
Louisiana
Maine
Maryland
Massachusetts
Michigan
Minnesota
Mississippi
Missouri
Montana
Nebraska
Nevada
New Hampshire
New Jersey
New Mexico
New York
North Carolina
North Dakota
Ohio
Oklahoma
Oregon
Pennsylvania
Rhode Island
South Carolina
South Dakota
Tennessee
Texas
Utah
Vermont
Virginia
Washington
West Virginia
Wisconsin
Wyoming

North Central Census Region
Minnesota
Kansas
Ohio
Iowa
Illinois
Wisconsin
Michigan
Indiana
North Dakota
Nebraska
Missouri
South Dakota

North Central Capitals
Pierre
Jefferson City
Lansing
Columbus
Springfield
St. Paul
Topeka
Indianapolis
Bismarck
Des Moines
Lincoln
Madison

Great Lakes
Lake Ontario
Lake Superior
Lake Erie
Lake Huron
Lake Michigan

Western Census Region
New Mexico
Hawaii
Montana
Oregon
Colorado
California
Arizona
Idaho
Utah
Washington
Alaska
Nevada
Wyoming

Western Capitals
Sacramento
Salt Lake City
Denver
Helena
Juneau
Salem
Santa Fe
Olympia
Carson City
Phoenix
Cheyenne
Boise
Honolulu

Extra Map Activities

Suggested activities for blank United States maps:

1. After students learn the names of the states, give each a blank map and directions to find their way to a mystery state. For example: Begin in Colorado. Go northeast (Nebraska), then directly north (South Dakota), then to the northwest (Montana), then directly west (Idaho). Students may write their own directions.
2. Use the blank U.S. map as a gameboard. Students first number states in the order they were admitted to the Union (see *Facts Plus* p. 94-101). Roll dice and proceed from Delaware to Hawaii, naming states along the way.

These lists of states and capitals may be cut out and glued to blank maps to make masters. Students label the states and capitals from memory. Spellings must be correct.

Southern Census Region

Oklahoma	Mississippi
South Carolina	Arkansas
Florida	Alabama
Louisiana	Virginia
West Virginia	Maryland
Texas	North Carolina
Delaware	Tennessee
Kentucky	Georgia

Southern Capitals
Columbia
Dover
Austin
Jackson
Tallahassee
Nashville
Frankfort
Annapolis
Charleston
Raleigh
Montgomery
Baton Rouge
Atlanta
Richmond
Little Rock
Oklahoma City

Teachers: Directions on p. 113

Northeast Census Region	**Northeast Capitals**
New York	Trenton
Maine	Boston
Massachusetts	Hartford
New Jersey	Montpelier
New Hampshire	Harrisburg
Rhode Island	Albany
Pennsylvania	Concord
Vermont	Augusta
Connecticut	Providence

Name________________________

Northeast Census Region

State	Capital	Population	Population Density	Per Capita Income	Area (square miles)
Connecticut					
Maine					
Massachusetts					
New Hampshire					
New Jersey					
New York					
Pennsylvania					
Rhode Island					
Vermont					

Teachers: Directions on p. 113 , answers on p. 123

Name ______________________________________

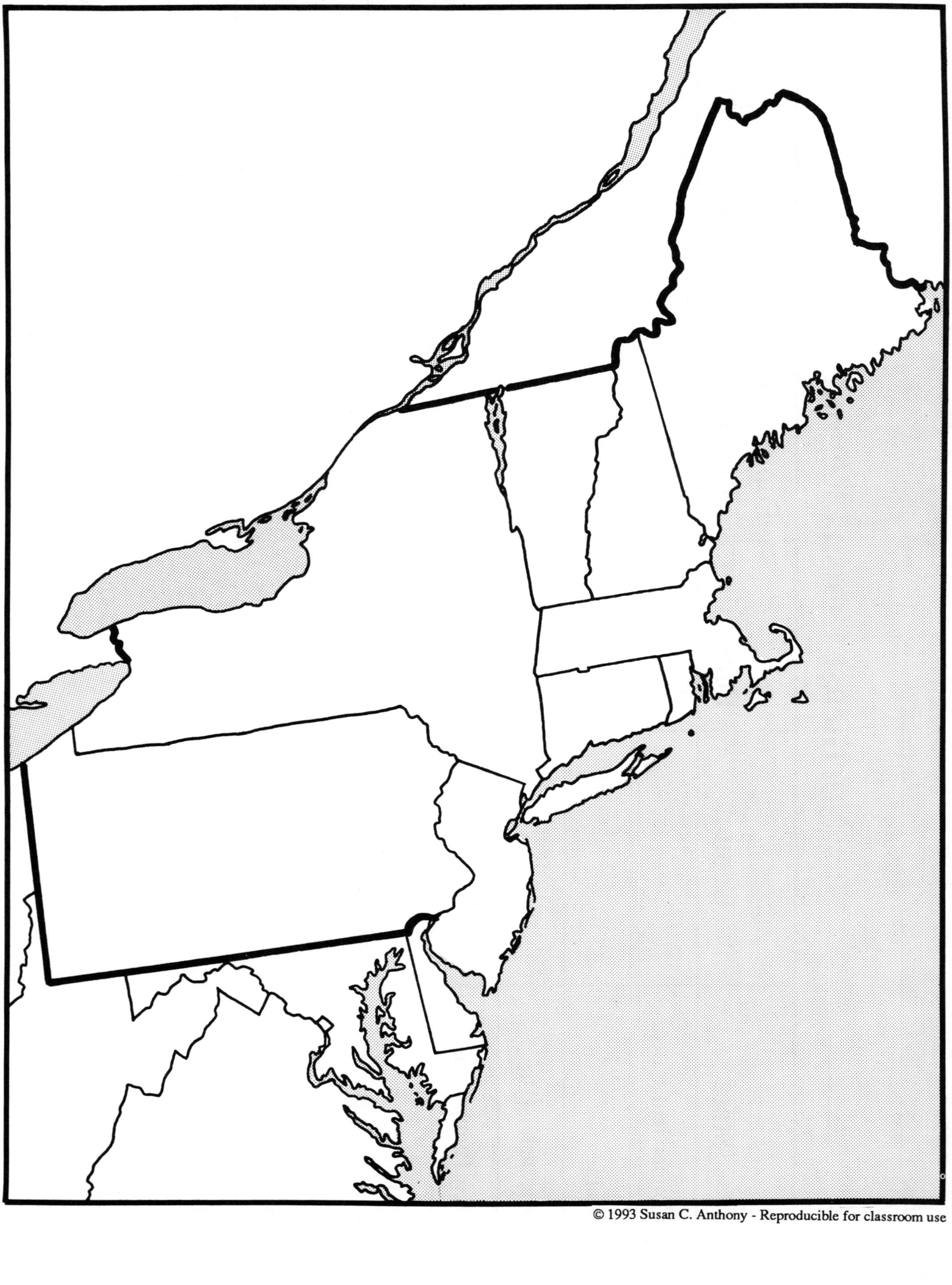

Southern Census Region

Name ______________________

State	Capital	Population	Population Density	Per Capita Income	Area (square miles)
Alabama					
Arkansas					
Delaware					
Florida					
Georgia					
Kentucky					
Louisiana					
Maryland					
Mississippi					
North Carolina					
Oklahoma					
South Carolina					
Tennessee					
Texas					
Virginia					
West Virginia					

Teachers: Directions on p. 113, answers on p. 123

Name ________________

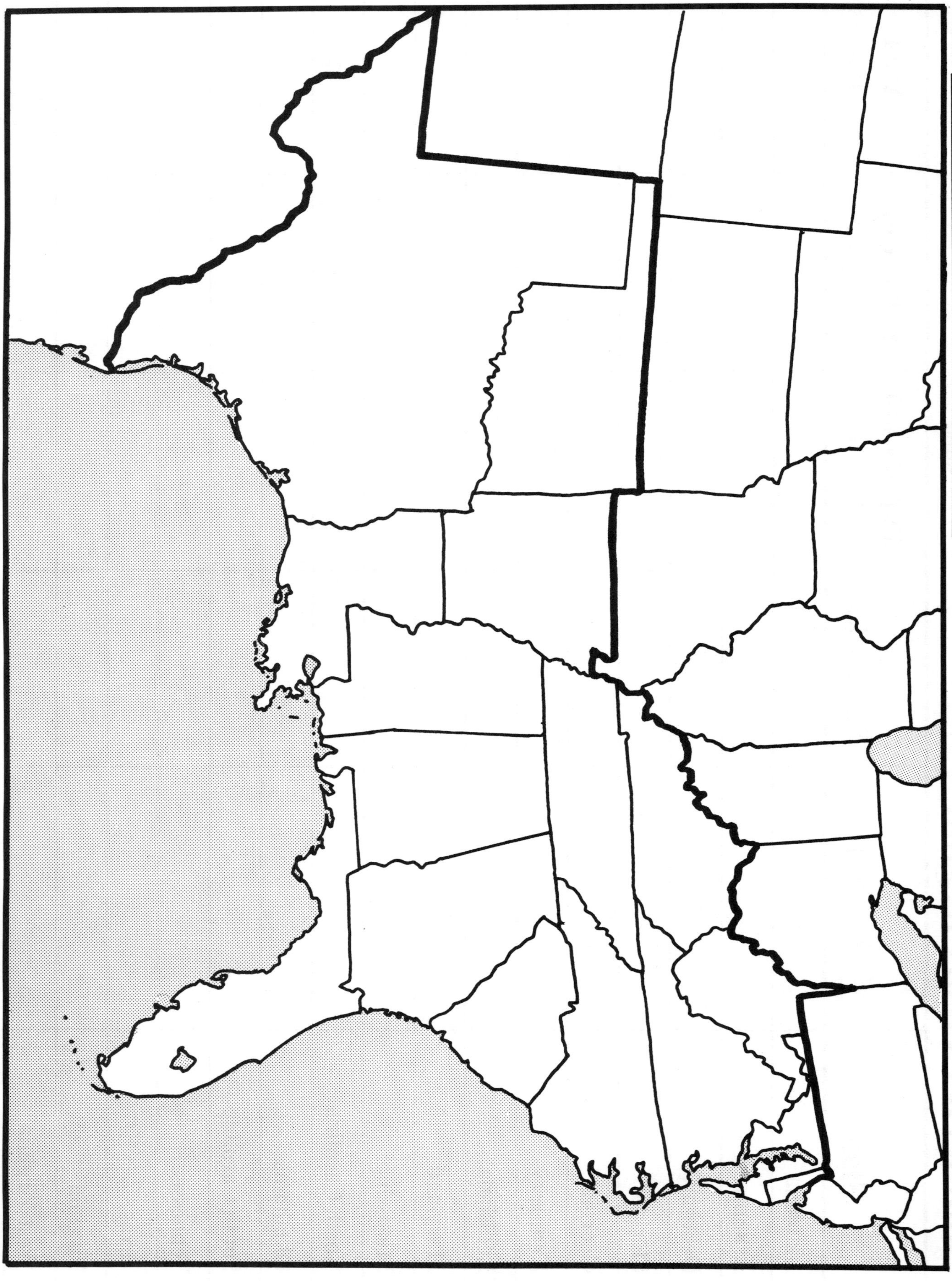

North Central Census Region

Name ______________________

State	Capital	Population	Population Density	Per Capita Income	Area (square miles)
Illinois					
Indiana					
Iowa					
Kansas					
Michigan					
Minnesota					
Missouri					
Nebraska					
North Dakoka					
Ohio					
South Dakota					
Wisconsin					

Teachers: Directions on p. 113, answers on p. 123

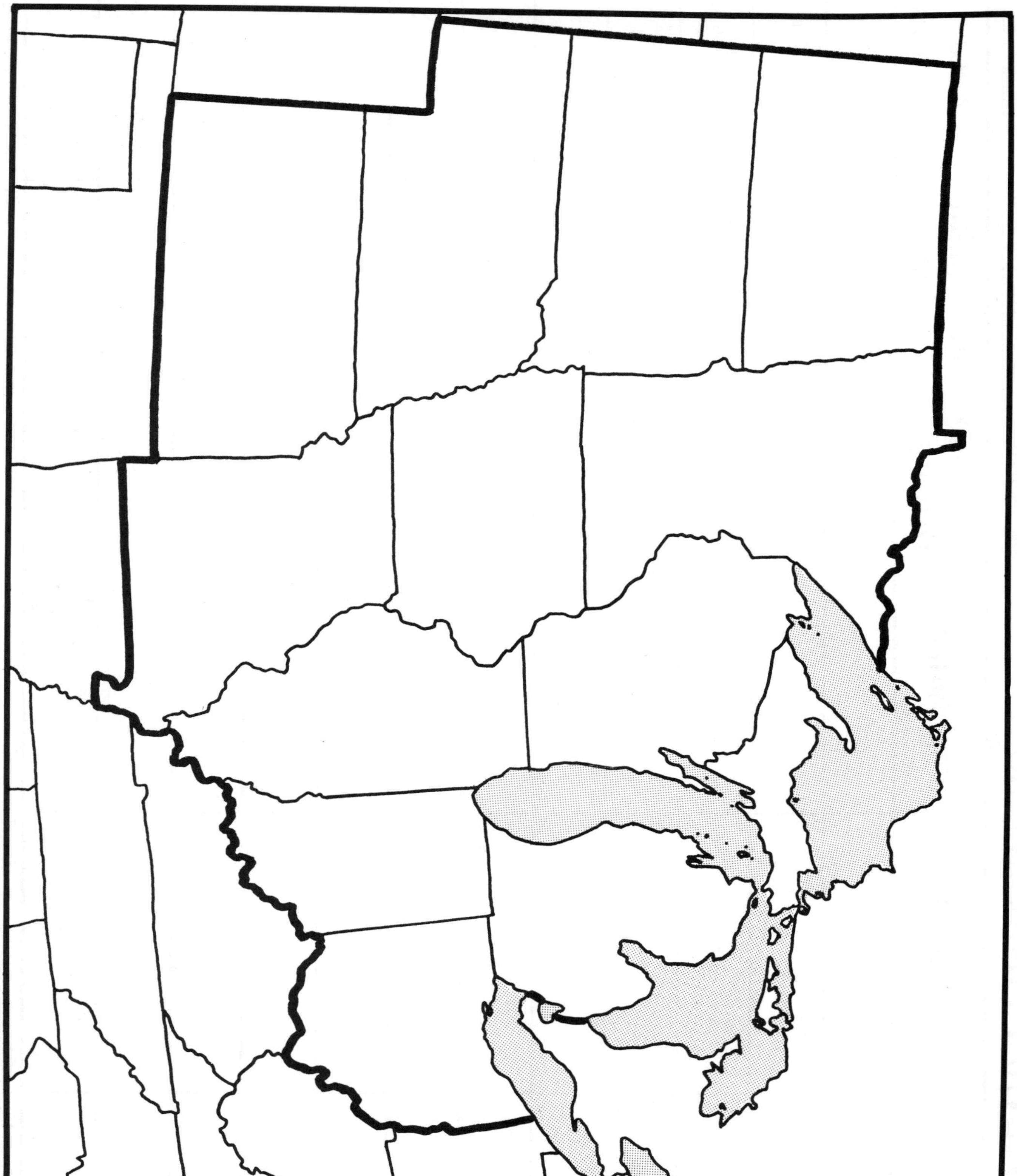

Name ______________________________

Western Census Region

Name ____________________

State	Capital	Population	Population Density	Per Capita Income	Area (square miles)
Alaska					
Arizona					
California					
Colorado					
Hawaii					
Idaho					
Montana					
Nevada					
New Mexico					
Oregon					
Utah					
Washington					
Wyoming					

Teachers: Directions on p. 113, answers on p. 123

Name ______________________________

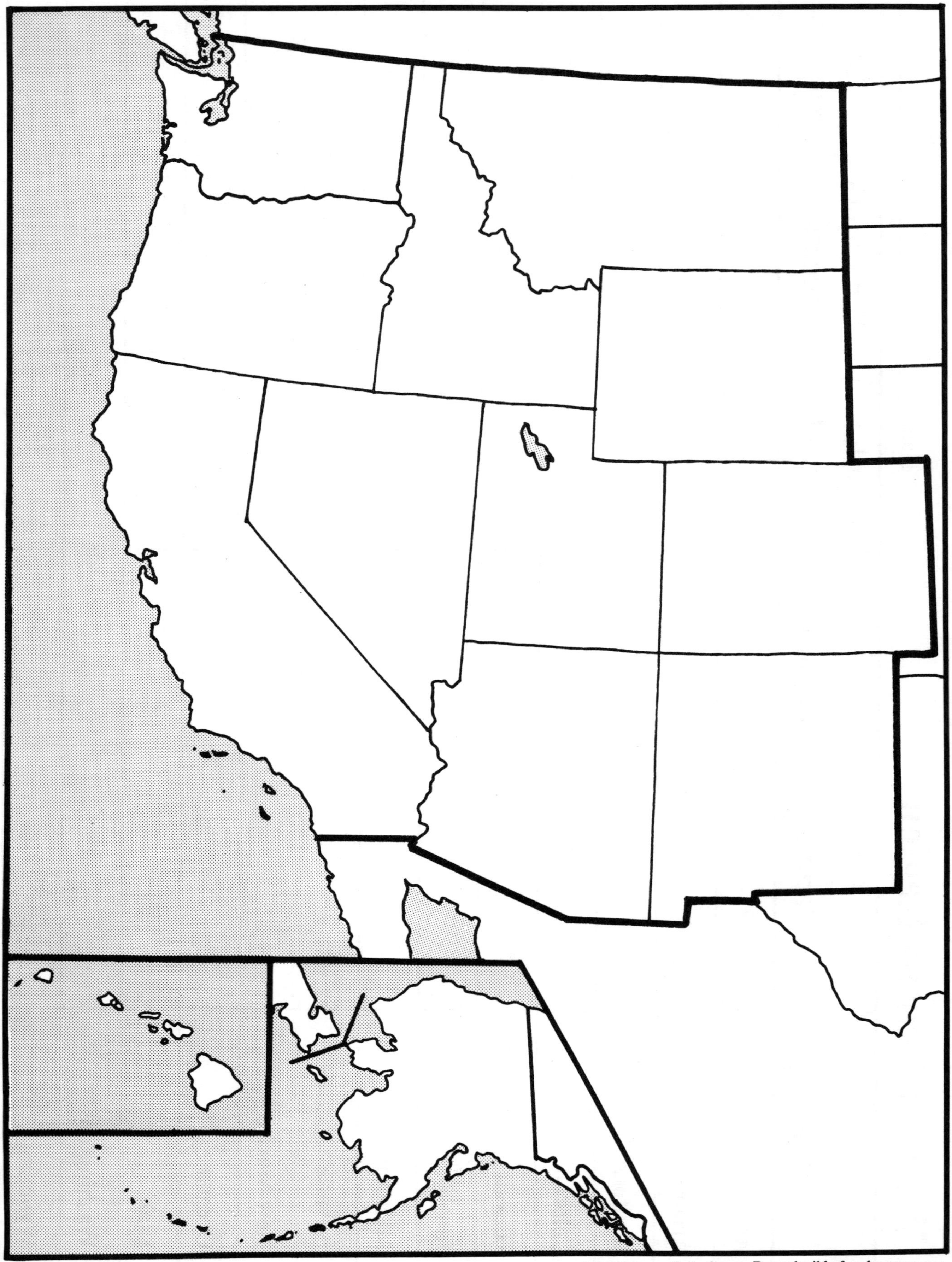

Northeast Census Region

KEY

State	Capital	Population	Population Density	Per Capita Income	Area (square miles)
Connecticut	Hartford	3,287,116	593	$24,683	5,544
Maine	Augusta	1,227,928	37	$16,248	35,387
Massachusetts	Boston	6,016,425	570	$22,174	10,555
New Hampshire	Concord	1,109,252	119	$20,267	9,351
New Jersey	Trenton	7,730,188	886	$23,778	8,722
New York	Albany	17,990,455	330	$21,073	54,475
Pennsylvania	Harrisburg	11,881,643	258	$17,269	46,058
Rhode Island	Providence	1,003,464	649	$17,950	1,545
Vermont	Montpelier	562,758	59	$16,371	9,615

Teachers: Directions on p. 113 , copy master on p. 1115

Southern Census Region

KEY

State	Capital	Population	Population Density	Per Capita Income	Area (square miles)
Alabama	Montgomery	4,040,587	77	$13,625	52,423
Arkansas	Little Rock	2,350,725	44	$12,901	53,182
Delaware	Dover	666,168	277	$18,483	2,489
Florida	Tallahassee	12,937,926	197	$17,647	65,758
Georgia	Atlanta	6,478,216	109	$16,053	59,441
Kentucky	Frankfort	3,685,296	91	$13,743	40,411
Louisiana	Baton Rouge	4,219,973	81	$12,921	51,843
Maryland	Annapolis	4,781,468	385	$21,013	12,407
Mississippi	Jackson	2,573,216	53	$11,724	48,434
North Carolina	Raleigh	6,628,637	123	$15,198	53,821
Oklahoma	Oklahoma City	3,145,585	45	$14,154	69,903
South Carolina	Columbia	3,486,703	109	$13,634	32,007
Tennessee	Nashville	4,877,185	116	$14,694	42,146
Texas	Austin	16,986,510	63	$15,702	286,601
Virginia	Richmond	6,187,358	145	$18,927	42,769
West Virginia	Charleston	1,793,477	74	$12,345	24,231

Teachers: Directions on p. 113, answers on p. 117

North Central Census Region

KEY

State	Capital	Population	Population Density	Per Capita Income	Area (square miles)
Illinois	Springfield	11,430,602	197	$18,824	57,918
Indiana	Indianapolis	5,544,159	152	$15,779	36,420
Iowa	Des Moines	2,776,755	49	$15,487	56,276
Kansas	Topeka	2,477,574	30	$16,498	82,282
Michigan	Lansing	9,295,297	96	$17,444	96,810
Minnesota	Saint Paul	4,375,099	50	$17,657	86,943
Missouri	Jefferson City	5,117,073	73	$16,292	69,709
Nebraska	Lincoln	1,578,385	20	$15,446	77,358
North Dakoka	Bismarck	638,800	9	$13,563	70,704
Ohio	Columbus	10,847,115	242	$16,373	44,828
South Dakota	Pierre	696,004	9	$13,685	77,121
Wisconsin	Madison	4,891,769	75	$16,449	65,503

Teachers: Directions on p. 113, copy master on p. 119

Western Census Region

KEY

State	Capital	Population	Population Density	Per Capita Income	Area (square miles)
Alaska	Juneau	550,043	0.8	$21,656	656,424
Arizona	Phoenix	3,665,228	32	$15,802	114,006
California	Sacramento	29,760,021	182	$19,929	163,707
Colorado	Denver	3,294,394	32	$17,553	104,100
Hawaii	Honolulu	1,108,229	101	$18,472	10,932
Idaho	Boise	1,006,749	12	$13,707	83,574
Montana	Helena	799,065	5	$14,078	147,046
Nevada	Carson City	1,201,833	11	$19,269	110,567
New Mexico	Santa Fe	1,515,069	12	$13,140	121,598
Oregon	Salem	2,842,321	29	$15,919	98,386
Utah	Salt Lake City	1,722,850	20	$13,079	84,904
Washington	Olympia	4,866,692	68	$17,647	71,303
Wyoming	Cheyenne	453,588	5	$14,508	97,818

Teachers: Directions on p. 113, copy master on p. 121

Name ______________________

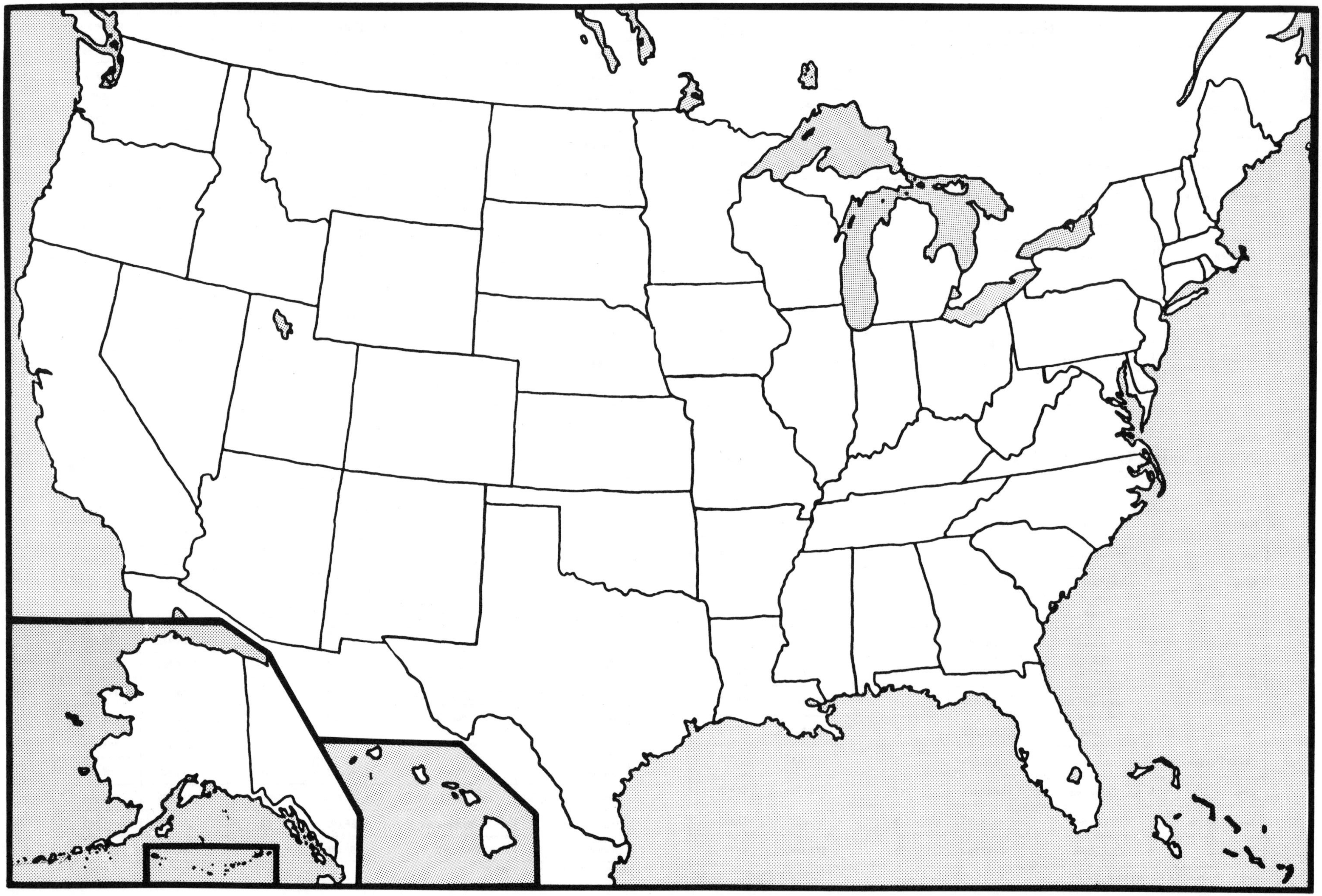

Name________________________________ Date__________________________

UNITED STATES POPULATION 1790-2000

Use a calculator to figure out population densities. Divide population by area and round to the nearest unit. Subtract to figure out increase over the previous census.

Year	Area	Population	Population Density	Increase over previous census	Percent increase
1790	891,364	3,929,214			
1800	891,364	5,308,483			35.1
1810	1,722,685	7,239,881			36.4
1820	1,792,552	9,639,453			33.1
1830	1,792,552	12,866,020			33.5
1840	1,752,552	17,069,453			32.7
1850	2,991,655	23,191,876			35.9
1860	3,021,295	31,443,321			35.6
1870	3,021,295	39,818,449			26.6
1880	3,021,295	50,155,783			26.0
1890	3,021,295	62,947,714			25.5
1900	3,021,295	75,994,575			20.7
1910	3,021,295	91,972,266			21.0
1920	3,021,295	105,710,620	35		14.9
1930	3,021,295	122,775,046	41		16.1
1940	3,021,295	131,669,275	44		7.2
1950	3,021,295	150,697,361	50		14.5
1960	3,618,770	179,323,175	50		18.5
1970	3,618,770	203,302,031	56		13.4
1980	3,618,770	226,545,805	63		11.4
1990	3,618,770	249,022,783	69		

On average, in the United States:

A baby is born every 8.5 seconds.
Someone dies every 16.5 seconds.
Someone immigrates every 79 seconds.
Someone emigrates every 23 minutes.
There is a net increase of about 250 persons per hour.

Teachers: Answers on p. 113

United States Population Growth, 1790 to 2000

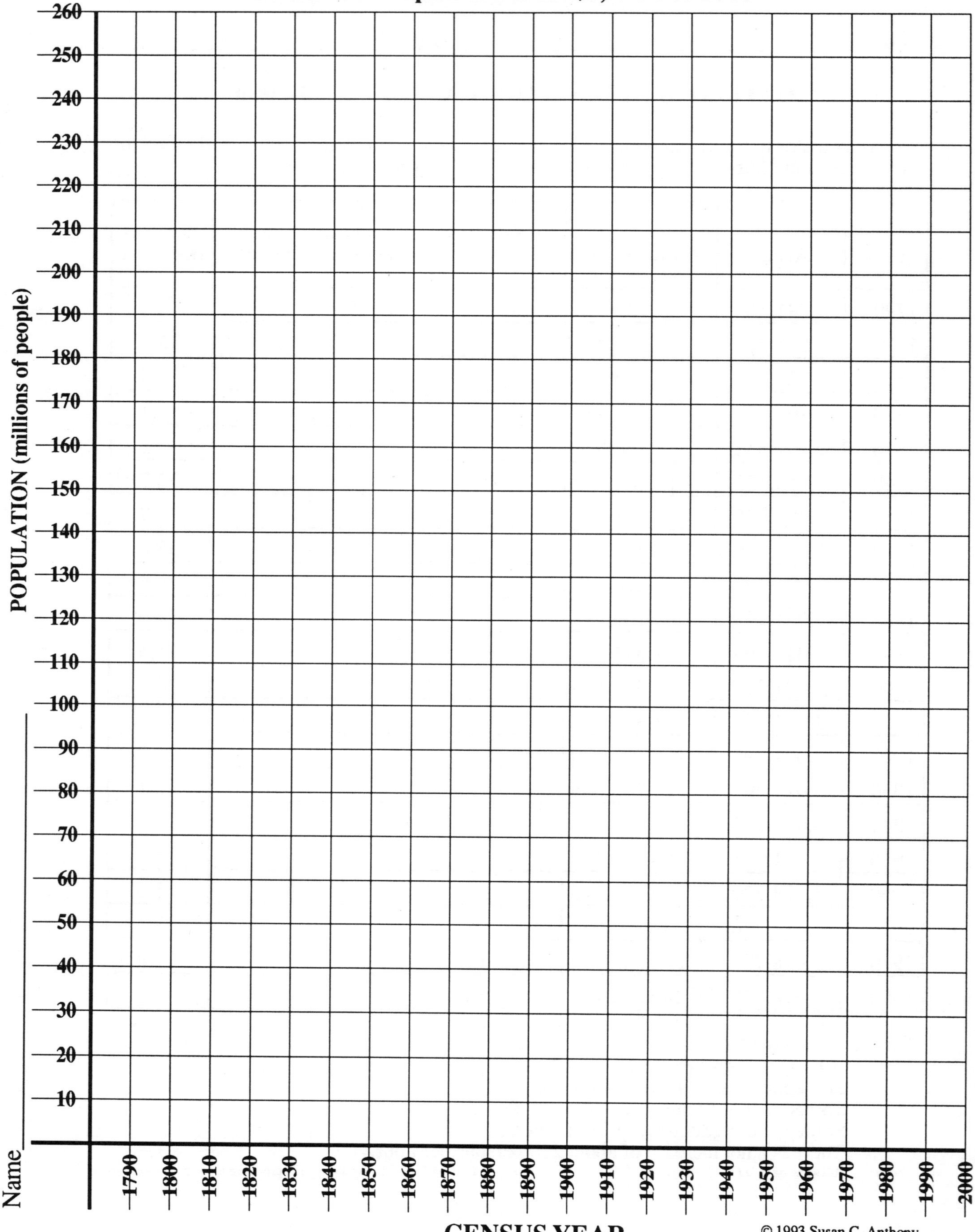

Name____________________

COUNTRY COMPARISONS

The charts, maps and graphs students generate in the following activities may be used as a lead-up to individual country research and reports. Besides learning the meaning of basic statistics used to compare nations, students look for patterns, make generalizations and hypotheses, and generate questions which lead them into in-depth research. The graphs make an excellent hall or bulletin board display. The base maps can be used for atlases students create.

Population Density Activities

Materials:

Optional: *Facts Plus,* calculator

Background information:

Population density is population divided by total area. The figures are rounded to the nearest whole number. Countries with high densities can be thought of as more crowded than those with low densities.

Suggested procedure:

1. Have students look up the area and population of the U.S. and China:
   United States area 3,787,425
   United States population 248,708,873
   China area 3,705,390
   China population 1,165,771,000
2. Note that, rounded, the areas of the United States and China are roughly equal. Define an area of the classroom to represent that area.
3. Have students divide the rounded U.S. population (250,000,000) by 50,000,000 (answer is 5), then choose 5 children, each to represent 50,000,000 Americans. Have the five stand in the area of the classroom previously defined to show the "population density" of the U.S.
4. Have students divide the rounded population of China (1,000,000,000) by 50,000,000 (answer is 20). Choose 20 students, each to represent 50,000,000 Chinese. Have them stand in the same area of the classroom to show the comparative "population density" of China.
5. Discuss the causes and effects for high and low population densities, such as crowding and demand for food, housing, schools, etc. What kinds of land will best support a high population density?
6. Show with a calculator how population densities are figured. Divide population by area and round to nearest whole number.
   U.S., 248,708,873 / 3,787,425 = 66
   China, 1,165,771,000 / 3,705,390 = 315
   Note: Hong Kong, a city in China administered by the British, is the most densely populated city in the world, with 242,000 people per square mile! 15,365 students would have to crowd into the same area of the classroom to show this density.
7. As a possible follow-up, have students find countries with population densities which are lower than the U.S. or higher than China. Search for the country with the lowest or highest population density in the world. Use calculators to figure densities.

Countries Questions

Materials:

Countries Questions worksheet (Activity Book p. 129, answers on p. 130)

Facts Plus for each student

Background information and procedure:

Make sure students understand all the terms used on pages 53-69. Terms are explained in depth in *Facts Plus* on page 230. Population density activities (above) may be used to clarify that concept. Students complete the worksheet on their own.

South America Graphs

Materials:

Facts Plus class set

Blank map of South America (Activity Book p. 144)

Copies of chart for South America (Activity Book p. 143, answers p. 148)

Copies of graphs (Activity Book p. 150, 151, 155, 157, and 158). Second and additional pages are *not* needed for South America.

Suggested procedure:

1. Students may first find South America on a globe or map and locate and label the countries on the blank map.
2. Students use *Facts Plus* to complete chart.
3. Using information from the chart, graph population growth rate, population density, per capita GNP, average life expectancy and infant mortality rate.
4. Select one good example of each graph to post on the front board side by side. Other students keep their graphs at their desks.
5. Have students look for patterns. Which countries are highest and lowest in various areas? Are there any countries which stand out as different? Bolivia and Uruguay are examples.
6. Look at the statistics: Compared to other countries in South America, Bolivia has a high population growth rate, low population density, low per capita GNP, low average life expectancy, and high infant mortality rate. Uruguay has low population growth rate, medium population density, high per capita GNP, high average life expectancy and low infant mortality rate. Which country would you rather live in? What factors could account for these differences?
7. Look for patterns and correlations. Are most countries which are high in one area high in another? Are there negative correlations, i.e. do countries which are low in one area tend to be high in another? As graphs for other continents are done, see if these correlations hold true.

Charts and Graphs

Note to teacher:

The charts and graphs on Activity Book p. 131 to 160 may be used in a variety of ways. For example, you may give students each a different chart. They complete their charts and graph *just* the population densities. Post all population density graphs side by side. Make observations and generate questions. Perhaps divide the class into seven groups and have each group complete the table and *all* graphs for their group of countries.

Materials:

Facts Plus class set

Copies of all charts (Activity Book p. 131 to 143)

Copies of population density graphs or all graphs (Activity Book p. 150 to 160), one graph for each indicator for each group of countries.

Suggested procedure:

1. Have students complete assigned charts and graphs.
2. Discuss as shown in previous activity.
3. Perhaps post all in a large grid on a wall.
4. Check correlations found in the South America graphs. Do they hold true?

Make Your Own Atlas

Materials:

Charts from previous activities

Blank world map (Activity Book p. 149)

Suggested procedure:

1. Begin by mapping infant mortality rate. Color countries with an IMR of 50 or less green, 51-100 yellow and 101 up red. Compare all maps and look for patterns.
2. Students may map other statistics by looking for highest and lowest numbers, making a key and coloring maps as was done for infant mortality rate.
3. Map anything else with any blank maps. Compile student-made maps into an atlas.

Name______________________________ Date________________________

COUNTRIES QUESTIONS

1. What language is spoken in Uruguay? __________________________
2. What is the population density of Laos? _________________________
3. What is the area of Belgium? _________________________________
4. What is the capital of Peru? __________________________________
5. What is the average life expectancy in Turkey? _________________
6. What is the per capita GNP in Sweden? _________________________
7. What is the currency in Guatemala? ____________________________
8. What is the infant mortality rate in China? ______________________
9. What is the population of India? ______________________________
10. What is the population growth rate of Kenya? ___________________
11. What is the population density of Algeria? ______________________
12. What is the location of Benin? _________________________________
13. What is the population growth rate of the United Kingdom? _______
14. What is the area of Israel? ____________________________________
15. What is the per capita GNP in Nepal? ___________________________
16. What is the average life expectancy in Paraguay? _______________
17. What is the location of San Marino? _____________________________
18. What language is spoken in Yemen? _____________________________
19. What is the population of the United States? ____________________
20. What is the capital of Egypt? __________________________________

The following questions are based on information found in *Facts Plus*, p. 70.

21. What are the Low Countries? __________________________________
____
22. Is Brunei in Southeast Asia? __________________________________
23. About how many countries are called Third World countries? _____
24. How many countries are in Central America? ____________________
25. In which ocean is Oceania? ____________________________________

Teachers: Lesson on p. 127, answers on p. 130

Name **KEY** Date____________

COUNTRIES QUESTIONS

1. What language is spoken in Uruguay? .... *Spanish*
2. What is the population density of Laos? *49*
3. What is the area of Belgium? ....*11,750 sq. mi.*
4. What is the capital of Peru? ....*Lima*
5. What is the average life expectancy in Turkey? *67*
6. What is the per capita GNP in Sweden? *$23,860*
7. What is the currency in Guatemala? .... *quetzal*
8. What is the infant mortality rate in China? *34*
9. What is the population of India? *882,575,000*
10. What is the population growth rate of Kenya? *3.7%*
11. What is the population density of Algeria? *28*
12. What is the location of Benin? .... *Western Africa*
13. What is the population growth rate of the United Kingdom? *0.3%*
14. What is the area of Israel? .... *8,020 sq. mi.*
15. What is the per capita GNP in Nepal? *$170*
16. What is the average life expectancy in Paraguay? *67*
17. What is the location of San Marino? ....*Southern Europe*
18. What language is spoken in Yemen? .... *Arabic*
19. What is the population of the United States? *248,708,873*
20. What is the capital of Egypt? .... *Cairo*

The following questions are based on information found in *Facts Plus,* p. 70.

21. What are the Low Countries? .....*Netherlands, Belgium, Luxembourg*
22. Is Brunei in Southeast Asia? ....*Yes*
23. About how many countries are called Third World countries? *120*
24. How many countries are in Central America? *7*
25. In which ocean is Oceania? ....*Pacific Ocean*

Teachers: Lesson on p. 127, copy master on p. 129

Name______________________________

AFRICA

Country	Population Growth Rate	Population Density	Per Capita GNP	Average Life Expectancy	Infant Mortality Rate
Algeria					
Central African Republic					
Ethiopia					
Guinea-Bissau					
Kenya					
Libya					
Mauritania					
Morocco					
Mozambique					
Nigeria					
Rwanda					
South Africa					
Sudan					
Tanzania					
Zaire					

Teachers: Lesson on p. 128, answers on p. 147

Name ____

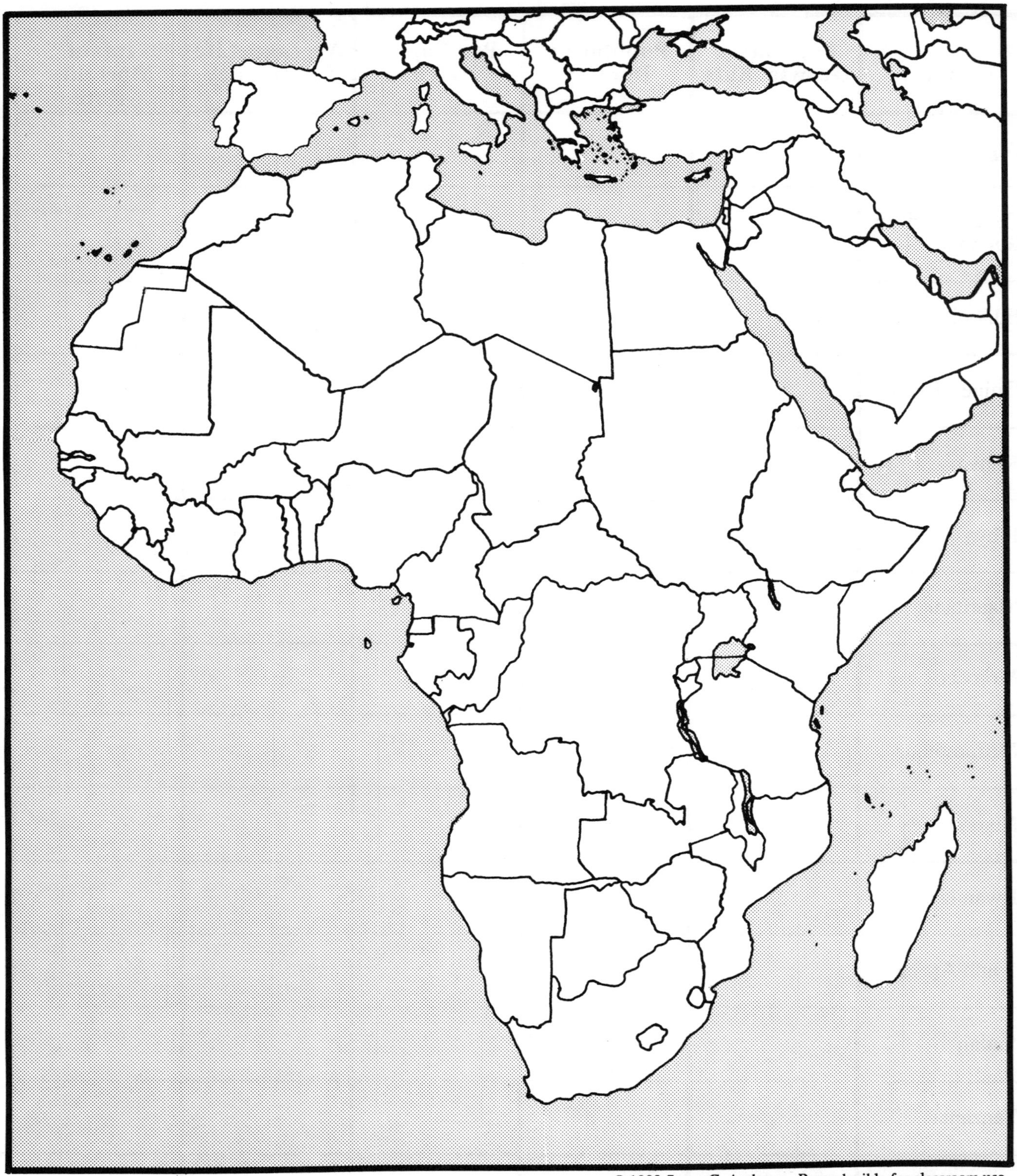

Name______________________________

ASIA

Country	Population Growth Rate	Population Density	Per Capita GNP	Average Life Expectancy	Infant Mortality Rate
Afghanistan					
Bangladesh					
China					
India					
Indonesia					
Japan					
Mongolia					
Myanmar					
Nepal					
Pakistan					
Philippines					
Singapore					
Sri Lanka					
Thailand					
Vietnam					

Teachers: Lesson on p. 128, answers on p. 147

Name ________________________________

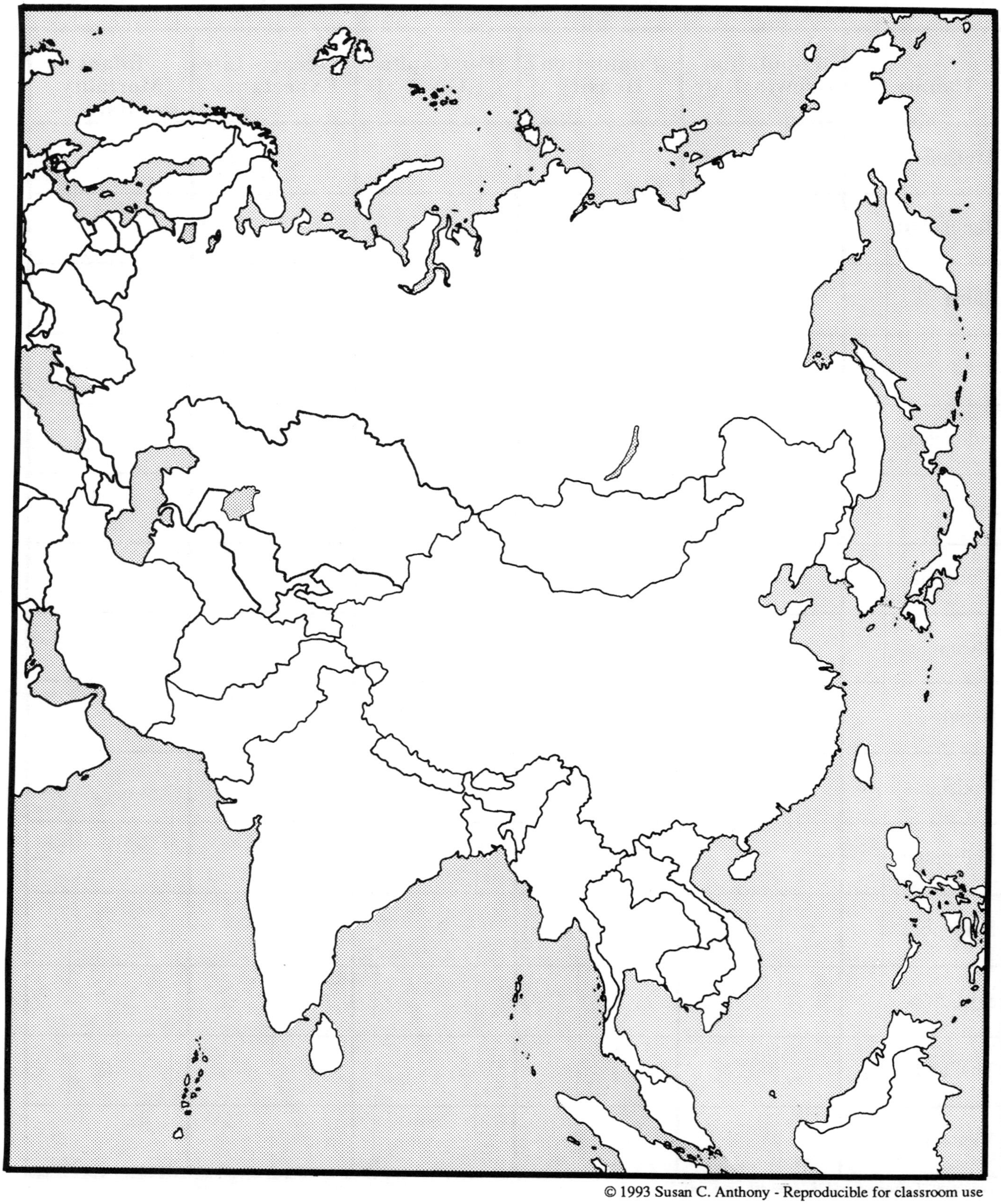

Name______________________________

FORMER SOVIET UNION

Country	Population Growth Rate	Population Density	Per Capita GNP	Average Life Expectancy	Infant Mortality Rate
Armenia					
Azerbaijan					
Belarus					
Estonia					
Georgia					
Kazakhstan					
Kyrgyzstan					
Latvia					
Lithuania					
Moldova					
Russia					
Tajikistan					
Turkmenistan					
Ukraine					
Uzbekistan					

Teachers: Lesson on p. 128, answers on p. 147

Name______________________________

EASTERN EUROPE

Country	Population Growth Rate	Population Density	Per Capita GNP	Average Life Expectancy	Infant Mortality Rate
Albania					
Bosnia-Herzegovina					
Bulgaria					
Croatia					
Czechoslovakia					
Hungary					
Macedonia					
Poland					
Romania					
Slovenia					
Yugoslavia					

Teachers: Lesson on p. 128, answers on p. 147

Name______________________________

EUROPE

Country	Population Growth Rate	Population Density	Per Capita GNP	Average Life Expectancy	Infant Mortality Rate
Austria					
Belgium					
Denmark					
Finland					
France					
Germany					
Greece					
Italy					
Netherlands					
Norway					
Portugal					
Spain					
Sweden					
Switzerland					
United Kingdom					

Teachers: Lesson on p. 128, answers on p. 148

Name ________________________________

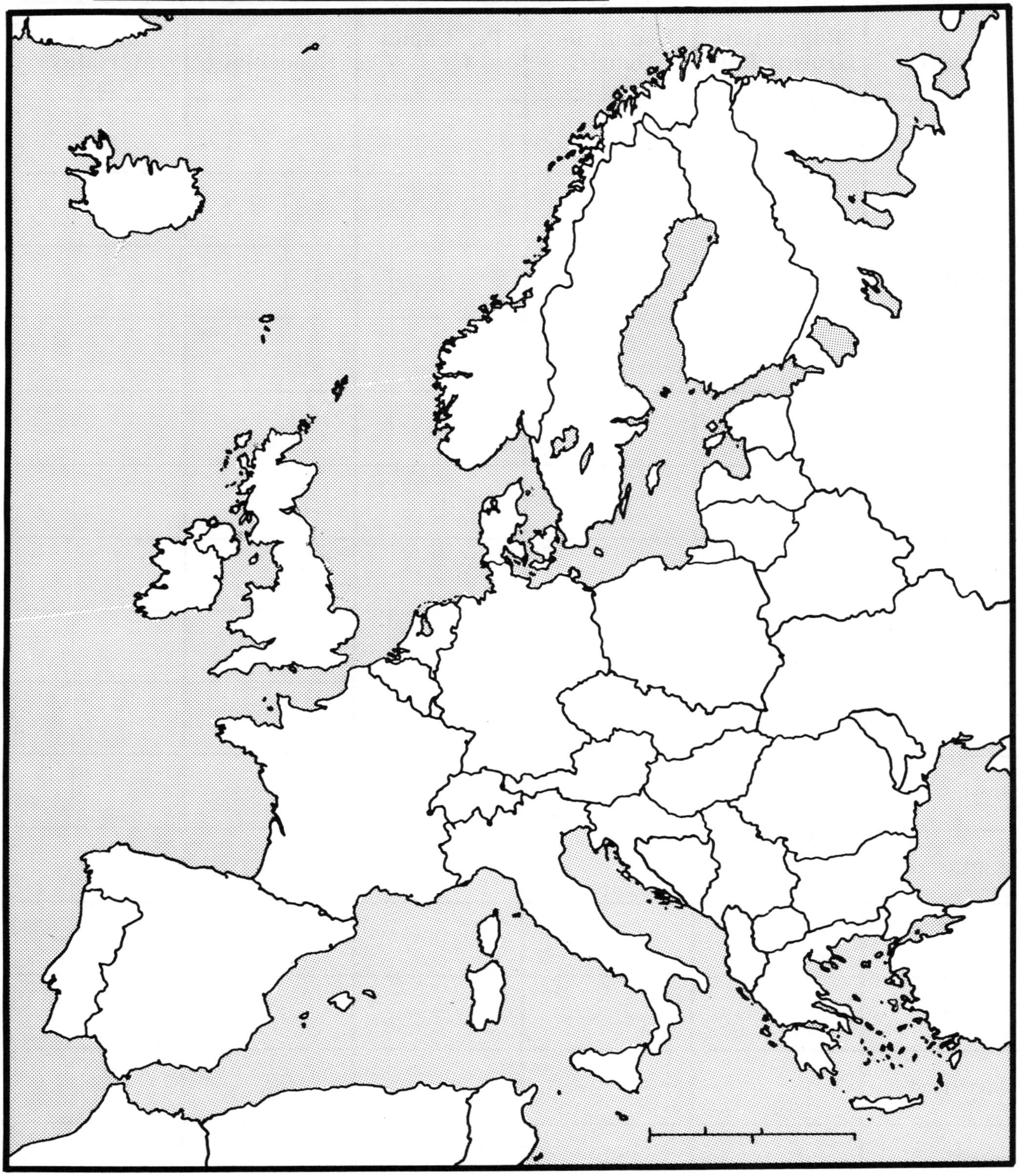

Name____________________________

MIDDLE EAST

Country	Population Growth Rate	Population Density	Per Capita GNP	Average Life Expectancy	Infant Mortality Rate
Cyprus					
Egypt					
Iran					
Iraq					
Israel					
Jordan					
Kuwait					
Lebanon					
Oman					
Qatar					
Saudi Arabia					
Syria					
Turkey					
United Arab Emirates					
Yemen					

Teachers: Lesson on p. 128, answers on p. 148

Name ____________________

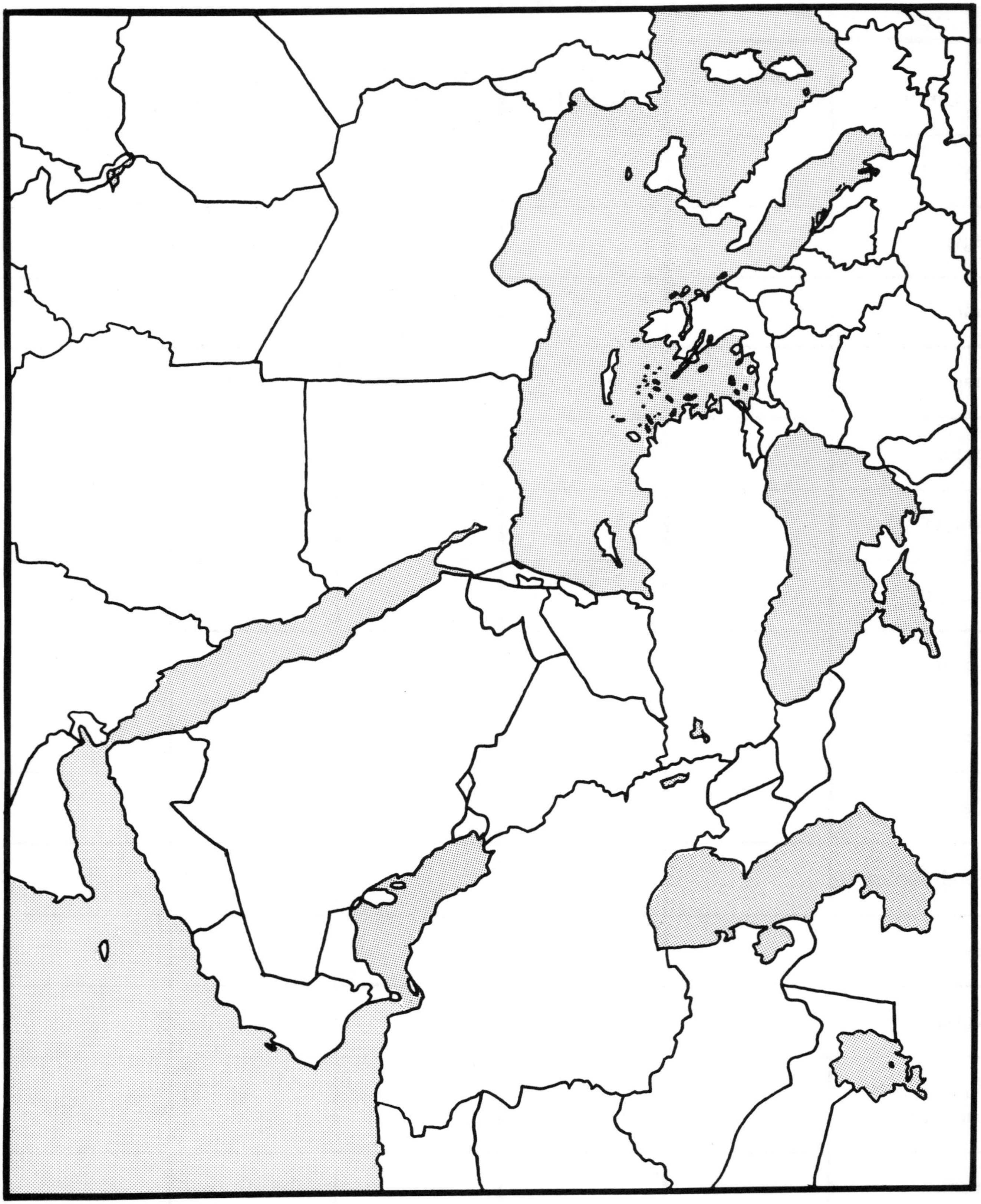

Name_____________________________

NORTH AMERICA

Country	Population Growth Rate	Population Density	Per Capita GNP	Average Life Expectancy	Infant Mortality Rate
Bahamas					
Belize					
Canada					
Costa Rica					
Cuba					
Dominican Republic					
El Salvador					
Guatemala					
Haiti					
Honduras					
Jamaica					
Mexico					
Nicaragua					
Panama					
United States					

Teachers: Lesson on p. 128, answers on p. 148

Name ________________________________

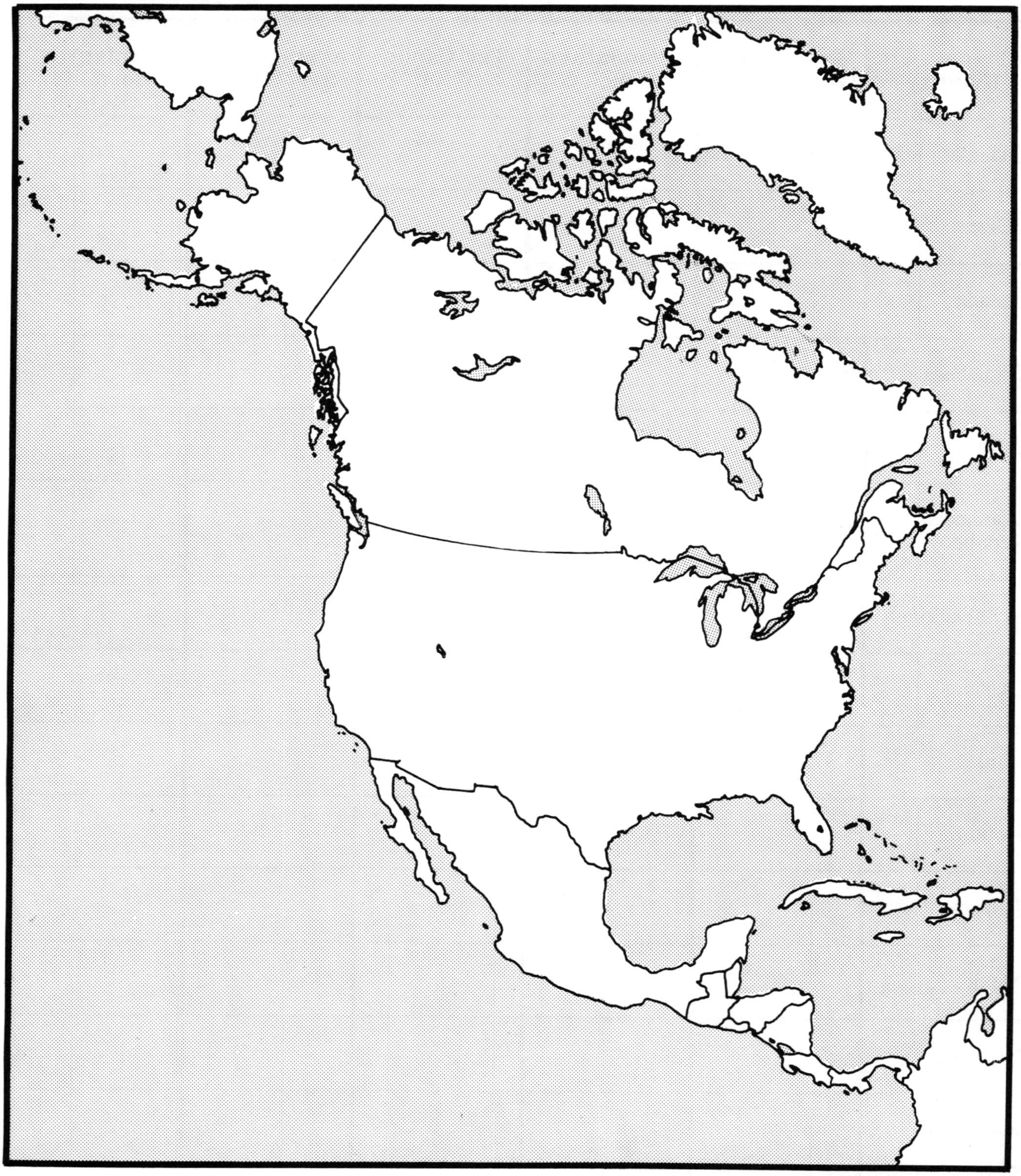

Name______________________________

SOUTH AMERICA

Country	Population Growth Rate	Population Density	Per Capita GNP	Average Life Expectancy	Infant Mortality Rate
Argentina					
Bolivia					
Brazil					
Chile					
Colombia					
Ecuador					
Guyana					
Paraguay					
Peru					
Suriname					
Uruguay					
Venezuela					

Teachers: Lesson on p. 128, answers on p. 148

Name ____

Name______________________________

Country	Population Growth Rate	Population Density	Per Capita GNP	Average Life Expectancy	Infant Mortality Rate

Choose any region or group of countries

Name ___________________________________

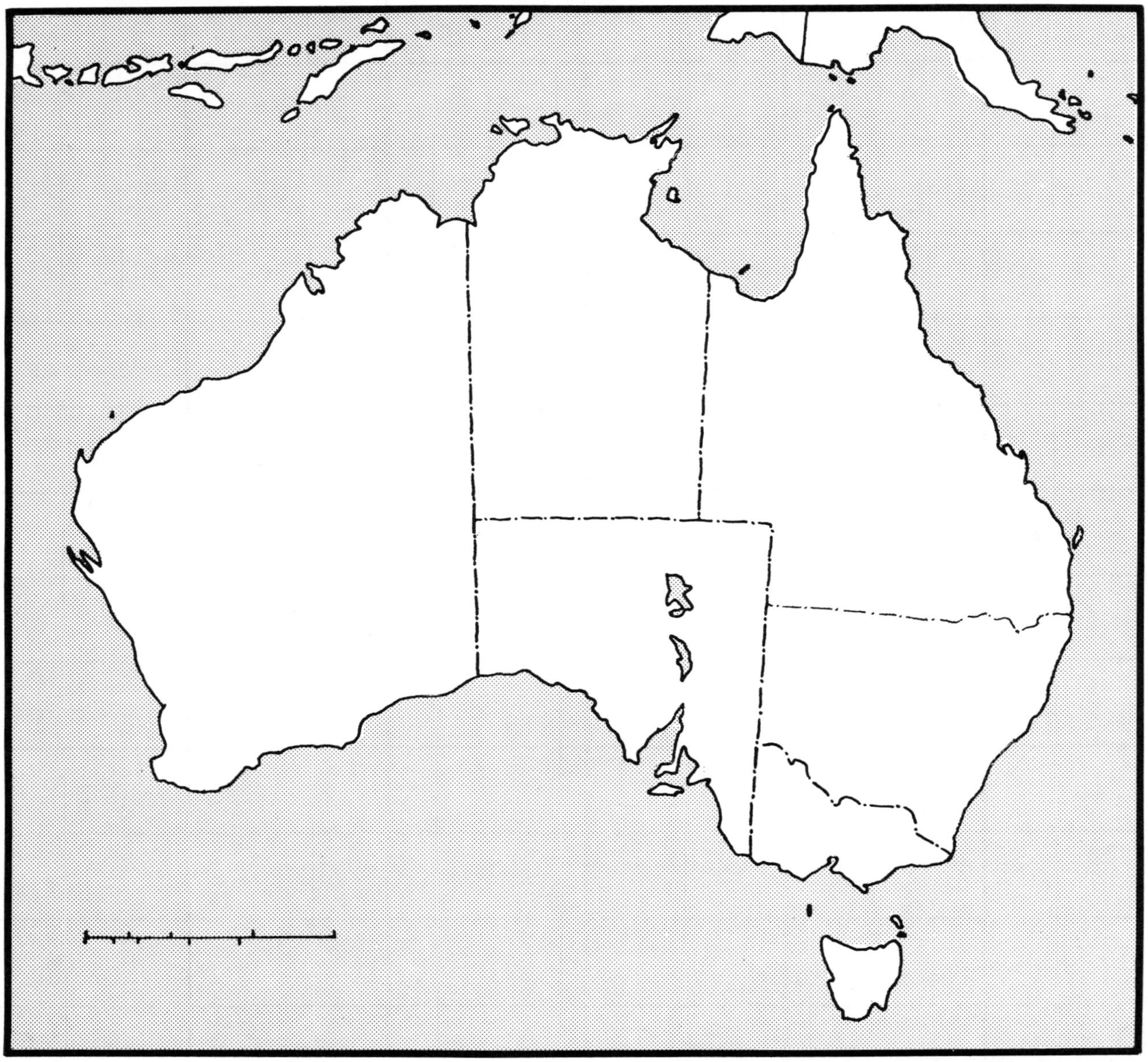

AFRICA

KEY

Country	Population Growth Rate	Population Density	Per Capita GNP	Average Life Expectancy	Infant Mortality Rate
Algeria	2.4%	28	$2,060	66	61
Central African Republic	2.6%	13	$390	47	141
Ethiopia	2.8%	115	$120	47	139
Guinea-Bissau	2.0%	72	$180	42	151
Kenya	3.7%	116	$370	61	62
Libya	3.0%	7	$5,410	68	64
Mauritania	2.8%	5	$500	48	122
Morocco	2.4%	152	$950	63	73
Mozambique	2.7%	54	$80	48	136
Nigeria	3.0%	253	$370	48	114
Rwanda	3.4%	759	$310	50	117
South Africa	2.6%	88	$2,520	64	52
Sudan	3.1%	27	$420	52	87
Tanzania	3.5%	75	$120	52	105
Zaire	3.1%	42	$230	52	83

Teachers: Lesson on p. 128, copy master on p. 131

ASIA

KEY

Country	Population Growth Rate	Population Density	Per Capita GNP	Average Life Expectancy	Infant Mortality Rate
Afghanistan	2.6%	67	$200	41	172
Bangladesh	2.4%	2,004	$200	53	120
China	1.3%	315	$370	70	34
India	2.0%	695	$350	58	91
Indonesia	1.7%	249	$560	61	70
Japan	0.3%	865	$25,430	79	5
Mongolia	2.8%	4	$880	65	64
Myanmar	1.9%	163	$280	58	72
Nepal	2.5%	365	$170	50	112
Pakistan	3.1%	392	$380	57	109
Philippines	2.4%	550	$730	65	54
Singapore	1.4%	12,347	$12,310	75	7
Sri Lanka	1.5%	696	$470	70	19
Thailand	1.4%	284	$1,420	67	39
Vietnam	2.2%	544	$215	64	45

Teachers: Lesson on p. 128, copy master on p. 133

FORMER SOVIET UNION

KEY

Country	Population Growth Rate	Population Density	Per Capita GNP	Average Life Expectancy	Infant Mortality Rate
Armenia	1.8%	305	---	72	35
Azerbaijan	2.0%	214	---	71	45
Belarus	0.3%	128	---	72	20
Estonia	0.2%	91	---	71	25
Georgia	0.9%	204	---	72	33
Kazakhstan	1.4%	16	---	69	44
Kyrgyzstan	2.2%	59	---	69	35
Latvia	0.1%	109	---	70	19
Lithuania	0.4%	148	---	72	18
Moldova	0.8%	336	---	69	35
Russia	0.2%	23	---	70	30
Tajikistan	3.2%	100	---	70	73
Turkmenistan	2.7%	20	---	65	93
Ukraine	0.1%	224	---	71	22
Uzbekistan	2.7%	123	---	69	64

Teachers: Lesson on p. 128, copy master on p. 135

EASTERN EUROPE

KEY

Country	Population Growth Rate	Population Density	Per Capita GNP	Average Life Expectancy	Infant Mortality Rate
Albania	1.9%	296	$1,200	73	31
Bosnia-Hercegovina	0.8%	211	---	72	15
Bulgaria	0.0%	207	$2,210	72	15
Croatia	0.1%	208	---	72	10
Czechoslovakia	0.2%	318	$3,140	72	11
Hungary	-0.2%	288	$2,780	70	15
Macedonia	1.0%	194	---	72	35
Poland	0.4%	318	$1,700	72	16
Romania	0.1%	253	$1,640	70	26
Slovenia	0.3%	245	---	73	9
Yugoslavia	0.5%	370	---	72	24

Teachers: Lesson on p. 128, copy master on p. 136

EUROPE

KEY

Country	Population Growth Rate	Population Density	Per Capita GNP	Average Life Expectancy	Infant Mortality Rate
Austria	0.1%	243	$19,240	76	7
Belgium	0.2%	855	$15,440	76	8
Denmark	0.1%	311	$22,090	75	8
Finland	0.3%	39	$26,070	75	6
France	0.4%	269	$19,480	77	7
Germany	-0.1%	585	$16,200	75	8
Greece	0.1%	202	$6,000	76	10
Italy	0.1%	499	$16,850	77	9
Netherlands	0.5%	1,055	$17,330	77	7
Norway	0.4%	34	$23,120	77	7
Portugal	0.1%	295	$4,890	75	11
Spain	0.2%	198	$10,920	77	8
Sweden	0.3%	50	$23,860	78	6
Switzerland	0.3%	431	$32,790	78	7
United Kingdom	0.3%	611	$16,070	76	8

Teachers: Lesson on p. 128, copy master on p. 137

MIDDLE EAST

KEY

Country	Population Growth Rate	Population Density	Per Capita GNP	Average Life Expectancy	Infant Mortality Rate
Cyprus	1.1%	200	$8,040	76	11
Egypt	2.4%	144	$600	59	73
Iran	3.3%	94	$2,450	65	43
Iraq	3.7%	109	$1,940	67	67
Israel	1.5%	653	$10,970	77	9
Jordan	3.4%	100	$1,240	71	39
Kuwait	3.0%	200	$13,680	74	16
Lebanon	2.1%	856	$700	68	46
Oman	3.5%	19	$5,220	66	44
Qatar	2.5%	114	$15,860	72	26
Saudi Arabia	3.5%	19	$6,230	64	65
Syria	3.8%	192	$990	65	48
Turkey	2.2%	197	$1,630	67	59
United Arab Emirates	2.8%	78	$19,860	71	25
Yemen	3.5%	51	$640	50	124

Teachers: Lesson on p. 128, copy master on p. 139

NORTH AMERICA

KEY

Country	Population Growth Rate	Population Density	Per Capita GNP	Average Life Expectancy	Infant Mortality Rate
Bahamas	1.5%	49	$11,510	73	26
Belize	3.1%	26	$1,970	70	32
Canada	0.8%	7	$20,450	77	7
Costa Rica	2.4%	163	$1,910	77	15
Cuba	1.1%	245	$2,000	76	11
Dominican Republic	2.3%	397	$820	68	61
El Salvador	2.9%	675	$1,100	65	55
Guatemala	3.1%	231	$900	63	61
Haiti	2.9%	600	$370	55	106
Honduras	3.2%	126	$590	64	69
Jamaica	2.0%	591	$1,510	73	17
Mexico	2.3%	115	$2,490	69	47
Nicaragua	3.1%	82	$830	62	61
Panama	1.9%	82	$1,830	73	21
United States	0.8%	66	$21,700	76	9

Teachers: Lesson on p. 128, copy master on p. 141

SOUTH AMERICA

KEY

Country	Population Growth Rate	Population Density	Per Capita GNP	Average Life Expectancy	Infant Mortality Rate
Argentina	1.2%	31	$2,370	69	26
Bolivia	2.7%	18	$620	61	89
Brazil	1.9%	46	$2,680	65	69
Chile	1.8%	47	$1,940	74	17
Colombia	2.0%	78	$1,240	71	37
Ecuador	2.4%	91	$960	67	57
Guyana	1.8%	10	$370	64	52
Paraguay	2.7%	29	$1,110	67	34
Peru	2.2%	45	$1,160	62	76
Suriname	2.0%	7	$3,050	70	31
Uruguay	0.8%	46	$2,560	72	20
Venezuela	2.5%	54	$2,560	71	24

Teachers: Lesson on p. 128, copy master on p. 143

Name ______________________________

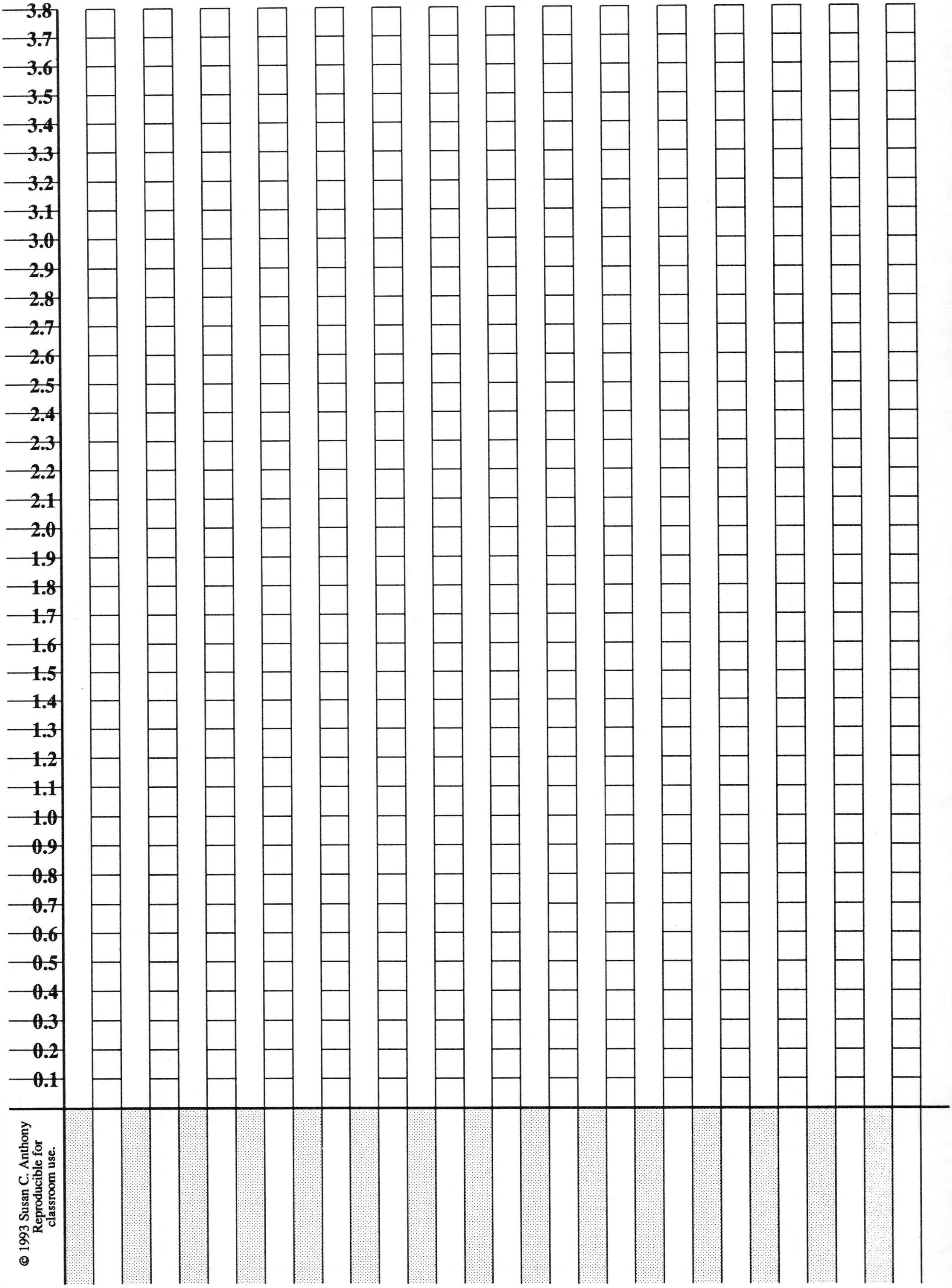
POPULATION GROWTH RATE (%)
3.8
3.7
3.6
3.5
3.4
3.3
3.2
3.1
3.0
2.9
2.8
2.7
2.6
2.5
2.4
2.3
2.2
2.1
2.0
1.9
1.8
1.7
1.6
1.5
1.4
1.3
1.2
1.1
1.0
0.9
0.8
0.7
0.6
0.5
0.4
0.3
0.2
0.1

Name________________________

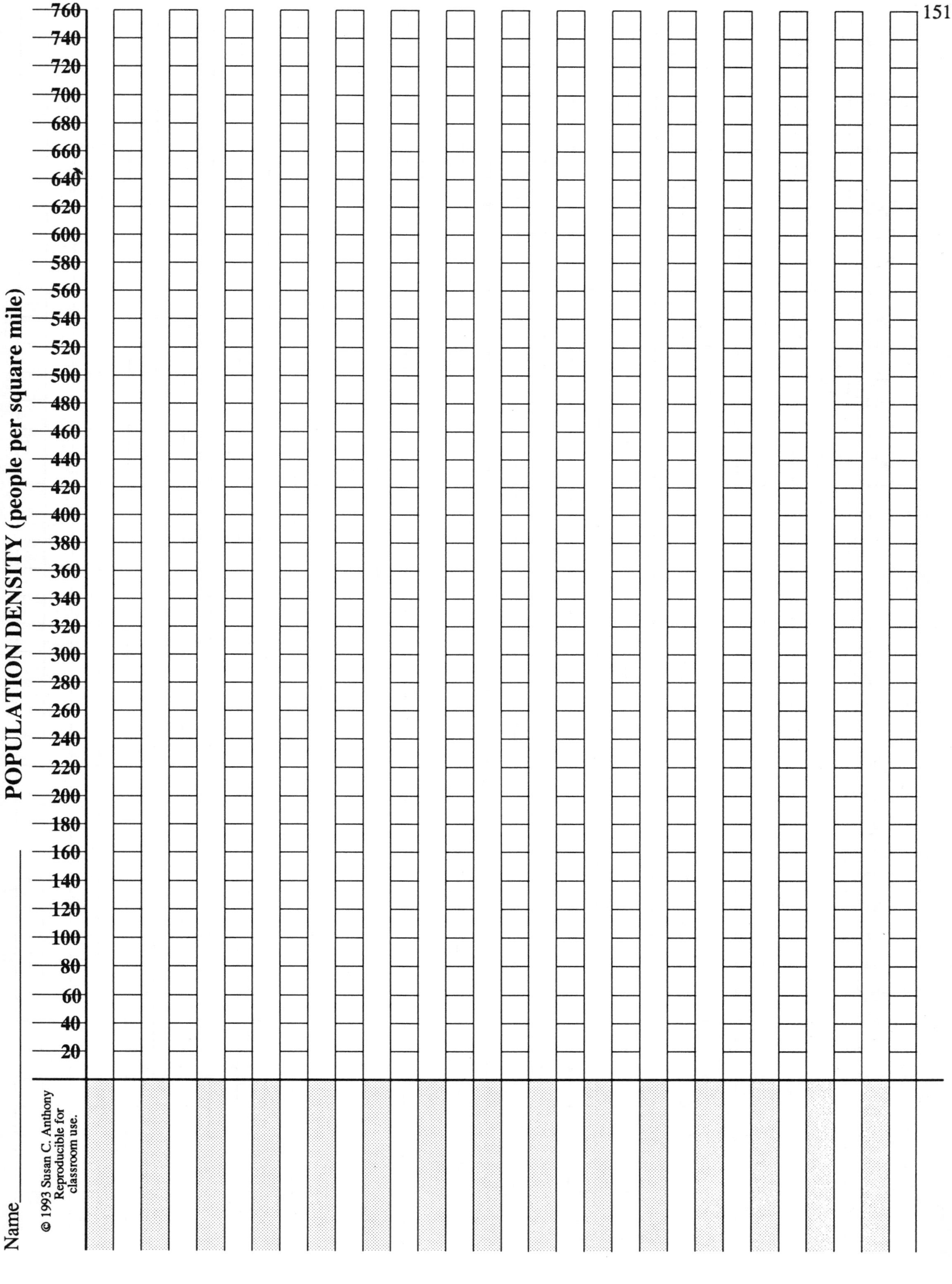
POPULATION DENSITY (people per square mile)
760
740
720
700
680
660
640
620
600
580
560
540
520
500
480
460
440
420
400
380
360
340
320
300
280
260
240
220
200
180
160
140
120
100
80
60
40
20

Name________________

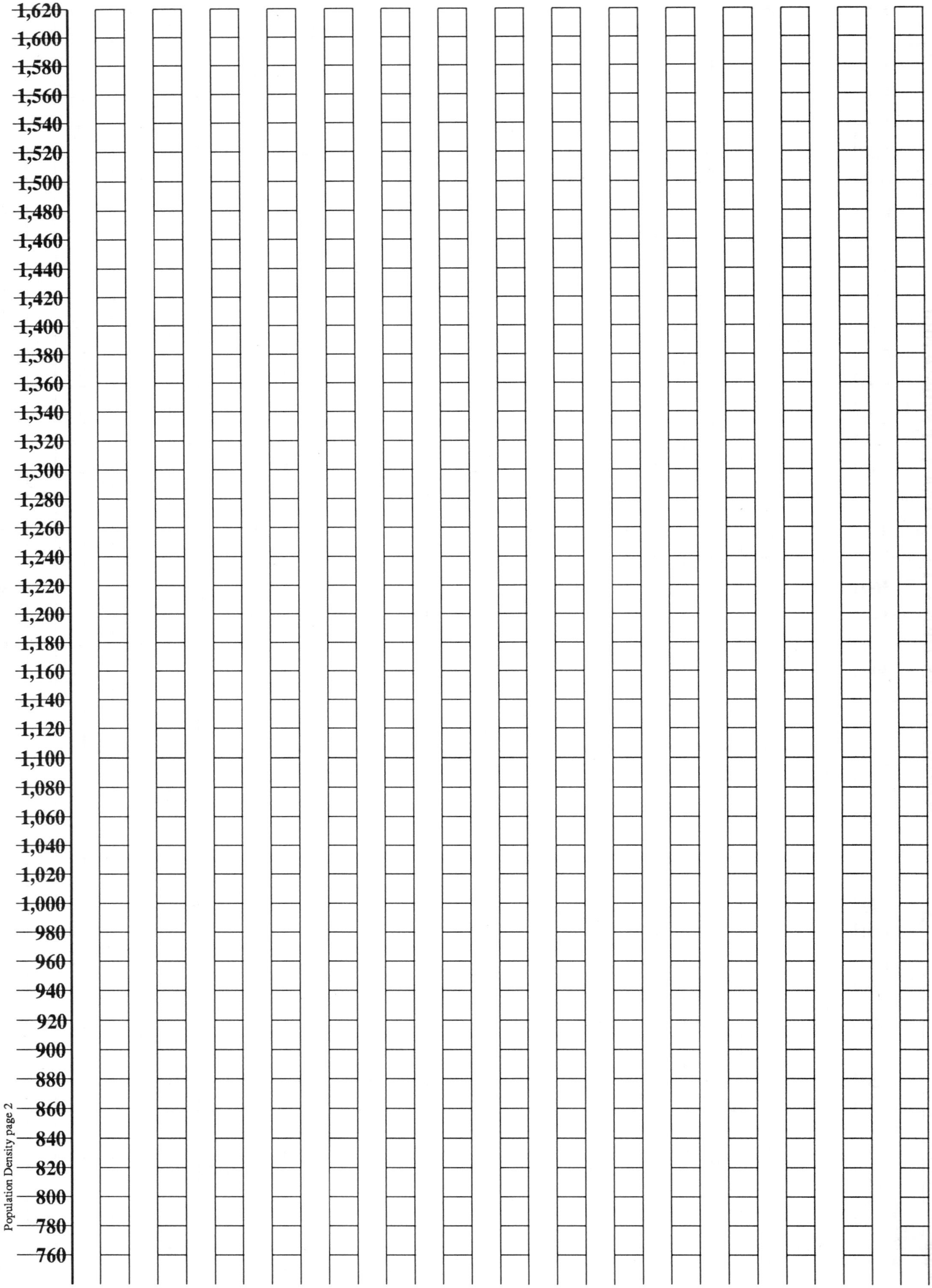
1,620
1,600
1,580
1,560
1,540
1,520
1,500
1,480
1,460
1,440
1,420
1,400
1,380
1,360
1,340
1,320
1,300
1,280
1,260
1,240
1,220
1,200
1,180
1,160
1,140
1,120
1,100
1,080
1,060
1,040
1,020
1,000
980
960
940
920
900
880
860
840
820
800
780
760
Population Density page 2

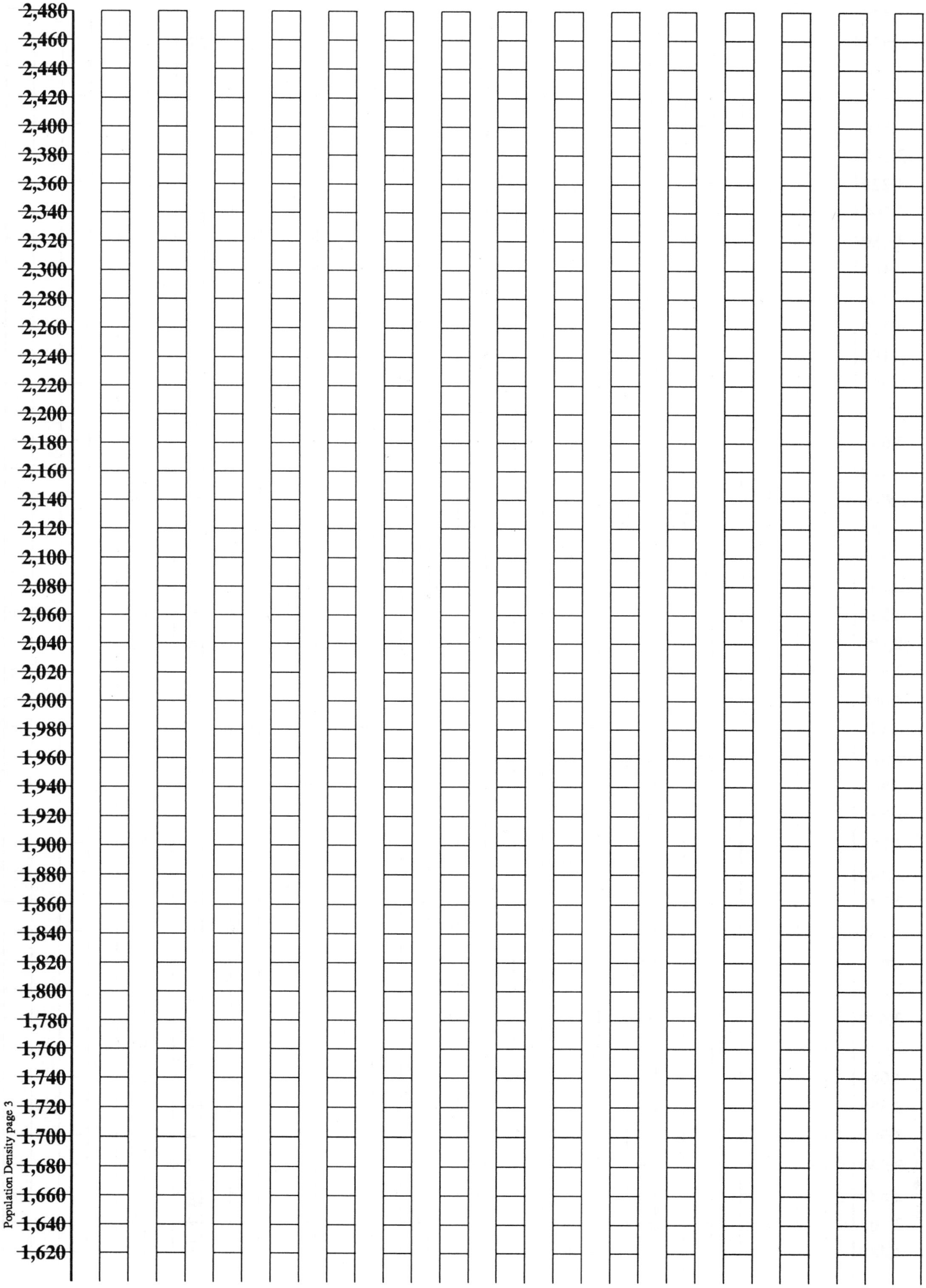
2,480
2,460
2,440
2,420
2,400
2,380
2,360
2,340
2,320
2,300
2,280
2,260
2,240
2,220
2,200
2,180
2,160
2,140
2,120
2,100
2,080
2,060
2,040
2,020
2,000
1,980
1,960
1,940
1,920
1,900
1,880
1,860
1,840
1,820
1,800
1,780
1,760
1,740
1,720
1,700
1,680
1,660
1,640
1,620
Population Density page 3

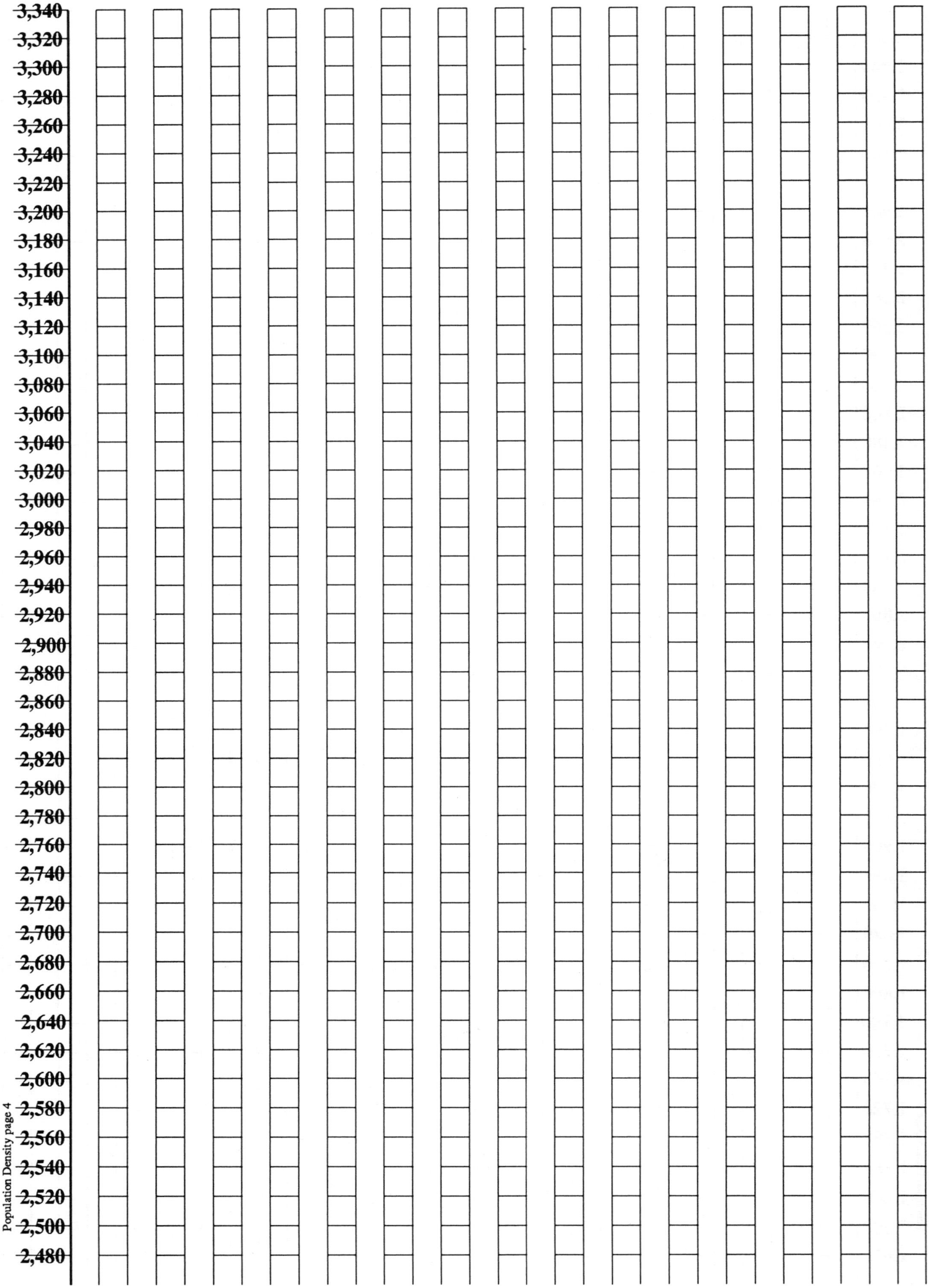
3,340
3,320
3,300
3,280
3,260
3,240
3,220
3,200
3,180
3,160
3,140
3,120
3,100
3,080
3,060
3,040
3,020
3,000
2,980
2,960
2,940
2,920
2,900
2,880
2,860
2,840
2,820
2,800
2,780
2,760
2,740
2,720
2,700
2,680
2,660
2,640
2,620
2,600
2,580
2,560
2,540
2,520
2,500
2,480
Population Density page 4

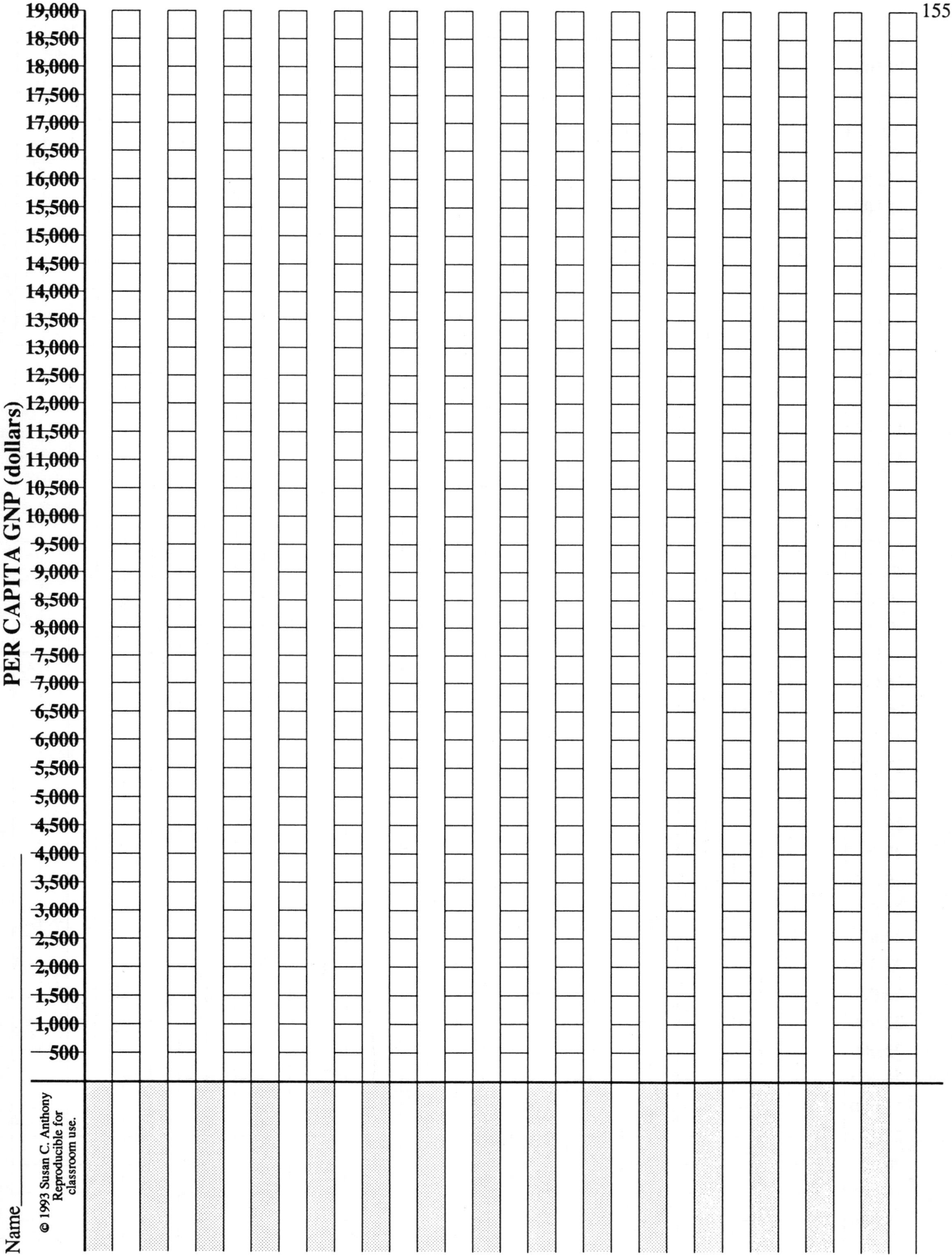
PER CAPITA GNP (dollars)
19,000
18,500
18,000
17,500
17,000
16,500
16,000
15,500
15,000
14,500
14,000
13,500
13,000
12,500
12,000
11,500
11,000
10,500
10,000
9,500
9,000
8,500
8,000
7,500
7,000
6,500
6,000
5,500
5,000
4,500
4,000
3,500
3,000
2,500
2,000
1,500
1,000
500

Name____________________

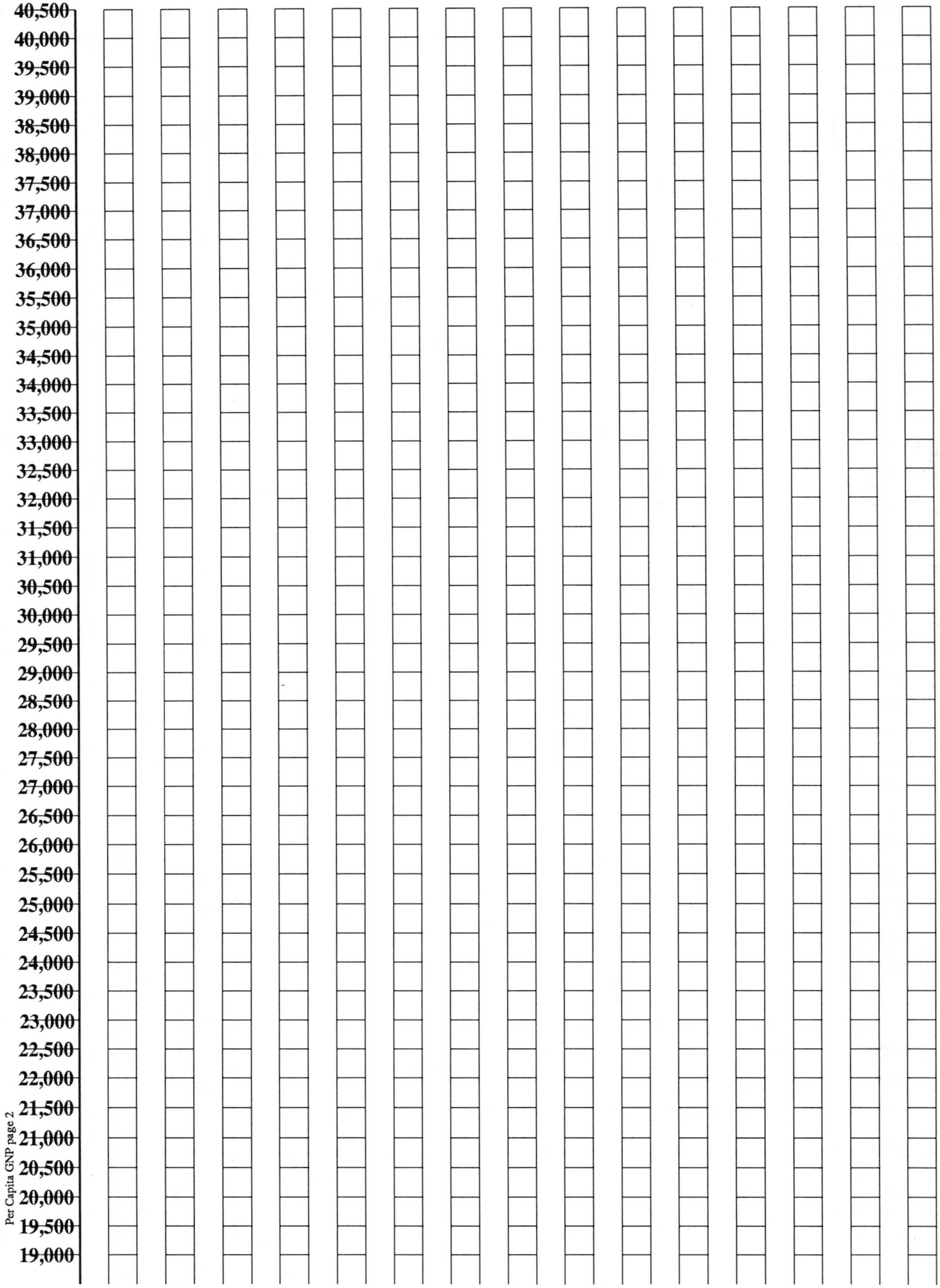
40,500
40,000
39,500
39,000
38,500
38,000
37,500
37,000
36,500
36,000
35,500
35,000
34,500
34,000
33,500
33,000
32,500
32,000
31,500
31,000
30,500
30,000
29,500
29,000
28,500
28,000
27,500
27,000
26,500
26,000
25,500
25,000
24,500
24,000
23,500
23,000
22,500
22,000
21,500
21,000
20,500
20,000
19,500
19,000
Per Capita GNP page 2

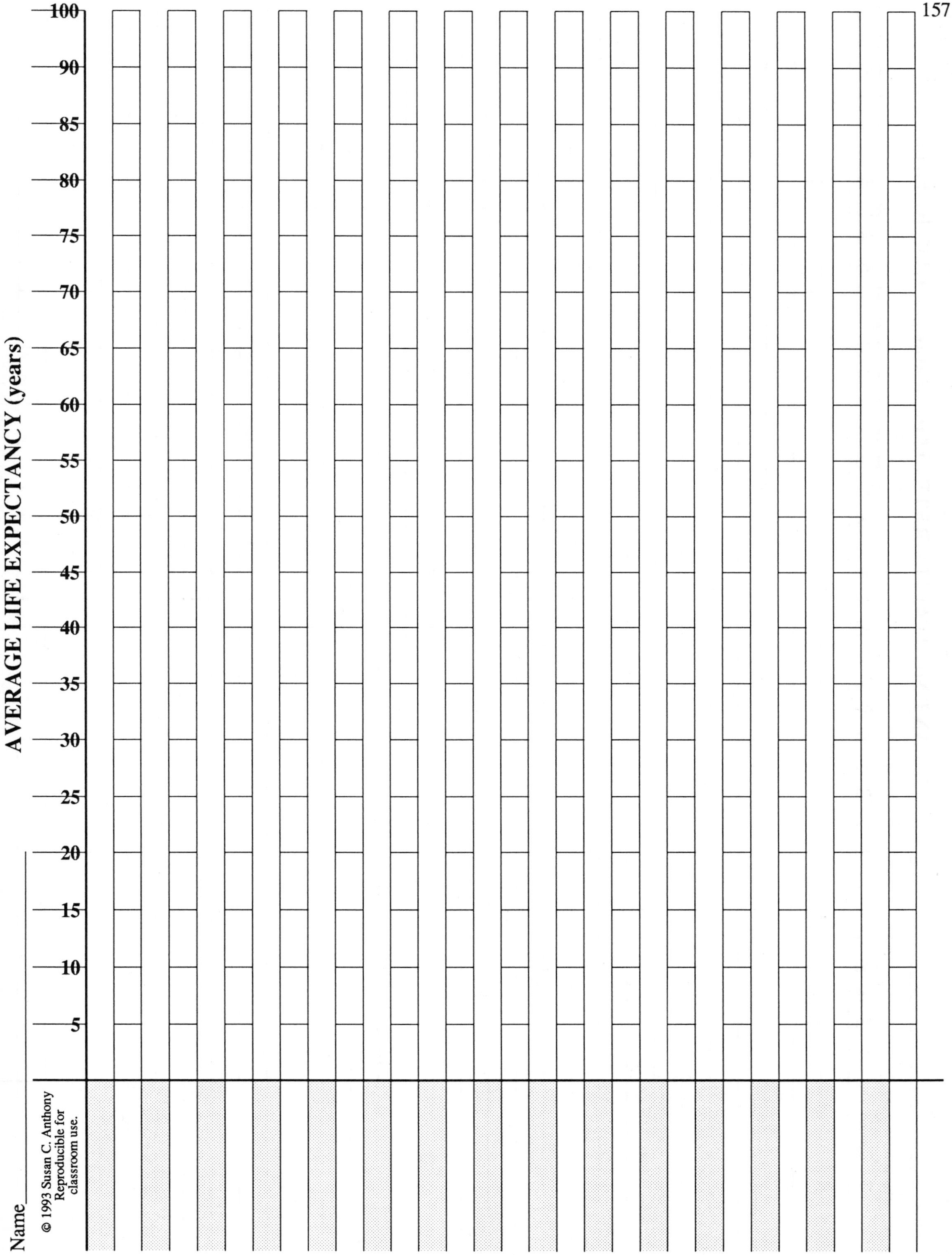
AVERAGE LIFE EXPECTANCY (years)
100
90
85
80
75
70
65
60
55
50
45
40
35
30
25
20
15
10
5

Name______________

Name________________________________

INFANT MORTALITY RATE (infant deaths per 1,000 live births)

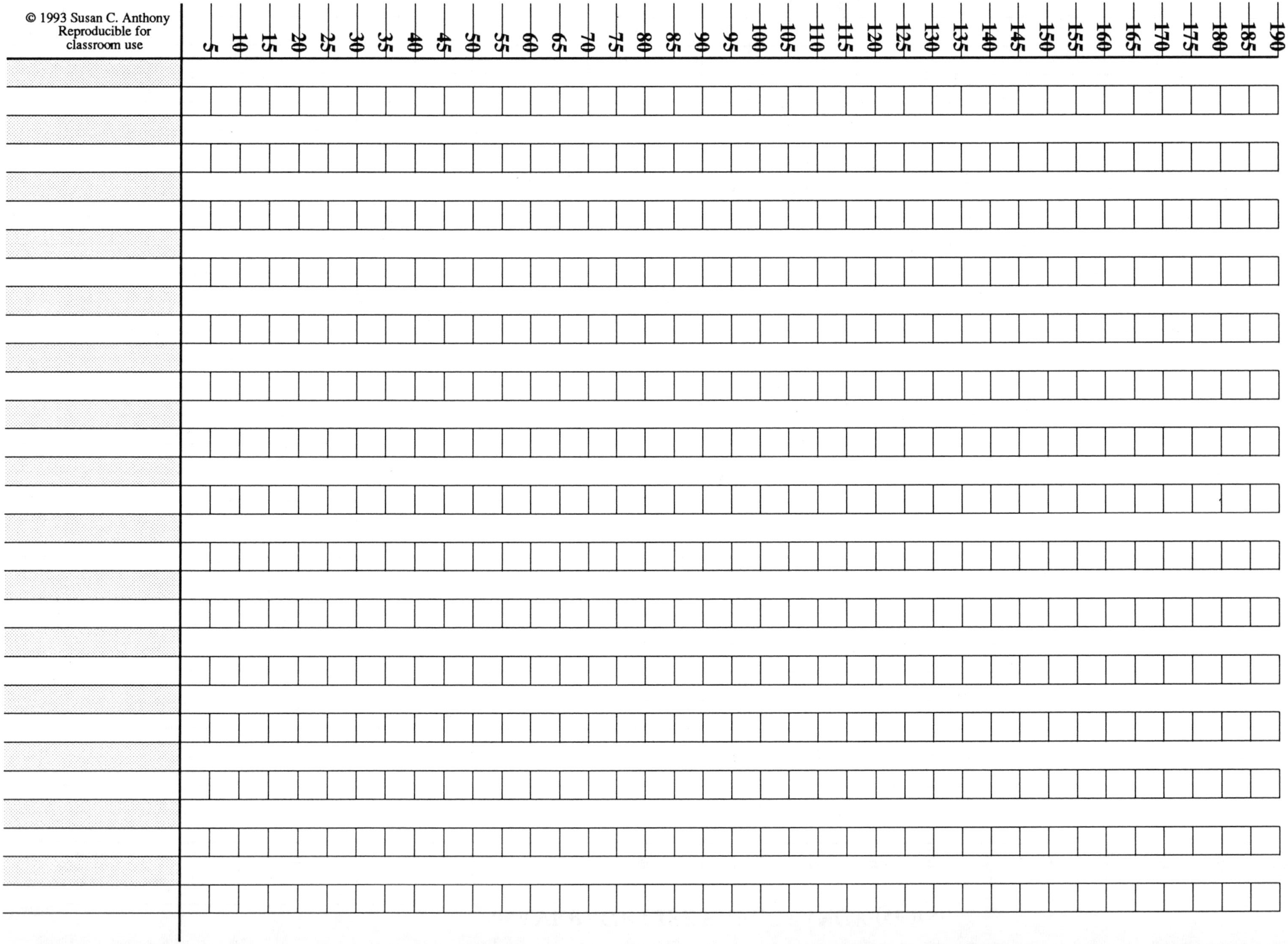

Name________

160

PASSPORT TO THE WORLD

The following activity challenges students to "visit" and learn about as many countries of their choice as desired. Students apply for and receive passports which are stamped when they "enter" (begin a study of) and "exit" (complete a study of) any country of choice. After initial classroom instruction and introductory activities, students can proceed independently at home or in school. The activity may be used for up to the entire school year.

Countries Questions

Materials:

Countries Questions worksheet (Activity Book p. 129, answers on p. 130)

Facts Plus for each student

Background information and procedure:

Make sure students understand all the terms used on pages 53-69. Terms are explained in depth in *Facts Plus* on page 230. Population density activities (Activity Book page 127) may be used to clarify that concept. Students complete the worksheet on their own.

Introduction to Time Zones

Materials:

Facts Plus p. 2-3

Copies of the worksheet on this page to the right, or write it on the board.

Optional: Globe, large world map showing time zones

Background information:

Have students read pages 2 and 3 of *Facts Plus* for information on time and time zones. Perhaps use a globe and a light source to illustrate why the time is different in different parts of the world. Remember **W E** (going west it gets earlier) and **E L** (going east it gets later). Have students use the time zones map on p. 3 of *Facts Plus* to figure out the time at each meridian. Rulers may help.

Answers: 1) 11:00 a.m., 2) 1:00 p.m., 3) 7:00 a.m., 4) 5:00 p.m., 5) 3:00 a.m., 6) 12:00 a.m., 7) 6:00 a.m., 8) 8:00 p.m., 9) 5:00 a.m., 10) 3:00 p.m.

Time Conversions

Materials:

Time Conversion Circle (Act. Book p. 164)

Brads and scissors for assembly

Time Zones of Capital Cities chart (Activity Book p. 165-166)

Time Zones Conversion Worksheet (Activity Book p. 167)

Optional: World map showing time zones

Suggested procedure:

Pass out the Time Conversion Circle. Have students assemble theirs and put their names on them. Assist them in following directions and using the Time Zones of Capital Cities chart to complete the worksheet. Collect the time conversion circles and charts for later use.

Name ______________________

TIME ZONES

On the map on page 3 of *Facts Plus,* it is 12:00 p.m. at 0° longitude (Greenwich Mean Time). What time is it at:

1. 15°W ____________
2. 15°E ____________
3. 75°W ____________
4. 75° E ____________
5. 135° W ____________
6. 180° ____________
7. 90° W ____________
8. 120°E ____________
9. 105°W ____________
10. 45°E ____________

Currency Conversion

Materials:

Currency Exchange Chart (Activity Book p. 168 or copy of the latest rates printed in *The Wall Street Journal)*

Currency Exchange Worksheet (Activity Book p. 169, answers p. 170)

Optional: calculators, samples of foreign money, current newspaper

Background information:

Each country issues its own *currency* (money in the form of bills and coins). *Facts Plus* page 212 shows all United States currency. Most merchants in other countries do not accept U.S. dollars so they must be exchanged for local currency in order to purchase food, pay for a taxi, etc. Generally, money can be exchanged at the airport or at a bank. In some countries, especially Third World countries, people on the street may approach travelers and offer to exchange money on the *black market*. Although the rate may be better than at a bank, this is illegal and risky. All but 27 of the world's countries have a black market. There is no black market in the United States.

The *exchange rate* shows the value of one currency in relation to another. Some basic units of money, such as the British pound, are worth more than the dollar. Most are worth less. Some are worth much less! A dollar is worth 7864 Turkish lira, for example. That means there are more than 78 lira to a penny! Exchange rates change every day. Newspapers publish rates for the major currencies in the daily business section.

The United States dollar is a form of *hard currency*. At one time, this meant that it could be exchanged for gold. Now it means that its value is expected to remain the same or increase as compared with other currencies. The British pound, the German deutsche mark, the French franc and the Japanese yen are also hard currencies. Hard currency is easily changed into other currencies. *Soft currency* is worth little or nothing outside the country which issued it because it cannot be exchanged. It may even be illegal to take bills or coins out of these countries.

In the Currency Exchange Chart, the equivalent of $1.00 worth of foreign money has been calculated. To figure how much you would receive for $50, multiply by 50.

Suggested procedure:

1. Read the background information aloud.
2. Pass out the Chart, the Worksheet, and calculators if available. Without calculators, students must multiply with decimals.
3. Work at least the first 2-3 problems as a group until students understand.
4. Allow students to finish the worksheet. First look up all rates, then do all calculations.
5. Collect the charts as they'll be needed again.

Class "Trip" to Mexico

Materials:

Question sheet (Activity Book p. 171, answers on p. 172)

Facts Plus for each student

Time Conversion Circles (from previous activity, Activity Book p. 164)

Time Zones of Capital Cities chart (from previous activity, Act. Book p. 165-166)

Currency Exchange Chart (from previous activity, Activity Book p. 167)

Optional: Large world map or globe, atlases

Background information:

No passport is required for travel to Mexico. This activity is to familiarize students with what will be required in the Passport Activity.

Suggested procedure:

This should be teacher directed. No more than 10 questions a day should be done because of the initial instruction required. See Activity Book p. 172 for tips on instruction.

Sample bonus sentences:

Mexico has a volcano named Paricutin which started in a cornfield in 1943. (p. 30)

The Rio Grande River is the border between the U.S. and Mexico. (p. 50)

Passport Applications

Materials:

Passport Applications (Activity Book p. 173) or use real applications

Passports (Activity Book p. 176-178, assembled in advance)

Students should bring in two photographs. School photos are perfect.

Optional: An authentic United States passport, a way to measure height

Note to the teacher:

This activity gives students experience with the same application form they will fill out if they ever apply for a real passport. If a classroom economy is in place, the teacher may wish to charge a fee for the passport. Although teachers may adapt this activity to fit their own needs, the intent is not that every child should necessarily have a passport or participate beyond the introductory activities. Students who need extra challenge may enjoy being part of a special group of "world travelers" if rewards are structured to recognize their additional efforts.

Background Information:

To get a real passport, an applicant must supply proof of U.S. citizenship (generally a birth certificate), proof of identity (a picture ID), two photographs and a fee of $65.00. Anyone born in the United States or to parents who are citizens of the U.S. is automatically a citizen.

Suggested procedure:

1. Pass out the applications. Explain the difference between "mailing address" and "permanent address." If student does not have a social security number, enter all zeros. Occupation is "Student."
2. Students complete the application.
3. The teacher may read and explain the following "Acts or Conditions" then have the students take the oath printed on the application and sign. In real life, false statements are punishable by fines or imprisonment.

Acts or Conditions

"I have not, since acquiring United States citizenship, been naturalized as a citizen of a foreign state; taken an oath or made an affirmation or other formal declaration of allegiance to a foreign state; entered or served in the armed forces of a foreign state; accepted or performed the duties of any office, post, or employment under the government of a foreign state or political subdivision thereof; made a formal renunciation of nationality either in the United States or before a diplomatic or consular officer of the United States in a foreign state; or been convicted by a court or court martial of competent jurisdiction of committing any act of treason against, or attempting by force to overthrow, or bearing arms against, the United States, or conspiring to overthrow, put down, or to destroy by force, the Government of the United States, or having been naturalized, within one year after such naturalization, returned to the country of my birth or any other foreign country to take up a permanent residence."

Passport Activity

Materials:

Folder for each participating student with:
- Passport
- Time Conversion Circle
- Time Zones of Capital Cities chart
- Currency Exchange Chart
- Question sheets for countries visited
- See Activity Book p. 174 for more instructions on making folders

Facts Plus and calculators

Teacher materials:
- Copies of question sheets, p. 171, or teachers may set other requirements
- Stamp for passports (Have stamp made from master on Activity Bk. p. 174)
- Gold stars to put in passport to reward bonus or super bonus work

Suggested procedure:

1. When student chooses a country, give her a question sheet and stamp the passport.
2. When a student completes the question sheet and/or activities, stamp "departed."
3. Color the country on blank map in folder on possibly on large map in classroom.

TIME CONVERSION CIRCLE

To assemble:

1) Cut out each circle.
2) Fasten the smaller circle on top of the larger one with a brad through the center.

To use:

1) Determine your local time zone and locate it on the inner circle. Center its line on the the hour nearest the local time on the outer circle.
2) Determine the standard time meridian or zone number of the place you wish to call. Find the zone number or meridian and read the time it is in that place on the outer dial.

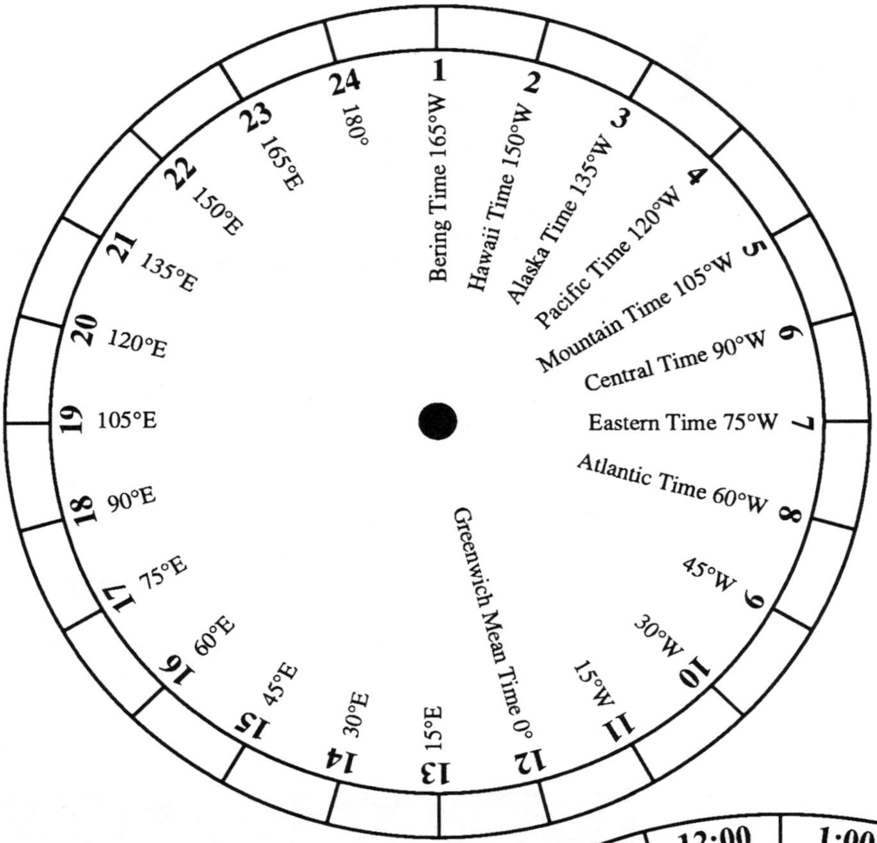

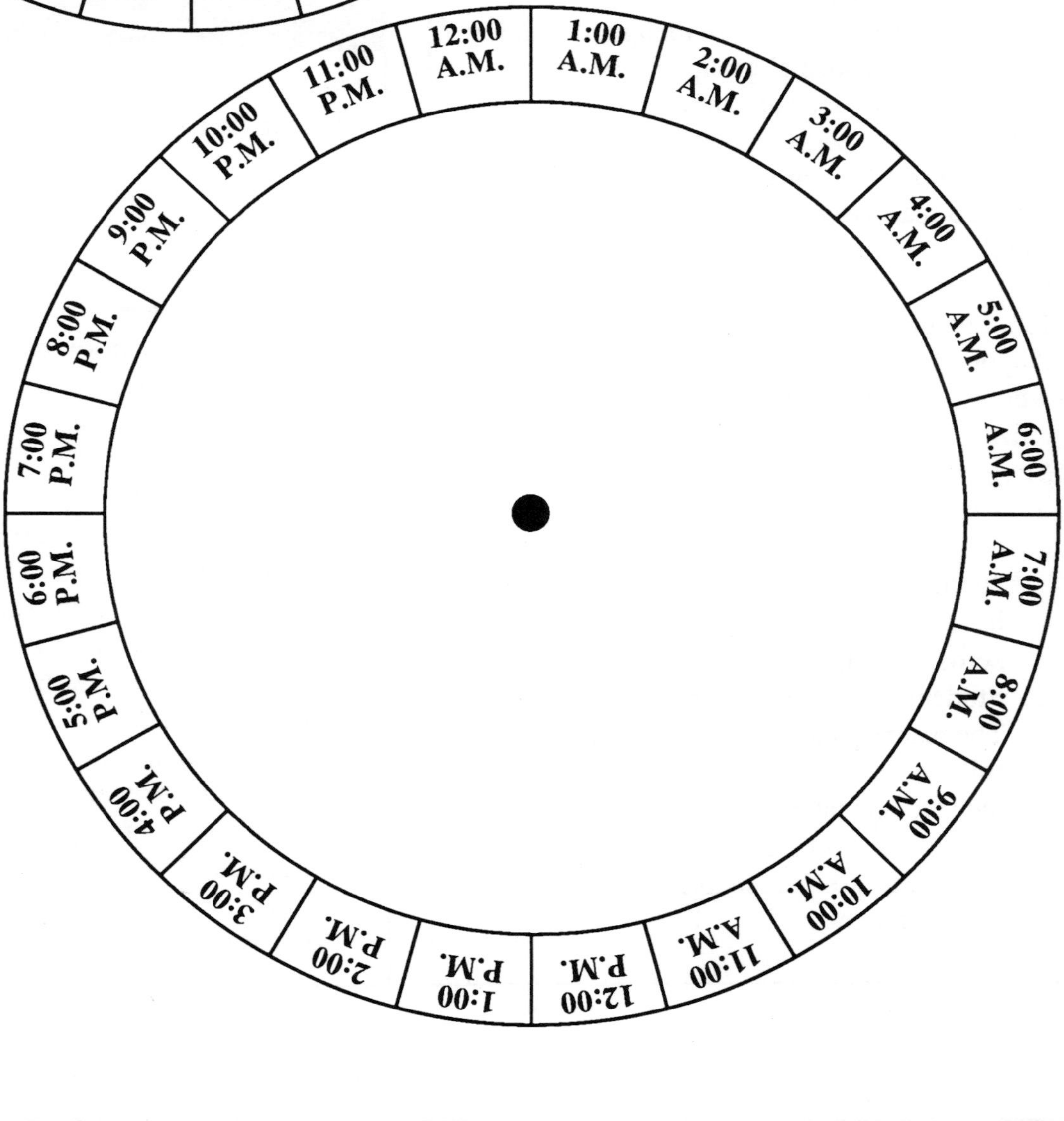

Name ____________________

Teachers: Lessons on p. 161, 162, 163

TIME ZONES OF CAPITAL CITIES

Note: The meridian at the left is at the center of the standard time zone used by the capital city shown.

60°E ..... Afghanistan—Kabul + ½ hr.
15°E ..... Albania—Tiranë
15°E ..... Algeria—Algiers
15°E ..... Andorra—Andorra la Vella
15°E ..... Angola—Luanda
60°W ..... Antigua & Barbuda—St. John's
45°W ..... Argentina—Buenos Aires
60°E ..... Armenia—Yerevan
150°E ..... Australia—Canberra
15°E ..... Austria—Vienna
60°E ..... Azerbaijan—Baku
75°W ..... Bahamas—Nassau
60°E ..... Bahrain—Manama
90°E ..... Bangladesh—Dhaka
60°W ..... Barbados—Bridgetown
45°E ..... Belarus—Minsk
15°E ..... Belgium—Brussels
90°W ..... Belize—Belmopan
15°E ..... Benin—Porto-Novo
90°E ..... Bhutan—Thimphu + ½ hr.
60°W ..... Bolivia—La Paz
15°E ..... Bosnia-Hercegovina—Sarajevo
30°E ..... Botswana—Gaborone
45°W ..... Brazil—Brasília
120°E ..... Brunei—Bandar Seri Begawan
30°E ..... Bulgaria—Sofia
0° ..... Burkina Faso—Ouagadougou
30°E ..... Burundi—Bujumbura
105°E ..... Cambodia—Phnom Penh
15°E ..... Cameroon—Yaoundé
75°W ..... Canada—Ottawa, Ontario
15°W ..... Cape Verde—Praia
15°E ..... Central African Republic—Bangui
15°E ..... Chad—N'Djamena
60°W ..... Chile—Santiago
120°E ..... China—Beijing
75°W ..... Colombia—Bogotá
45°E ..... Comoros—Moroni
15°E ..... Congo—Brazzaville
90°W ..... Costa Rica—San José
0° ..... Côte D'Ivoire—Abidjan
15°E ..... Croatia—Zagreb
75°W ..... Cuba—Havana
30°E ..... Cyprus—Nicosia
15°E ..... Czechoslovakia—Prague
15°E ..... Denmark—Copenhagen
45°E ..... Djibouti—Djibouti
60°W ..... Dominica—Roseau
60°W ..... Dominican Republic—Santo Domingo
75°W ..... Ecuador—Quito
30°E ..... Egypt—Cairo
90°W ..... El Salvador—San Salvador
15°E ..... Equatorial Guinea—Malabo
45°E ..... Estonia—Tallinn
45°E ..... Ethiopia—Addis Ababa
180° ..... Fiji—Suva
30°E ..... Finland—Helsinki
15°E ..... France—Paris
15°E ..... Gabon—Libreville
0° ..... Gambia—Banjul
60°E ..... Georgia—Tblisi
15°E ..... Germany—Berlin
0° ..... Ghana—Accra
30°E ..... Greece—Athens
60°W ..... Grenada—St. George's
90°W ..... Guatemala—Guatemala City
0° ..... Guinea—Conakry
0° ..... Guinea-Bissau—Bissau
45°W ..... Guyana—Georgetown
75°W ..... Haiti—Port-au-Prince
90°W ..... Honduras—Tegucigalpa
15°E ..... Hungary—Budapest
0° ..... Iceland—Reykjavík
75°E ..... India—New Delhi + ½ hr.
105°E ..... Indonesia—Jakarta
45°E ..... Iran—Teheran + ½ hr.
45°E ..... Iraq—Baghdad
0° ..... Ireland—Dublin
30°E ..... Israel—Jerusalem
15°E ..... Italy—Rome
75°W ..... Jamaica—Kingston
135°E ..... Japan—Tokyo
30°E ..... Jordan—Amman
90°E ..... Kazakhstan—Alma-Ata
45°E ..... Kenya—Nairobi
165°E ..... Kiribati—Tarawa
135°E ..... Korea, North—P'yongyang
135°E ..... Korea, South—Seoul
45°E ..... Kuwait—Kuwait City
90°E ..... Kyrgyzstan—Bishkek
105°E ..... Laos—Vientiane
45°E ..... Latvia—Riga
30°E ..... Lebanon—Beirut
30°E ..... Lesotho—Maseru

0° ..... Liberia—Monrovia
30°E ..... Libya—Tripoli
15°E ..... Liechtenstein—Vaduz
45°E ..... Lithuania—Vilnius
15°E ..... Luxembourg—Luxembourg
15°E ..... Macedonia—Skopje
45°E ..... Madagascar—Antananarivo
30°E ..... Malawi—Lilongwe
105°E ..... Malaysia—Kuala Lumpur + ½ hr.
75°E ..... Maldives—Malé
0° ..... Mali—Bamako
15°E ..... Malta—Valletta
0° ..... Mauritania—Nouakchott
60°E ..... Mauritius—Port Louis
90°W ..... Mexico—Mexico City
45°E ..... Moldova—Kishinëv
15°E ..... Monaco—Monaco
120°E ..... Mongolia—Ulaanbaatar
0° ..... Morocco—Rabat
30°E ..... Mozambique—Maputo
90°E ..... Myanmar—Yangon + ½ hr.
30°E ..... Namibia—Windhoek
165°E ..... Nauru—Yaren + ½ hr.
90°E ..... Nepal—Kathmandu
15°E ..... Netherlands—Amsterdam
180° ..... New Zealand—Wellington
90°W ..... Nicaragua—Managua
15°E ..... Niger—Niamey
15°E ..... Nigeria—Lagos
15°E ..... Norway—Oslo
60°E ..... Oman—Muscat
75°E ..... Pakistan—Islamabad
75°W ..... Panama—Panama City
150°E ..... Papua New Guinea—Port Moresby
60°W ..... Paraguay—Asunción
75°W ..... Peru—Lima
120°E ..... Philippines—Manila
15°E ..... Poland—Warsaw
0° ..... Portugal—Lisbon
45°E ..... Qatar—Doha
30°E ..... Romania—Bucharest
45°E ..... Russia—Moscow
30°E ..... Rwanda—Kigali
60°W ..... St. Kitts and Nevis—Basseterre
60°W ..... St. Lucia—Castries
60°W ..... St. Vincent & the Grenadines—Kingstown
15°E ..... San Marino—San Marino
0° ..... São Tomé & Principé—São Tomé
45°E ..... Saudi Arabia—Riyadh*
0° ..... Senegal—Dakar
60°E ..... Seychelles—Victoria
0° ..... Sierra Leone—Freetown
105°E ..... Singapore—Singapore + ½ hr.
15°E ..... Slovenia—Ljubljana
165°E ..... Solomon Islands—Honiara
45°E ..... Somalia—Mogadishu
30°E ..... South Africa—Cape Town
15°E ..... Spain—Madrid
75°E ..... Sri Lanka—Colombo + ½ hr.
30°E ..... Sudan—Khartoum
60°W ..... Suriname—Paramaribo + ½ hr.
30°E ..... Swaziland—Mbabane
15°E ..... Sweden—Stockholm
15°E ..... Switzerland—Bern
45°E ..... Syria—Damascus
120°E ..... Taiwan—Taipei
75°E ..... Tajikistan—Dushanbe
45°E ..... Tanzania—Dar es Salaam
105°E ..... Thailand—Bangkok
0° ..... Togo—Lomé
180° ..... Tonga—Nuku'alofa
60°W ..... Trinidad & Tobago—Port-of-Spain
15°E ..... Tunisia—Tunis
45°E ..... Turkey—Ankara
75°E ..... Turkmenistan—Ashkhabad
180° ..... Tuvalu—Funafuti
45°E ..... Uganda—Kampala
45°E ..... Ukraine—Kiev
60°E ..... United Arab Emirates—Abu Dhabi
0° ..... United Kingdom—London
75°W ..... United States—Washington, D.C.
45°W ..... Uruguay—Montevideo
90°E ..... Uzbekistan—Tashkent
165°E ..... Vanuatu—Port-Vila
60°W ..... Venezuela—Caracas
105°E ..... Vietnam—Hanoi
180° ..... Western Samoa—Apia
45°E ..... Yemen—San'a'
15°E ..... Yugoslavia—Belgrade
15°E ..... Zaire—Kinshasa
30°E ..... Zambia—Lusaka
30°E ..... Zimbabwe—Harare

*Saudi Arabia uses sun time, rather than a standard time zone.
Source: *The World Book Great Geographical Atlas*

Teachers: Lessons on p. 161, 162, and 163

Name________________________________ Date________________________________

TIME ZONE CONVERSION WORKSHEET

These conversions will give you a general idea of the time in the foreign city. Because of Daylight Saving and the fact that some countries do not use standard time zones, the actual time in the foreign city may be different.

YOUR LOCAL TIME ZONE AND ITS CENTRAL MERIDIAN________________________________

FOREIGN CITY & COUNTRY	CENTRAL MERIDIAN OF ITS TIME ZONE	TIME THERE	YOUR LOCAL TIME
Budapest, Hungary			2:00 p.m.
San José, Costa Rica			12:00 noon
Moscow, Russia			7:00 a.m.
Canberra, Australia			9:00 p.m.
Teheran, Iran			3:00 a.m.
Taipei, Taiwan			6:00 p.m.
Panama City, Panama			1:00 a.m.
Rabat, Morocco			3:00 p.m.
Washington, D.C., USA			5:00 p.m.
Tokyo, Japan			10:00 a.m.
Cape Town, South Africa			11:00 p.m.
Hanoi, Vietnam			4:00 a.m.
Stockholm, Sweden			7:00 p.m.
Wellington, New Zealand			6:00 a.m.
Lima, Peru			1:00 p.m.
Berlin, Germany			11:00 a.m.
Jakarta, Indonesia			3:00 p.m.
Jerusalem, Israel			10:00 p.m.
Asunción, Paraguay			1:00 a.m.
Panama City, Panama			6:00 p.m.

Challenge: When you finish, figure out what time it is at home when it is noon in each of these cities.

Teachers: Lesson plan on p. 161, answers vary by local time zone

CURRENCY EXCHANGE CHART

Note: The numbers at the left show the amount of local currency equal in value to one U.S. dollar.

1,162.50	afghani
21.47	Algerian dinar
8,849.56	austral
1.39	Australian dollar
10.56	Austrian schilling
1.00	Bahamian dollar
.38	Bahrani dinar
25.32	baht
1.00	balboa
2.01	Barbadian dollar
30.90	Belgian franc
2.00	Belizean dollar
5.00	birr
4.03	boliviano
76.30	bolívar
1.61	Bruneian dollar
208.72	Burundi franc
1.25	Canadian dollar
62.63	Cape Verdean escudo
486.00	cedi
254.48	CFA franc
375.33	Chilean peso
791.19	Colombian peso
8.75	colón
136.37	Costa Rican colón
5.43	córdoba
7,510.20	cruziero
1.32	Cuban peso
.40	Cypriot pound
8.30	dalasi
1.50	deutsch mark
177.72	Djibouti franc
240.00	dobra
12.77	Dominican peso
194.65	drachma
2.70	East Caribbean dollar
3.31	Egyptian pound
3.67	Emirian dirham
1.52	Fijian dollar
79.61	forint
5.09	French franc
10.52	gourde
1,555.00	guaraní
5,000.00	Guinea-Bisseau peso
812.29	Guinean franc
125.49	Guyanese dollar
28.38	Indian rupee
2,044.00	Indonesian rupiah
1.55	inti
.31	Iraqi dinar
1,437.00	Iranian rial
.56	Irish pound
1,326.75	Italian lira
23.28	Jamaican dollar
.68	Jordanian dinar
34.21	Kenyan shilling
.96	kina
27.84	koruna
5.78	krone
57.20	króna
.29	Kuwaiti dinar
4.17	kwacha
550.00	kwanza
5.97	kyat
2,170.00	Lebanese pound
110.00	lek
5.92	lempira
500.00	leone
430.00	leu
23.28	lev
1.00	Liberian dollar
.28	Libyan dinar
2.91	lilangeni
2.91	loti
30.90	Luxembourg franc
1,827.37	Malagasy franc
11.52	Maldivian rufiyaa
.27	Maltese lira
4.75	markka
15.49	Mauritian rupee
2,725.53	metical
3.106	Mexican peso
8.08	Moroccan dirham
19.45	naira
46.63	Nepalese rupee
1.69	Netherlands guilder
1.85	New Zealand dollar
10,875.00	new dong
2.52	new Israeli shekel
715.00	new kip
23.30	new Taiwan dollar
3,328.00	new Uruguayan peso
28.38	ngultrum
2.15	North Korean won
6.12	Norwegian krone
.39	Omani rial
106.00	ouguiya
1.39	pa'anga
25.12	Pakistani rupee
107.20	peseta
24.63	Philippine peso
133.78	Portuguese escudo
.59	pound sterling
2.17	pula
3.64	Qatari riyal
5.27	quetzal
2.91	rand
16.50	rial
2,000.00	riel
2.50	ringgit
368.00	ruble
141.23	Rwandan franc
3.75	Saudi riyal
5.07	Seychelles rupee
1.61	Singapore dollar
2.94	Solomon Islands dollar
2,620.00	Somali shilling
782.80	South Korean won
44.25	Sri Lankan rupee
1,882.50	sucre
100.00	Sudanese pound
1.79	Suriname guilder
5.66	Swedish krona
1.34	Swiss franc
104.75	Syrian pound
38.95	taka
2.46	tala
322.73	Tanzanian shilling
4.55	Trinidad/Tobago dollar
40.00	tughrik
.85	Tunisian dinar
7,864.61	Turkish lira
1,173.73	Ugandan shilling
113.76	vatu
16.50	Yemeni riyal
120.98	yen
5.55	yuan
200.00	Yugoslav dinar
1,150,017.00	zaire
213.90	Zambian kwacha
5.18	Zimbabwean dollar
14,640.00	zloty

Source: Wall Street Journal 10/26/92. Rates are rounded.

Teachers: Lessons on p. 162 and 163

Name______________________________ Date________________________

CURRENCY EXCHANGE WORKSHEET

Note: This worksheet requires multiplication of decimal numbers.

Question	$1.00 (from chart)	Answer
1. How many French francs would you get for $100?		
2. How many Netherlands guilders would you get for $10?		
3. How many rubles would you get for $65?		
4. How many naira (Nigeria) would you get for $500?		
5. How many Australian dollars would you get for $225?		
6. How many Egyptian pounds would you get for $45?		
7. How many yen (Japan) would you get for $128?		
8. How many deutsch marks would you get for $740?		
9. How many Indian rupees would you get for $86?		
10. How many lempira (Honduras) would you get for $350?		
11. How many krone (Denmark) would you get for $197?		
12. How many pounds sterling would you get for $371?		
13. How many drachma (Greece) would you get for $22?		
14. How many zloty (Poland) would you get for $100?		
15. How many pesetas (Spain) would you get for $275?		
16. How many Dominican pesos would you get for $510?		
17. How many guaraní (Paraguay) would you get for $25?		
18. How many Zambian kwachas would you get for $72?		
19. How many Kenyan shillings would you get for $98?		
20. How many South Korean wons would you get for $48?		
21. How many Colombian pesos would you get for $33?		
22. How many Saudi riyals would you get for $425?		
23. How many yuan (China) would you get for $1,000?		
24. How many quetzal (Guatemala) would you get for $65?		
25. How many CFA francs would you get for $550?		

Teachers: Lesson on p. 162, answers on p. 170

Name **KEY** Date

CURRENCY EXCHANGE WORKSHEET

Note: This worksheet requires multiplication of decimal numbers.

Question	$1.00 (from chart)	Answer
1. How many French francs would you get for $100?	*5.09*	*509.00*
2. How many Netherlands guilders would you get for $10?	*1.69*	*16.90*
3. How many rubles would you get for $65?	*368.00*	*23,920.00*
4. How many naira (Nigeria) would you get for $500?	*19.45*	*9,725.00*
5. How many Australian dollars would you get for $225?	*1.39*	*312.75*
6. How many Egyptian pounds would you get for $45?	*3.31*	*148.95*
7. How many yen (Japan) would you get for $128.00?	*120.98*	*15,485.44*
8. How many deutsch marks would you get for $740?	*1.50*	*1,110.00*
9. How many Indian rupees would you get for $86?	*28.38*	*2,440.68*
10. How many lempira (Honduras) would you get for $350?	*5.92*	*2,097.00*
11. How many krone (Denmark) would you get for $197?	*5.78*	*1,138.66*
12. How many pounds sterling would you get for $371?	*.59*	*218.89*
13. How many drachma (Greece) would you get for $22?	*194.65*	*4,282.30*
14. How many zloty (Poland) would you get for $100?	*14,640.00*	*1,464,000*
15. How many pesetas (Spain) would you get for $275?	*107.20*	*29,480.00*
16. How many Dominican pesos would you get for $510?	*12.77*	*6,512.70*
17. How many guaraní (Paraguay) would you get for $25?	*1,555.00*	*38,875.00*
18. How many Zambian kwachas would you get for $72?	*213.90*	*15,400.80*
19. How many Kenyan shillings would you get for $98?	*34.21*	*3,352.58*
20. How many South Korean wons would you get for $48?	*782.80*	*37,574.40*
21. How many Colombian pesos would you get for $33?	*791.19*	*26,109.27*
22. How many Saudi riyals would you get for $425?	*3.75*	*1,593.75*
23. How many yuan (China) would you get for $1,000?	*5.55*	*5,550.00*
24. How many quetzal (Guatemala) would you get for $65?	*5.27*	*342.55*
25. How many CFA francs would you get for $550?	*254.48*	*139,964.00*

Teachers: Lesson on p. 162, copy master on p. 169

Name ______________________ **Date of Entry** ______________________
Country ______________________ **Date of Departure** ______________________

List *Facts Plus* pages with information on this country: ______________________

1. What is the general location of the country? ______________________
2. What is the latitude and longitude? ______________________
3. Locate the country on a map or globe.
4. Is the country in the eastern or western hemisphere? ______________________
5. Is the country in the northern or southern hemisphere? ______________________
6. Is the country in a tropical, temperate or arctic area? ______________________
7. If it's in a temperate or arctic zone, in what month does summer begin? __________
8. Is the country landlocked? ______ If not, what is one body of water which forms a boundary? ______________________
9. What countries border this country? ______________________
10. Your plane lands in the capital city. What is its name? ______________________
11. You want to call home to tell your family you arrived safely. What is the central meridian of the time zone used by the capital city? ______________________
12. The best time to catch your family at home is at 8:00 p.m. their time. What time should you call from your country? ______________________
13. What is the basic unit of money called? ______________________
14. How much local currency can be exchanged for $1.00? ______________________
15. How much local money will you get when you exchange $150.00? __________
16. What is the area of this country? ______________________
17. How much smaller or larger is it than your state? ______________________
18. How many years can the average person expect to live in this country? __________
19. How much longer or shorter is that than the U.S. life expectancy? __________
20. What is the infant mortality rate in this country? ______________________
21. Is hunger and starvation a basic issue in this country? ______________________
22. What major languages are spoken in this country? ______________________
23. What is the per capita GNP in this country? ______________________
24. How much more or less is this than the per capita GNP in the U.S.? __________
25. What is the population of this country? ______________________
26. What is the population growth rate? ______________________
27. What is the population density in this country? ______________________
28. How much more or less is this than the density in your state? __________
29. Is this country a member of the United Nations? ______________________
30. What regions or groups of countries does this country belong to, if any? __________

____

Bonus: On the back, write a sentence for each additional piece of information you find about this country in *Facts Plus* or other reference sources.

Teachers: Lessons on p. 162 and 163, answers for Mexico on p. 172

Name **KEY**　　　**Date of Entry** Date study began
Country Mexico　　　**Date of Departure** Date study ended

Facts Plus pages with information on Mexico: ___62-63, 30, 50, 70, 75, 76, 90, 105, 191, 131

1. What is the general location of the country? ....*North America (p. 63)*
2. What is the latitude and longitude? ....*23°N 102°W (p. 63)*
3. Locate the country on a map or globe. ....Use map, globe, or *Facts Plus* p. 131 and 134.
4. Is the country in the eastern or western hemisphere? ...*Western* Refer to *Facts Plus* p. 142 and a globe if available.
5. Is the country in the northern or southern hemisphere?..*Northern*
6. Is the country in a tropical, temperate or arctic area? *Temperate and tropical.* Read *Facts Plus* p. 26 for background information. Find the equator, Tropic of Cancer, Tropic of Capricorn, Arctic Circle and Antarctic Circle on a globe and in *Facts Plus* p. 134-135. Some countries, including Mexico, are in more than one zone.
7. If it's in a temperate or arctic zone, in what month does summer begin?........*June* Refer to *Facts Plus* p. 14. Seasons in the southern hemisphere are reversed. Tropical zones do not have 4 seasons.
8. Is the country landlocked? *No* If not, what is one body of water which forms a boundary? *The Gulf of Mexico and the Pacific Ocean.* "Landlocked" means surrounded by land with no coastline.
9. What countries border this country? ....*The United States, Belize, Guatemala (p. 131)*
10. Your plane lands in the capital city. What is its name?..................................*Mexico City (p. 62)*
11. You want to call home to tell your family you arrived safely. What is the central meridian of the time zone used by the capital city? ....*90°W* Use the Time Zones of Capital Cities chart
12. The best time to catch your family at home is at 8:00 p.m. their time. What time should you call from your country? ....*11:00 p.m.* Use the Time Zones Conversion Circle
13. What is the basic unit of money called? ....*Mexican peso (p. 62)*
14. How much local currency can be exchanged for $1.00? .....*3.106* Use Currency Exchange Chart. The old Mexican peso was worth 3,106.10. Both old and new are being used (since 1/1/93).
15. How much local money will you get when you exchange $75.00? ....*232.95 pesos* Multiply 75 x 3.106.
16. What is the area of this country? ....*761,600 sq. mi. (p. 62)*
17. How much smaller or larger is it than your state? .....Answers vary. State areas on pages 94-101.
18. How many years can the average person expect to live in this country?...............*69 years (p. 63)*
19. How much longer or shorter is that than the U.S. life expectancy?..*7 years shorter* Subtract U.S. life expectancy of 76 (p. 68) minus 69. Label with "years" and "shorter" or "longer."
20. What is the infant mortality rate in this country? ....*47 (p. 63)*
21. Is hunger and starvation a basic issue in this country? ..*No* Read about infant mortality rate on p. 231 of *Facts Plus*. If the IMR is more than 50, this answer is "yes." If 50 or less, "no."
22. What major languages are spoken in this country?..*Spanish (p. 62)*
23. What is the per capita GNP in this country?...*$2,490 (p. 63)*
24. How much more or less is this than the per capita GNP in the U.S.? ....*$19,210 less* Subtract Mexico's per capita GNP from that of the U.S. on *Facts Plus* p. 68 ($21,700)
25. What is the population of this country? ....*87,715,000 (p. 63)*
26. What is the population growth rate?...*2.3% (p. 63)*
27. What is the population density in this country?..*115 (p. 63)*
28. How much more or less is this than the density in your state? ..Answers vary. State densities on p. 94-101.
29. Is this country a member of the United Nations? ....*Yes (p. 70)*
30. What regions or groups of countries does this country belong to, if any? ....*None*

Bonus: *Teachers: Sample bonus sentences on p. 162*

APPLICATION FOR UNITED STATES PASSPORT

1. NAME First Name ______ Middle Name ______

Last Name ______

Photo

2. MAILING ADDRESS

Street ______

City, State, ZIP Code ______

Country ______

3. SEX ☐ Male ☐ Female

4. PLACE OF BIRTH (City, State, Country) ______

5. DATE OF BIRTH Month ___ Day ___ Year ___

6. SOCIAL SECURITY # ______

7. HEIGHT Feet ___ Inches ___

8. COLOR OF HAIR ______

9. COLOR OF EYES ______

10. (Area Code) HOME PHONE ______

11. (Area Code) WORK PHONE ______

12. OCCUPATION ______

13. PERMANENT ADDRESS (Street, City, State, ZIP Code) ______

14. FATHER'S NAME Birthplace Birth Date U.S. Citizen ☐ Yes ☐ No

15. MOTHER'S MAIDEN NAME Birthplace Birth Date U.S. Citizen ☐ Yes ☐ No

16. TRAVEL PLANS ***(Not Mandatory)*** Departure Date Length of Stay

Countries ______

17. HAVE YOU EVER BEEN ISSUED A U.S. PASSPORT? ☐ Yes ☐ No

18. HAVE YOU EVER BEEN MARRIED? ☐ Yes ☐ No

19. IN CASE OF EMERGENCY, NOTIFY ***(Person Not Traveling With You)*** Relationship ______

Full Name ______

Address ______ (Area Code) Phone Number ______

20. Do not sign application until requested to do so by person administering oath.

I have not, since acquiring United States citizenship, performed any of the acts listed under "Acts or Conditions." I solemnly swear (or affirm) that the statements made on this application are true and the photograph attached is a true likeness of me.

(Sign in presence of person authorized to accept application.) ______

Teachers: Lesson on p. 163

Note to teachers: Activity explained on p. 163. Cut-outs on these pages can be used to make up the student folders, which may be laid out as shown here:

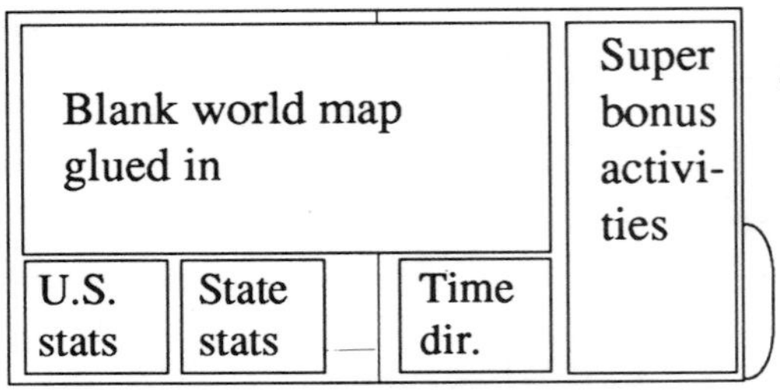

State statistics are on pages 94-101 of Facts Plus. Permission granted to copy your state's statistics for this activity.

On the right is a master for a stamp for use with the passports. Cut this out and take it to a local stamp shop. When using stamp, fill in name of country and date.

The bearer of this passport entered/departed

____

on the following date: _________

UNITED STATES

Capital: Washington, D.C.
Area: 3,787,425 sq. mi.
Language: English
Currency: U.S. dollar
Population: 248,708,873
Population Growth Rate: 0.8%
Population Density: 66
Per Capita GNP: $21,700
Average Life Expectancy: 76
Infant Mortality Rate: 9
Location: North America
Latitude-Longitude: 38°N 97°W

TIME CONVERSION CIRCLE

My local time zone__________________

Directions for use:

1) Determine your local time zone and locate it on the inner circle. Center its line on the hour nearest the local time on the outer circle.
2) Determine the standard time meridian or zone number of the place you wish to call. Find the zone number or meridian and read the time it is in that place on the outer dial.

SUPER BONUS ACTIVITIES

Draw and color the country's flag.

Trace a map of the country and fill in the capital and major cities, names of bordering countries, major rivers and physical features, or whatever is of interest to you.

Draw the traditional costume of the country.

Draw a picture of the basic unit of money.

Make a poster with photos of the country. Check with a travel agent.

Read an encyclopedia article about the country.

Read a book about the country.

Find and share with the class an example of the music of the country.

Bring in objects from the country to share.

Make a travel brochure. Use an actual travel brochure to get ideas about how to put one together. Advertise the best things about the country.

Invite a person who has been to the country to share photos, objects and stories with the class. Schedule this with your teacher.

Bring in newspaper clippings with news about events in the country.

Make a time line of the major events in the history of the country.

Show or write about how holidays are celebrated in the country.

Write a short report about the country.

Teachers: Activity is explained on p. 163. To assemble passport, copy p. 175-178 two-sided. Cut on dotted lines, fold and staple.

PASSPORT

United States of America

GENERAL INFORMATION

VISAS. IT IS THE RESPONSIBILITY OF THE PASSPORT BEARER TO OBTAIN THE NECESSARY VISAS.

LE TITULAIRE DU PASSEPORT EST SEUL RESPONSABLE DE L'OBTENTION DES VISAS REQUIS.

IMMUNIZATIONS. Under the International Health Regulations, a country may require International Certificates of Vaccination against Yellow Fever and Cholera. Because smallpox has been eradicated, smallpox vaccination should NOT be given. Check with health care providers or your records to ensure measles, mumps, rubella, polio, diphtheria, tetanus, and pertussis immunizations are up to date. Prophylactic medication for malaria and certain other preventative measures are advisable for some travelers. NO immunizations are required to return to the United States. Pertinent information is included in "Health Information for International Travel," U.S. Government Printing Office, Washington, D.C. 20402 or may be obtained from your local health department or physician.

HEALTH INSURANCE. Persons considering foreign travel should determine what health insurance coverage, if any, they have while outside the United States. Medicare does not cover health care costs outside the United States except under limited circumstances in Canada and Mexico.

CUSTOMS SERVICE. The pamphlet, "Know Before You Go," gives you current pertinent information about Customs requirements, and how they apply to articles acquired abroad. Obtain a copy from your nearest Customs Office or from the U.S. Customs Service, P.O. Box 7407, Washington, D.C. 20044. The transportation of currency or bearer instrument, regardless of the amount, is legal; however, if you take out of or bring into the United States more than $5,000 (U.S. or foreign currency, travelers checks, money orders, or other bearer monetary instruments), you are required by U.S. law to file a report with the U.S. Customs Service.

TREASURY. The unlicensed purchase or importation of Cuban, North Korean, Vietnamese, or Cambodian goods is prohibited except for goods with a foreign market value of $100 or less imported as accompanied baggage directly from those countries. Certain transactions involving travel to Cuba are prohibited. For more information, contact the Office of Foreign Assets Control, Treasury Department, Washington, D.C. 20220.

AGRICULTURE. Your reentry into the United States will be speeded if you bring with you NO foreign meat, other animal products, birds, animals, fruits, vegetables, plants, soil, or other agricultural items. It is unlawful to import foreign agricultural items without permission since they may carry destructive plant or animal pests and diseases. For specific information, write "Quarantines," PPQ, APHIS, U.S. Department of Agriculture, 6505 Belcrest Road, Hyattsville, Maryland 20782.

The Secretary of State of the United States of America hereby requests all whom it may concern to permit the citizen/national of the United States named herein to pass without delay or hindrance and in case of need to give all lawful aid and protection.

Le Secrétaire d'Etat des Etats-Unis d' Amérique prie par les présentes toutes autorités compétentes de laisser passer le citoyen ou ressortissant des Etas-Unis titulaire du présent passeport, sans délai ni difficulté et, en cas de besoin, de lui accorder toute aide et protection légitimes.

____

SIGNATURE OF BEARER

Teachers: This activity is explained on p. 163

UNITED STATES OF AMERICA

Surname ____________________

Given names ____________________

Nationality ____________________

Date of birth ____________________

Sex ____________________

Place of birth ____________________

Date of issue ____________________

Date of expiration ____________________

Issued by ____________________

Photo

Passport Number

____

IMPORTANT INFORMATION

THIS PASSPORT IS THE PROPERTY OF THE UNITED STATES GOVERNMENT. IT MUST BE SURRENDERED UPON DEMAND MADE BY AN AUTHORIZED REPRESENTATIVE OF THE U.S. GOVERNMENT.

LOSS, THEFT OR DESTRUCTION OF PASSPORT should be reported immediately to local police authorities and to the Passport Services, Washington, D.C. 20520, or, if overseas, to the nearest American embassy or consulate. Your passport is a valuable citizenship and identity document. It should be carefully safeguarded. Its loss could cause you unnecessary travel complications as well as significant expense.

ALTERATION OR MUTILATION OF PASSPORT. This passport must not be altered or mutilated in any way. Alteration may make it INVALID and, if willful, may subject you to prosecution (Title 18, U.S. Code, Section 1543). Only authorized officials of the United States or of foreign countries, in connection with official matters, may place stamps or make statements, notations or additions in this passport. You may amend or update personal information for your own convenience on page four.

EXPIRATION. The expiration date is given on the inside front cover.

LOSS OF NATIONALITY. You may lose your U.S. nationality by being naturalized in, or by taking an oath or making a declaration of allegiance to a foreign state; or by serving in the armed forces or accepting employment under the government of a foreign state; or by making a formal renunciation of nationality either in the United States or before a diplomatic or consular officer of the United States while abroad. For detailed information, consult the nearest American embassy or consulate.

DUAL NATIONALS. A person is considered a dual national when he owes allegiance to more than one country at the same time. A claim to allegiance may be based on facts of birth, marriage, parentage or naturalization. A dual national may, while in the jurisdiction of the other country which considers that person its national, be subject to all of its laws, including being conscripted for military service. Dual nationals who encounter problems should contact the nearest American embassy or consulate.

WHEN TRAVELING IN DISTURBED AREAS you should keep in touch with the nearest American embassy or consulate.

IF YOU RESIDE ABROAD or when traveling to remote areas you should register at the nearest American embassy or consulate.

NOTICE

THIS PASSPORT MUST NOT BE USED BY ANY PERSON OTHER THAN THE PERSON TO WHOM ISSUED OR IN VIOLATION OF THE CONDITIONS OR RESTRICTIONS PLACED THEREIN OR IN VIOLATION OF THE RULES REGULATING THE ISSUANCE OF PASSPORTS. ANY WILLFUL VIOLATION OF THESE LAWS AND REGULATIONS WILL SUBJECT THE OFFENDER TO PROSECUTION UNDER TITLE 18, UNITED STATES CODE.

FOR YOUR PROTECTION, PENCIL IN THE NAMES AND ADDRESSES BELOW.

PLEASE KEEP THESE ENTRIES UP TO DATE.

BEARER'S ADDRESS IN THE UNITED STATES:

____

____

IN CASE OF DEATH OR ACCIDENT, NOTIFY THE NEAREST AMERICAN EMBASSY OR CONSULATE AND THE INDIVIDUAL NAMED BELOW:

NAME ____________________

ADDRESS ____________________

____

TELEPHONE ____________________

Visas

Entries	*Departures*

Visas

Entries *Departures*

Visas

Entries *Departures*

Visas

Entries *Departures*

Visas

Entries *Departures*

Teachers: Activity is explained on p. 163. To make a larger passport, make extra copies of p. 177-178.

Teachers: This activity is explained on p. 163

Visas

Entries	*Departures*

Visas

Entries	*Departures*

Visas

Entries	*Departures*

Visas

Entries	*Departures*

ODDS AND ENDS

This very *short* section consists of reproducible pages I couldn't bear to leave out because I found them useful when I was teaching, and had difficulty locating them in other sources. I hope they'll be helpful to you!

Memorization Challenges

Materials:

Copies of Memorization Challenges, Activity Book p. 180 for participating students

Large grid to post with challenges across the top and student names down the side

Rewards such as play money to be used in classroom auctions

Background:

Before challenging students to learn all countries of a continent or the world, teach all students the location of continents and some key countries. My students loved the classroom map game described on this page.

Suggested uses:

Challenge students to memorize challenges they choose during free time or at home. Provide rewards. Although not all students will choose to participate, everyone will want to do at least a few of the easy challenges if rewards are appropriate and motivational.

Periodic Table

Activity Book p. 181. Look for patterns. Color in known elements, elements listed on p. 34 of *Facts Plus* or radioactive elements. Use the Periodic Table to decipher chemical formulas such as those on p. 35 of *Facts Plus*.

Keyboard

Activity Book p. 182. Color the keyboard. Possibly color fingernails to match or use colored stickers. Students practice "typing" using paper keyboards or available computers.

Classroom Map Game

Materials:

Large wall maps (see Activity Book p. iv for specific suggestions)

Coffee can containing slips of paper with names of continents, oceans, seas, countries, etc. which students have studied using blank maps such as that on Activity Book p. 149 (world map)

Stopwatch

Background:

This game reviews locations of places such as those listed below. I teach a group of places a week and continually review everything. (1) Continents, (2) Oceans, (3) Sahara Desert, Greenland, Sinai Peninsula, Arabian Peninsula, (4) Rocky Mountains, Appalachians, Andes, Alps, Himalayas, (5) Rivers: Mississippi, Amazon, Nile, Congo, (6) Seas: Bering, Caribbean, Mediterranean, Black, Red, (7) Hudson Bay, Gulf of Mexico, Persian Gulf, Panama Canal, Suez Canal, (8) Central America, Middle East, Far East, Southeast Asia, Pacific Northwest, (9) Canada, United States, Mexico, Cuba, Brazil, Argentina, (10) United Kingdom, Spain, France, Germany, Italy, Greece, (11) Morocco, Egypt, Nigeria, Kenya, South Africa, (12) Israel, Saudi Arabia, Iran, Iraq, Kuwait, (13) Russia, India, Nepal, China, South Korea, (14) Japan, Philippines, Vietnam, Australia, New Zealand.

Suggested procedure:

Divide the class into two teams. Students from alternating teams come up one at a time, draw a slip of paper and have 10 seconds to locate the place on the wall map. Success earns a point for the team. Students at their desks can use *Facts Plus* p. 134-135 for practice.

Name_________________________________

MEMORIZATION CHALLENGES

- ❑ Gettysburg Address (125)
- ❑ I Have a Dream (125)
- ❑ Poem on the Statue of Liberty (127)
- ❑ Presidents (130)
- ❑ Braille alphabet (165)
- ❑ American manual alphabet (165)
- ❑ Phonetic alphabet (165)
- ❑ International Morse code (165)
- ❑ Preamble to U.S. Constitution (114)

- ❑ Paragraph from the Declaration of Independence beginning, "When in the course of human events. . ." (112)

- ❑ Paragraph from the Declaration of Independence beginning, "We hold these truths to be self-evident. . ." and ending, ". . .their Safety & Happiness."

- ❑ North American countries (131)
  Bahamas, Belize, Canada, Costa Rica, Cuba, Dominican Republic, El Salvador, Guatemala, Haiti, Honduras, Jamaica, Mexico, Nicaragua, Panama, Puerto Rico (U.S.), United States

- ❑ South American countries (136)
  Argentina, Bolivia, Brazil, Chile, Colombia, Ecuador, French Guiana (France), Guyana, Paraguay, Peru, Suriname, Uruguay, Venezuela

- ❑ European countries (138)
  Austria, Belgium, Denmark, Finland, France, Germany, Iceland, Ireland, Italy, Liechtenstein, Luxembourg, Netherlands, Norway, Portugal, Spain, Sweden, Switzerland, United Kingdom

- ❑ European countries (138)
  Albania, Belarus, Bosnia-Hercegovina, Bulgaria, Croatia, Czechoslovakia, Estonia, Greece, Hungary, Latvia, Lithuania, Macedonia, Moldova, Poland, Romania, Slovenia, Ukraine, Yugoslavia

- ❑ Former Soviet Union (139)
  Armenia, Azerbaijan, Belarus, Estonia, Georgia, Kazakhstan, Kyrgyzstan, Latvia, Lithuania, Moldova, Russia, Tajikistan, Turkmenistan, Ukraine, Uzbekistan

- ❑ Northern African countries (137)
  Algeria, Benin, Cameroon, Central African Republic (C.A.R.), Chad, Djibouti, Egypt, Ethiopia, Gambia, Ghana, Guinea, Guinea-Bissau, Ivory Coast, Liberia, Libya, Mali, Mauritania, Morocco, Niger, Nigeria, Senegal, Sierra Leone, Sudan, Togo, Tunisia, Upper Volta

- ❑ Southern African countries (137)
  Angola, Botswana, Burundi, Congo, Equatorial Guinea, Gabon, Kenya, Lesotho, Madagascar, Malawi, Mozambique, Namibia, Rwanda, Somalia, South Africa, Swaziland, Tanzania, Uganda, Zaire, Zambia, Zimbabwe

- ❑ Middle Eastern countries (137)
  Bahrain, Cyprus, Egypt, Iran, Iraq, Israel, Jordan, Kuwait, Lebanon, Oman, Qatar, Saudi Arabia, Syria, Turkey, United Arab Emirates, Yemen

- ❑ Asian countries (139)
  Afghanistan, Bangladesh, Bhutan, Brunei, Cambodia, China, India, Indonesia, Iran, Japan, Laos, Malaysia, Mongolia, Myanmar, Nepal, North Korea, Pakistan, Philippines, Singapore, South Korea, Soviet Union, Sri Lanka, Taiwan, Thailand, Vietnam

Numbers in parentheses are *Facts Plus* page numbers.

Teachers: Ideas for use on p. 179

PERIODIC TABLE OF THE ELEMENTS

Name______________________________

Key: Atomic number — 1; Chemical symbol — H; Element name — Hydrogen; Atomic weight — 1.00797

PERIOD	1A	2A	3B	4B	5B	6B	7B	8B	8B	8B	1B	2B	3A	4A	5A	6A	7A	8A
1	1 H Hydrogen 1.00797																	2 He Helium 4.0026
2	3 Li Lithium 6.939	4 Be Beryllium 9.0122											5 B Boron 10.811	6 C Carbon 12.01115	7 N Nitrogen 14.0067	8 O Oxygen 15.9994	9 F Fluorine 18.998403	10 Ne Neon 20.183
3	11 Na Sodium 22.9898	12 Mg Magnesium 24.312											13 Al Aluminum 26.9815	14 Si Silicon 28.0855	15 P Phosphorus 30.9738	16 S Sulfur 32.064	17 Cl Chlorine 35.453	18 Ar Argon 39.948
4	19 K Potassium 39.0983	20 Ca Calcium 40.08	21 Sc Scandium 44.956	22 Ti Titanium 47.90	23 V Vanadium 50.942	24 Cr Chromium 51.996	25 Mn Manganese 54.9380	26 Fe Iron 55.847	27 Co Cobalt 58.9332	28 Ni Nickel 58.71	29 Cu Copper 63.54	30 Zn Zinc 65.37	31 Ga Gallium 69.72	32 Ge Germanium 72.59	33 As Arsenic 74.9216	34 Se Selenium 78.96	35 Br Bromine 79.909	36 Kr Krypton 83.80
5	37 Rb Rubidium 85.47	38 Sr Strontium 87.62	39 Y Yttrium 88.905	40 Zr Zirconium 91.22	41 Nb Niobium 92.906	42 Mo Molybdenum 95.94	43 Tc Technetium (97)	44 Ru Ruthenium 101.07	45 Rh Rhodium 102.905	46 Pd Palladium 106.4	47 Ag Silver 107.870	48 Cd Cadmium 112.41	49 In Indium 114.82	50 Sn Tin 118.69	51 Sb Antimony 121.75	52 Te Tellurium 127.60	53 I Iodine 126.9044	54 Xe Xenon 131.30
6	55 Cs Cesium 132.905	56 Ba Barium 137.33		72 Hf Hafnium 178.49	73 Ta Tantalum 180.948	74 W Tungsten 183.85	75 Re Rhenium 186.2	76 Os Osmium 190.2	77 Ir Iridium 192.2	78 Pt Platinum 195.09	79 Au Gold 196.967	80 Hg Mercury 200.59	81 Tl Thallium 204.37	82 Pb Lead 207.19	83 Bi Bismuth 208.980	84 Po Polonium (210)	85 At Astatine (210)	86 Rn Radon (222)
7	87 Fr Francium (223)	88 Ra Radium (226)																

57 La Lanthanum 138.91	58 Ce Cerium 140.12	59 Pr Praseodymium 140.907	60 Nd Neodymium 144.24	61 Pm Promethium (145)	62 Sm Samarium 150.35	63 Eu Europium 151.96	64 Gd Gadolinium 157.25	65 Tb Terbium 158.924	66 Dy Dysprosium 162.50	67 Ho Holmium 164.930	68 Er Erbium 167.26	69 Tm Thulium 168.934	70 Yb Ytterbium 173.04	71 Lu Lutetium 174.97
89 Ac Actinium (227)	90 Th Thorium 232.038	91 Pa Protactinium (231)	92 U Uranium 238.03	93 Np Neptumium 237	94 Pu Plutonium (244)	95 Am Americium (243)	96 Cm Curium (247)	97 Bk Berkelium (247)	98 Cf Californium (251)	99 Es Einsteinium (254)	100 Fm Fermium (257)	101 Md Mendelevium (258)	102 No Nobelium (255)	103 Lr Lawrencium (256)

Name_______________________

KEYBOARD

Outline the **home keys** in black on the keyboard below, as shown on the right. These are the keys your fingers will come back to, the place where they'll "rest." Next, carefully color *just the keys below* using the colors shown at the right: **G** for green, **O** for orange, **B** for blue, **Y** for yellow and **P** for pink. These show which fingers can "visit" which keys.

Green keys may be visited by pinkies.
Orange keys may be visited by ring fingers.
Blue keys may be visited by middle fingers.
Yellow keys may be visited by the left index finger.
Pink keys may be visited by the right index finger. The **space bar** may be visited by either thumb. Keys not colored are seldom used.

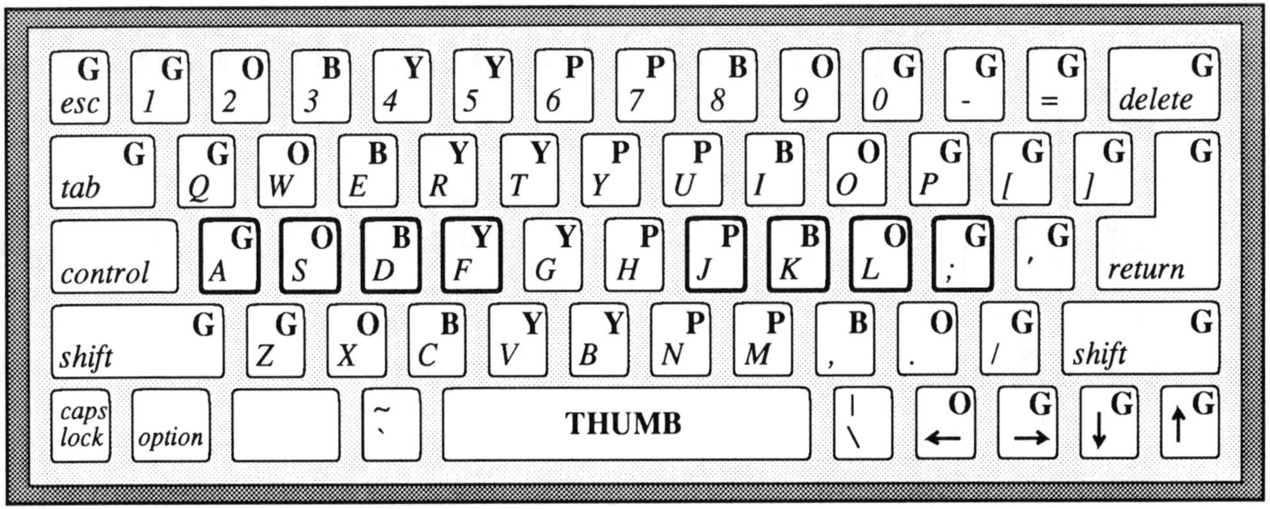

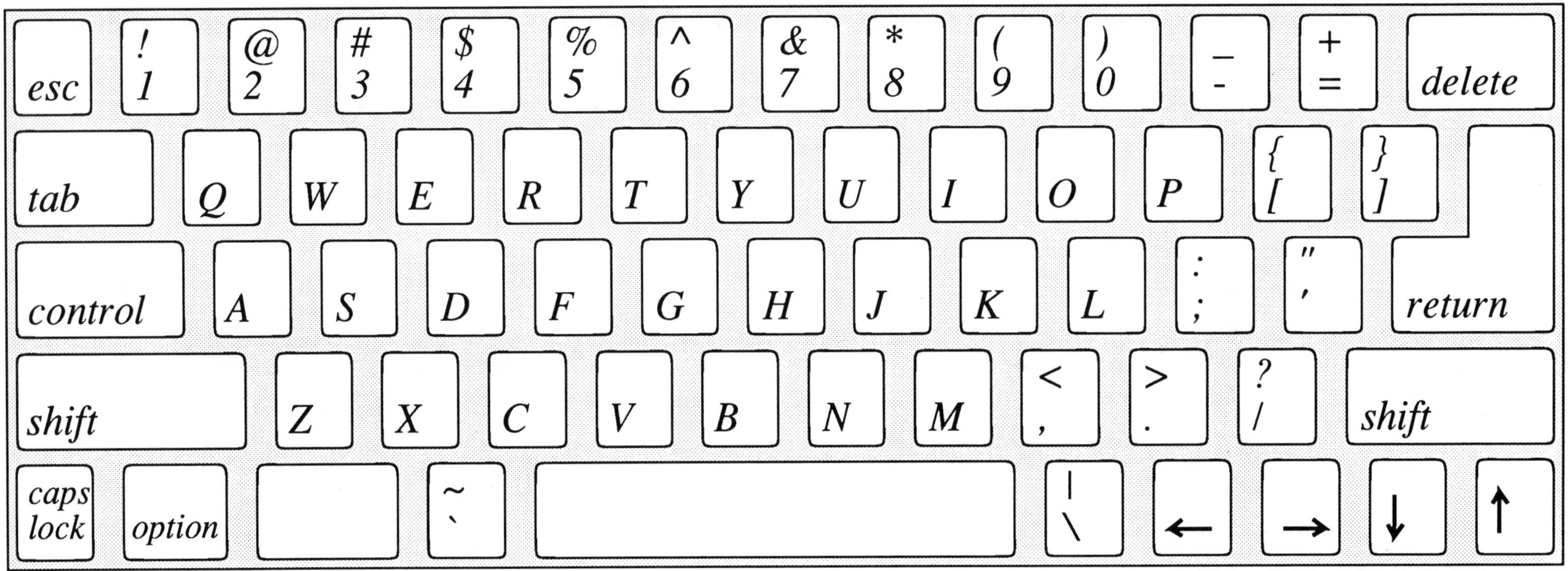